The BBC and national identity in Britain, 1922–53

Manchester University Press

STUDIES IN
POPULAR
CULTURE

General editor: Professor Jeffrey Richards

The BBC and national identity in Britain, 1922–53

THOMAS HAJKOWSKI

Manchester University Press
Manchester and New York

distributed exclusively in the USA by Palgrave Macmillan

Published by Manchester University Press
Oxford Road, Manchester M13 9NR, UK
and Room 400, 175 Fifth Avenue, New York, NY 10010, USA
www.manchesteruniversitypress.co.uk

Distributed in the United States exclusively by
Palgrave Macmillan, 175 Fifth Avenue, New York,
NY 10010, USA

Distributed in Canada exclusively by
UBC Press, University of British Columbia, 2029 West Mall,
Vancouver, BC, Canada V6T 1Z2

British Library Cataloguing-in-Publication Data
A catalogue record for this book is available from the British Library

Library of Congress Cataloging-in-Publication Data applied for

ISBN   978 0 7190 7994 3 *hardback*

First published 2010

Typeset in Adobe Garamond with Gill Sans display by
Special Edition Pre-press Services, www.special-edition.co.uk
Printed in Great Britain by
CPI Antony Rowe Ltd, Chippenham, Wiltshire

STUDIES IN
POPULAR
CULTURE

There has in recent years been an explosion of interest in culture and cultural studies. The impetus has come from two directions and out of two different traditions. On the one hand, cultural history has grown out of social history to become a distinct and identifiable school of historical investigation. On the other hand, cultural studies has grown out of English literature and has concerned itself to a large extent with contemporary issues. Nevertheless, there is a shared project, its aim, to elucidate the meanings and values implicit and explicit in the art, literature, learning, institutions and everyday behaviour within a given society. Both the cultural historian and the cultural studies scholar seek to explore the ways in which a culture is imagined, represented and received, how it interacts with social processes, how it contributes to individual and collective identities and world views, to stability and change, to social, political and economic activities and programmes. This series aims to provide an arena for the cross-fertilisation of the discipline, so that the work of the cultural historian can take advantage of the most useful and illuminating of the theoretical developments and the cultural studies scholars can extend the purely historical underpinnings of their investigations. The ultimate objective of the series is to provide a range of books which will explain in a readable and accessible way where we are now socially and culturally and how we got to where we are. This should enable people to be better informed, promote an interdisciplinary approach to cultural issues and encourage deeper thought about the issues, attitudes and institutions of popular culture.

Jeffrey Richards

Contents

General editor's foreword

In this extensively researched, judicious and revealing book, Thomas Hajkowski makes a compelling argument for recognition of the major role played by the BBC in constructing an inclusive and pluralistic British national identity in the first half of the twentieth century. He demonstrates convincingly that the BBC set out to promote both the empire and the monarchy as unifying institutions for the nation as a whole. Support for the empire was inculcated by twin methods: education (talks, documentaries) and entertainment (dramatizations of key imperial texts such as *The Four Feathers* and *Sanders of the River*). Close links were established with the Empire Day Movement and the Empire Marketing Board, and the BBC Empire Service was launched in 1932. This commitment to empire continued throughout the Second World War and on into the post-war decade. The monarchy was promoted by regular coverage of royal events, coronations, weddings, and overseas tours and by the introduction, in 1932, of the King's annual Christmas broadcast, which brought the voice of the monarch into every home in the empire.

But complementing this commitment to national unity, the BBC also cultivated the distinct identities of the constituent countries of the United Kingdom, particularly Scotland, Wales and Northern Ireland. Contrary to the received scholarly wisdom that regional identities were stifled and neutered by an ongoing policy of centralization and the imposition of a metropolitan southern English culture, Hajkowski demonstrates by reference to both policies and programmes that the regional services of the BBC developed and maintained vibrant independent voices.

The regional services in Scotland and Wales, largely staffed by Scots and Welsh people, produced regular programmes of indigenous music, dramatizations of iconic Scottish and Welsh novels, and documentaries on the history, culture and everyday life of the Scots and the Welsh. At the same time they stressed the full participation of Scotland and Wales in the empire and the wider national community. The situation in Northern Ireland was rather different. The BBC sought to stress the integration of Northern Ireland in the United Kingdom and largely avoided programmes about history, with its inevitable sectarian implications. But there was a sustained bid to create an Ulster identity with programmes on the landscape, culture and everyday life of the province. The result of these policies was the strong reinforcement of multiple identities, national and regional to which everyone could belong. Hajkowski's book fundamentally alters the way in which we should assess the history of the BBC and its role in British cultural life.

Jeffrey Richards

Acknowledgements

The research and writing of this book was made possible through the generosity of many institutions and people. I am grateful for having had the financial support of Northwestern University as well as a grant from the English-Speaking Union. In addition, a summer research grant from Misericordia University allowed me to revise this work from a dissertation into a book manuscript.

The support of friends and family were also vital to the completion of this book. Several research trips and conference presentations would have been impossible without the enthusiastic help of Tom Briggs, Sharon Turnbull, and Bill Turnbull. Thank you also to Lynn and Howard Marsh for welcoming me into your homes, in both London and Maryland.

My thanks to the staff at the National Archives, the British Library, the Archive Centre at King's College, Cambridge, the Churchill College Archives, the Mass Observation Archive, and the Library of Congress. I am particularly indebted to Jacqueline Kavanagh and the archivists at the BBC Written Archives Centre at Caversham. My research at the archive would have been significantly less productive and less pleasant without them. A special word of appreciation to Jeff Walden—I am grateful to have been the beneficiary of his vast knowledge of the Centre's holdings.

I would like to express my gratitude to the committee that oversaw the doctoral dissertation upon which this book is based: Alex Owen, James Schwoch, John Bushnell, and T. W. Heyck. Their comments and support were pivotal to both my completing the dissertation and revising it into a book manuscript. Thanks to my colleagues at Misericordia University, David Wright, Rebecca Steinberger, and Allan Austin, for reading and commenting on Chapter 4. Guy Ortolano, Mark Hampton, and Jamie Medhurst read selected chapters, which were enriched by their queries and comments. The readers at Manchester University Press provided numerous helpful suggestions and saved me from making a few embarrassing gaffes. Thanks to everyone at Manchester University Press who contributed to the preparation of this book and to Jeffrey Richards, for supporting its inclusion in the *Studies in Popular Culture* series. I would also like to recognize my earliest mentors, Seth Koven and Dermot Quinn, both of whom made a major impact on my understanding of history.

Portions of Chapters 1 and 2 appeared in Joel H. Wiener and Mark Hampton, eds., *Anglo-American Media Interactions* (Palgrave Macmillan, 2007), and are reproduced with permission of Palgrave Macmillan, as well as my article, "The BBC, the Empire, and the Second World War," *Historical Journal of Film, Radio and Television,* 22 (2002): 135–55 (Taylor & Francis). I would also like to thank the following for permission to reprint copyrighted material: the British Broadcasting Corporation, Rory Johnston, and Rory J. Brocklebank. Every effort has been made to trace copyright and contact copyright holders.

The original idea for this book goes back to a lunch I shared with T. W. Heyck at Clarke's, in Evanston. From that point on, Bill proved to be an ideal mentor and guide. This book would never have been completed without his provocative questions, criticisms, and continued encouragement. He saw the value of this project long before I did, and for that I am deeply grateful.

To my wife Kerri I can finally say that it only seemed like I would never finish this book. I cannot thank her enough for her deep reserves of patience and forbearance. I want Tommy, Alex, and Luke to know that they were always a welcome distraction, even if it did not always seem so at the time. Finally, I would like to dedicate this book to my parents, Ann and Robert Hajkowski.

Introduction

On New Year's Eve, 1945, William Haley, the Director-General of the BBC, composed a memo to Lindsay Wellington, Head of the BBC's Home Service and one of his top lieutenants. Haley had just completed his first full year as Director-General. He had led the BBC through the final stages of the Second World War and the difficult transition to peacetime broadcasting. Like many of us, he used the occasion of New Year's Eve to reflect on the past year and look forward to the future. Contemplating the position of broadcasting in Britain, Haley judged it "essential" that the BBC's flagship channel, the Home Service, "strike keynotes attuned to the national position and outlook," including "virility, a sense of endeavour, [and] courage." Noting that the war would "drop largely out of public thinking," he argued that the BBC needed to "inculcate a spirit of striving." The British people, he claimed, were "nowhere near finished in our island or world story." Haley advised Wellington to "constantly" project the empire and Commonwealth "as a great heritage" and produce stimulating programs on Britain's role in the world. He told Wellington that the Home Service ought to be "appreciably" different in the coming year because 1945 represented the "hindsight of a closing era." "Tomorrow," Haley concluded, was "the threshold of a new day."[1]

Haley's memo to Wellington reveals much about his values and frame of mind. Like most Britons, he regarded the Second World War as a watershed, a turning point on the road to a more equal and just Britain. His words to Wellington also reveal his underlying assumptions about the BBC: its unique role in society, its status as a national institution, and its special responsibility to its listeners, who together constituted the British nation. For Haley, the BBC was an instrument to reflect, but also to nourish and encourage, the best virtues of the British character. Haley's memorandum also prioritizes a particular set of ideas about British national identity: British pluck and determination, the empire, the "island story."

Yet Haley's words also reflect his fears about the BBC and post-war Britain. The war had seen the apogee of the BBC's prestige and influence, and Haley was concerned that peace might make it less significant in national life. Britain had prevailed over Germany, but it was a pyrrhic victory. Haley's emphasis on "virility" and "endeavor" reveals an uncertainty about Britain and the British, given the human, financial, and psychological costs of the war. And his invocation of empire on the cusp of Indian independence seems positively short-sighted. Indeed, Haley's directive that Wellington think of 1945 as the end of an era in British history while also encouraging him to construct Britishness around empire and Britain's global role was incongruous and would prove difficult to put into practice.

While Haley's memo reflects the historical moment of its creation, it also shows Haley grappling with an issue that concerned British broadcasters from the very beginnings of the BBC: the role of broadcasting in reflecting, defining, and projecting British national identity. How could the BBC best serve the nation? To what extent should the BBC embrace British nationalism? What should Britishness look (or rather sound) like? How would the BBC negotiate the multi-national character of the United Kingdom? Sometimes, as during the Second World War, broadcasters came up with explicit answers to these questions. At other times these concerns manifested themselves in more subtle, but no less important, ways. What it meant to be British, and broadcasting's part in fostering a particular type of Britishness, is the subject of this book.

During the second quarter of the twentieth century the British Broadcasting Corporation was the most important arena in which regional cultures interacted with and interrogated a normative English culture, buttressing the hybrid "dual identities" of contemporary Britain. Established in 1922 as the British Broadcasting Company, and then chartered as a public service corporation in 1927 with a monopoly over broadcasting, the BBC regarded itself as a guarantor of an enduring British culture and tradition. However, as historians, political scientists, and social theorists have established, national identity is not fixed, but rather constructed and reconstituted over time.[2] This was certainly true of Britain, a multi-national state that integrated its peripheries unevenly and with limited success. The BBC had to contend with a multitude of national identities, all claiming the right to be heard: British, English, Scottish, Welsh, Ulster, and Irish. Because Scotland, Wales, and Northern Ireland each had their own distinct history, culture, and institutions, which distinguished them from England, as well as each other, the BBC had to accommodate these "national regions" with their own networks and specialized programming, in addition to providing a unitary British network. In trying to define, reflect, and embody Britishness, the BBC did, in some ways, present a particular, Anglo-centric and middle-class image of "Britain." But this version of Britishness was undermined, and eventually collapsed, under the weight of increasingly confident regional broadcasters, social and political change, public opposition, and war. By the late 1930s the BBC was presenting its audiences with a pluralistic Britishness, one that reminded listeners of their common history, institutions, and values while recognizing the diversity of nations and cultures in Britain.

The first half of this book focuses on the BBC's treatment of two national, integrative, "British" institutions, the empire and the monarchy. It will demonstrate the extent to which the BBC championed the British imperial ideal in its programs, and constructed the monarchy as a guarantor of a peculiarly British individualism, freedom, and pluralism. Both empire and monarchy were multi-national institutions, with Scots in particular taking pride in their contributions to the empire, while the monarchy effectively used broadcasting, with the assistance of the BBC, to promote itself as a symbol of Britain's cultural diversity. The BBC's focus on empire and monarchy to represent British national identity was neither innovative nor risky; the BBC did not try to change fundamental ideas of what it meant to be British, but it did help to refashion these traditional symbols of Britishness during a period of significant social and political change.

The second half of the book turns to the work of the BBC in Scotland, Wales, and Northern Ireland, and examines the tensions between the BBC's efforts to project a uniform Britishness and its commitment to local and regional broadcasting in these areas. These chapters revise standard histories of regional broadcasting in Britain that interpret it as a form of cultural hegemony emanating from London. Although regional broadcasters tended to be poorly funded and occasionally bullied by the BBC's central administration, regional broadcasting in Britain, after a shaky start, received considerable leeway from BBC Head Office in London. The regional organization of the BBC—Scotland, Wales, and Northern Ireland each eventually had their own distinct BBC stations—forged "imagined communities" of Scots, Welsh, and Northern Irish listeners in these regions.[3] In an age of local and provincial newspapers on the one hand, and London or Hollywood dominated cinema on the other, the regional BBCs were the only truly "national" media in Scotland, Wales, and Northern Ireland. The most powerful cultural agencies in their regions, the regional BBCs provided news, talks, and creative programming designed specifically for regional listeners, and in the process created conditions amenable to the assertion of Scottish, Welsh, and Northern Irish identity.

Method and sources

This book takes programs, not policy, as its subject. The policies developed by the BBC's Board of Governors and its Directors-General created the framework within which the creative staff produced its broadcasts. But policy-making at the level of the Board of Governors or Control Board tells us little about the motives or intent of program-makers, and even less about what Britons actually heard through their headphones or radio speakers. Few listeners were aware of the BBC's policies or the intricacies of its organization, but millions listened to programs every day. Programs are key historical artifacts, at once the end product of policy and a link between institution and public, production and reception.[4] Analyzed within a social/historical context, programs provide valuable insights into the BBC's construction of British national culture and identity.

Radio programs are, of course, ephemeral; they cease to exist the moment they are broadcast. Fortunately, there is a wealth of material that enables researchers to reconstruct the programs of the early days of radio. The BBC published two journals, the *Radio Times* and the *Listener*. The latter reprinted broadcast talks and included articles and criticism, but it is the former that is the key to accessing BBC programs from the 1920–40s. In addition to providing a record of the BBC's schedule, the *Radio Times* included articles and summaries of important broadcasts. The *Radio Times* has been an under-utilized source, and this book makes use of the *Radio Times* to a greater extent than previous histories of broadcasting. Another invaluable resource is the scripts of the programs themselves: many remain extant, especially from the late 1930s forward. Scripts for features and plays typically include information about sound effects and the tone or manner of the speaker.

Beyond the scripts, and the often detailed program descriptions found in the *Radio Times*, the BBC Written Archives Centre contains hundreds of files on the development, from conception to broadcast, of individual programs and recurring series. These provide valuable insights into the intent of program-makers, clashes over program development, and reactions to programs after their transmission. Further, the BBC often enlisted the assistance of, or was cajoled into cooperating with, a variety of government ministries. As with internal BBC memoranda, the exchanges between government officials and program-makers reveal much about the development and goal of programs as well as the clashes between program-makers, the government, and the higher administration of the BBC.

Finally, the BBC's Listener Research reports provide insight into how the public received certain programs. Unfortunately, audience research only began in 1936, and it was not used extensively until the Second World War; hence historians know little about the popularity of earlier programs beyond what can be ascertained from listeners' letters, radio criticism in the press, and the opinion of BBC personnel themselves. Through random sampling, the Listener Research Department could determine the size of the audience of a given program, which they expressed as a percentage of the listening audience. Many reports also included a "listening barometer," based on a scale of 100, which measured how favorably audiences reacted to a particular broadcast. A program with a listening barometer in the 90s was considered a great success. Even with the listening barometer, though, Listener Research reports do not tell us why the audience did or did not like a particular program. The subject matter, its treatment, presentation, or whether or not the audience liked a particular speaker or actor, all played a role in audience reaction. Therefore, I make use of listener research data sparingly and with caution.[5] This book is first and foremost a study of program production.

Nations, national identity and Britain

The past two decades have seen the emergence of an extensive literature on the question of national identity. Scholars continue to debate the precise origins of the concept of the nation, and therefore of nationalism and national identity. Historians have discovered elements of nationalism in the Creole rebellions of Latin America, the French Revolution, Romanticism, and reactions to the Industrial Revolution. However, a number of broad arguments regarding nations, nationalism, and national identity are now widely accepted. First, nationalism and national identity entered the stage of history sometime in the eighteenth century; the nation is fundamentally a creation of the modern world. Second, as entities created in history, as opposed to primordial, eternal "things," nations are contingent. Because of this contingency, national identity, the "we feeling" of belonging to a particular nation, is ever shifting, both reflecting and constructing changing political and social realities.

The emergence of these critical and historically based theories of nations and nationalism owes much to the groundbreaking work of Eric Hobsbawm,

Ernest Gellner, and Benedict Anderson.[6] Anderson's work has been particularly influential, in large part because of his conception of the nation as an "imagined community." This is not to say, insists Anderson, that nations are counterfeit communities foisted on the peoples of Europe and the Americas by manipulative elites or abstract historical processes. Rather, the nation must be an imagined community "because the members of even the smallest nation will never know most of their fellow-members, meet them, or even hear them, yet in the minds of each lives the image of their communion."[7] "Communities are distinguished," Anderson continues, "not by their falsity/genuineness, but by the style in which they are imagined."[8]

The impact of Anderson's formulation on this study is threefold. First, it employs Anderson's idea that national identity is not absolute or exclusive. Nationalism may be a powerful and seductive force, but it does not automatically preclude class or regional loyalties: one may be British *and* working class, English *and* Mancunian. This is not to deny, however, that there are times when national, regional, local, class, and other identities clash, or that men and women, working class and middle class, or Scots and English, might experience and understand their national identity differently. Second, the notion of the "imagined community" invites scrutiny of other groupings that may be equally "imagined," such as the region or the locality. Any community beyond the smallest village must be, by Anderson's conceptualization, "imagined." Third, Anderson contends that the rise of national consciousness was intimately linked to the development of print capitalism, particularly the newspaper. Using the example of newspapers in colonial Latin America, Anderson writes: "the newspaper of Caracas quite naturally, and even apolitically, created an imagined community among a specific assemblage of fellow-readers, to whom *these* ships, brides, bishops and prices belonged."[9] Broadcasting, I argue, works in fundamentally the same way. The BBC reinforced British national identity in the United Kingdom merely by creating a community of "British listeners" from Land's End to Londonderry. Equally, the creation of the separate BBC networks to serve Scotland, Wales, and Northern Ireland created listening communities in those areas as well, contributing to the development of national consciousness in these regions.

In addition to Benedict Anderson, the work of Rogers Brubaker plays an influential part in the theoretical framework of this book. In *Nationalism Reframed*, Brubaker argues that nationality or "nation-ness" is not "an entity but … a contingent event."[10] National identity is not a thing that individuals have, but rather something they experience or perform at particular moments.

At some times national identity can be active and manifest; at other times it remains latent. Brubaker is particularly interested in how the practices of the modern state institutionalize nationality. Using the example of the Soviet Union, he argues that while officially the Soviet state was hostile to nationalism, its practices, such as the creation of ethnically-based Soviet Republics (now the successor states of the Soviet Union) and Autonomous Socialist Republics and the internal passport system, which identified citizens by ethnicity, forged a sense of national—not class—identity amongst the Soviet people. Ironically, the policies of the Soviet state fostered the nationalist revival that would play a pivotal role in its own dissolution.[11] In a similar fashion, the BBC helped to institutionalize Scottish, Welsh, and Northern Irish identities through the creation of regional broadcasting networks to serve these areas. The BBC was not a state institution, but it was, like the old Soviet government, officially opposed to minority nationalism. And yet its regional structure and programs could not help but give new significance to Scottishness and Welshness. In Northern Ireland, the fact that the BBC was formed only a year after the partition of Ireland made it a central institution in the creation of a modern "Ulster" identity and the building of the statelet.

The most influential study of nation-building and national identity in Britain remains Linda Colley's *Britons*. Using Anderson's concept of the imagined community, Colley argues that a sense of Britishness was forged during the eighteenth century and came to coexist with local and regional identities. "Identities are not like hats," notes Colley, "human beings can and do put on several at a time."[12] Colley rejects arguments that claim that the development of Britain consisted of an English core dominating a Celtic periphery or the blending of the national cultures of Great Britain.[13] For Colley, Protestantism, capitalism, and a century of warfare with France gave rise to a new British national identity in the eighteenth century, and imperial expansion and contact with colonial peoples sustained this sense of Britishness into the twentieth century.[14]

Colley's synthesis, combined with several political and social changes in contemporary Britain, most notably devolution in Scotland, Wales, in Northern Ireland, rekindled interest in nationalism, nation-building, and national identity in Britain. In the wake of Colley, scholarly attention focused on the early-modern period and the fashioning of Britishness in the wake of the Act of Union with Wales in 1536, the union of the crowns under James I and VI, and the Act of Union with Scotland in 1707.[15] However, recent years have seen the publication of a number of studies that take into account the manifestations of

Britishness and Englishness in the modern era, and particularly the twentieth century.[16] In his *Britishness Since 1870*, Paul Ward argues that the preponderance of this scholarship presents Britishness as an identity in terminal decline during the twentieth century. According to this interpretation, the peoples of the United Kingdom never fully embraced Britishness; it remained a frail and perhaps even suspect form of identity. In so far as it did exist, the decline of Protestant Christianity, the unraveling of the empire, economic challenges, and Margaret Thatcher's assault on the welfare state combined to critically undermine Britishness, leading to political devolution, and perhaps, the disintegration of the British state.[17] In contradistinction, Ward posits Britishness as an extraordinarily resilient form of identity, in large part because of its flexibility and adaptability. "Britishness," he writes, "has more often than not been compatible with a huge variety of other identities, and that has been one reason for its continuing hold."[18] It is Ward's conceptualization of Britishness most closely mirrors the work of BBC radio from the 1920s to the 1950s. Throughout this period the BBC adjusted and refined its representation of Britishness, or rather the symbols of Britishness—empire and monarchy—while also recognizing, albeit at times insufficiently, the diversity of the British Isles.

In addition to the growing body of literature on national identity, this book draws on another thread of recent scholarship that has led historians to reconsider older narratives of the British past, the "four nations" approach to British history. In a groundbreaking 1975 article J. G. A. Pocock made a "plea" for an explicitly "British" history that would give due consideration to and explore the interactions of the distinct nations of the British Isles.[19] Critical of scholars who elided the difference between "England" and "Britain," Pocock called for a "plural history of a group of cultures situated along an Anglo-Celtic frontier."[20] This study adopts both the methodology and the mood of the four nations approach to British history pioneered by Pocock, Hugh Kearney, and T. W. Heyck.[21] The chapters on empire and monarchy focus not just on the BBC's support for these symbols of Britishness but also on how the Corporation constructed these institutions as representations of a multi-ethnic Britain. I also devote a chapter each to broadcasting in Scotland, Wales, and Northern Ireland. In each of these national regions radio broadcasting developed differently from the way it did in the BBC as a whole. Similarly, each region has its own broadcasting history, distinct from the other two. We cannot understand the role of radio in constructing national identity without taking into account its work in the regions. Finally, the book emphasizes the interactions, conflicts, and contradictions of British national identity (as well as Scottish,

Welsh, and Irish identity) as they played out within the BBC and between the BBC and the listening public. Many of the clashes that took place between Head Office and the BBC's regional stations were, at root, about matters of national identity.

Both historians of broadcasting and scholars of national identity have been slow to recognize the importance of radio in producing and disseminated Britishness. Asa Briggs's monumental, five-volume *History of Broadcasting in the United Kingdom* admirably strove for totality.[22] In addition to the organization and development of radio, Briggs examines the relationship between the BBC and the government, technological change, the manufacture and marketing of receivers, and the impact of radio on social habits and leisure. However, Briggs ultimately produces a top-down, institutional history of the BBC. Briggs, Raphael Samuel notes, "is fascinated by career structures, on policy makers, [and] on the merger or subdivision of [BBC] departments."[23] As a consequence, Briggs's *History* gives short shrift to certain aspects of broadcasting. Reflecting on the first four volumes of his *History*, Briggs himself expresses some regret that he did not fully take into account "cultural factors" and "the evolution of the BBC … examining local, regional, and national orientations."[24] Subsequently, some histories of the BBC broach questions of radio and national identity, but their treatment is limited, and primarily in the context of broader analyses. Paddy Scannell's and David Cardiff's seminal *A Social History of British Broadcasting* includes a chapter on national identity and provides an excellent overview of the development of the BBC's regional policy, but their book examines a whole range of interactions between radio and society, from the meaning of public service broadcasting to the coverage of international affairs.[25] Siân Nicholas's *Echo of War* admirably traces the BBC's representation of the British nation, as well as Germany, the Soviet Union, and the United States.[26] Yet, the chronological scope of her work is necessarily narrow and, like Scannell and Cardiff, Nicholas discusses national identity as one of a broad range of developments within broadcasting during the war. Both *A Social History of British Broadcasting* and *Echo of War* deeply enrich our understanding of the BBC's historic construction of national identity, as my own footnotes will attest, but the historical development of national identity in Britain has become a key issue in recent historiographic debates, and this development demands a more comprehensive treatment of radio's role in making Britishness. Some histories of the regional BBCs provide valuable analysis of how the BBC promoted or undermined national identity in the regions, especially John Davies's excellent history of the BBC in Wales and Gillian McIntosh's chapter on the BBC in Northern Ireland in her book *The Force of Culture*.[27] Others refer to issues of culture and identity only fleetingly.[28] Similarly, while some recent studies of British national identity have, to their credit, considered the work of the BBC,[29] others only offer brief, intermittent remarks about broadcasting.[30] The *Radio Times*, the *Listener*, and the BBC's Written Archive Centre remain under-utilized resources for the study of national identity in Britain.

A sketch history of the BBC

The British Broadcasting Company was created in 1922.[31] The original company represented a consortium of radio manufacturers; the company's purpose was not to provide a public service but rather to produce entertaining programs that would entice Britons to buy radio sets. A Board of Governors directed the company, and the Postmaster General was given responsibility for government oversight of the new medium.[32] The Board of Governors made its first order of business the appointment of a general manager. Their decision to appoint to the post J. C. W. Reith, a young Scot with no experience in broadcasting, proved momentous. Through his determination, energy, longevity, and vision, Reith forged the BBC into a national institution.[33]

Under Reith's leadership, radio developed quickly into a national service. When the BBC completed work on its nine main stations and ten relay stations in 1924, approximately 70 per cent of the population of Great Britain was within the range of a BBC transmitter. Between 1922 and 1955 the number of radio license holders steadily increased, attesting to the popularity of radio, as well as its availability to nearly all Britons. In 1922 the government issued approximately 36,000 licenses; by 1930 that number had grown to 3,075,828. This number trebled by 1946, reaching a total of 11,546,925.[34] And the diffusion of radio ownership, in terms of both class and region, was impressive. To take 1939 as an example, about 4,200,000 of the 9,082,666 wireless licenses were taken out by individuals with incomes between £2 10s and £4 a week, while an additional 2,000,000 licenses were issued to individuals with an even smaller weekly income. Geographically, the Midlands had the highest number of license holders per capita, eight out of every ten families. But even in remote Northern Scotland some 40,000 families took out 14,000 licenses.[35]

Reith envisioned British broadcasting as a public service, answerable neither to the government nor to the listeners, but only to a higher cultural ideal. "Our responsibility," he wrote in 1924, "is to carry into the greatest possible number of homes everything that is best in every department of human knowledge … and to avoid the things which are, or may be, hurtful."[36] His first great triumph was the transformation of the BBC into a public corporation in 1927, supported by a license fee paid by radio owners, thereby liberating radio from the market system and direct government intervention. The government did wield a significant amount of indirect control over the BBC: the government determined the amount of the license fee, and the Prime Minister appointed the Board of Governors. The government also retained the right to take control of the BBC in a national emergency. It has never exercised this power, but the threat of government takeover could cow the BBC into submission.[37] Nevertheless, Britain has never suffered state-controlled radio.

Reith also ensured that the BBC did not have to answer to the public by vigorously defending the BBC's monopoly. The monopoly, originally established to protect the radio manufacturers from competition, gave the BBC enormous cultural power. British listeners had two choices: listen to the BBC or turn off the wireless. The lack of competition gave the BBC the luxury of pursuing a high-minded policy of cultural uplift.[38] The license fee also made the BBC independent of commercial considerations, allowing it to pursue of policy of mixed programming ("something for everyone") designed to cater to minority listeners and expose the masses to highbrow, or at least middlebrow, culture. By the time Reith left broadcasting in 1938 to assume the chairmanship of Imperial Airways, the BBC had evolved into a national institution, in the words of David Cardiff and Paddy Scannell, "as thoroughly typical and representative as the Bank of England—safe, responsible, reliable, the guarantor of the nation's cultural capital."[39]

The Second World War fundamentally altered the BBC. The Corporation closed its regional broadcasting networks (creating one unified Home Service), ceased television broadcasting, and endured increased government oversight for the duration. More important were the long-term changes induced by the war. The BBC more than doubled its staff from 1939 to 1945, an increase in personnel that made change inevitable. Overseas broadcasting expanded enormously, and was paid for directly out of government revenues. Because program-makers needed to evaluate the effectiveness of propaganda, audience research blossomed during the war and became an integral part of the BBC apparatus. The war also revolutionized the BBC's presentation of the news. Reporters in the field provided thrilling descriptions of the fighting, supplemented by recorded material from the war zone. The vividness and immediacy of the BBC's news coverage allowed Britons to connect their own sacrifices on the Home Front to the military effort against Germany.

Most significantly, the war forced the BBC to abandon many of the practices associated with Reith's vision of public service broadcasting. Overall,
programs became lighter, quicker, and in the eyes of some, more "American."
In addition, the BBC adopted "fixed point" broadcasting; the same program
would be broadcast at the same time on the same day each week. Reith dis-
dained fixed-point broadcasting because, concomitant with his idea of the
BBC's mission, he wanted to surprise listeners with programs they might not
normally listen to in order to expose them to high culture. In 1940 the BBC
introduced the Forces Programme, originally intended to entertain the British
Expeditionary Force in France. It featured a much narrower mix of items than
the Home Service, focusing largely on "light" programs such as dance music,
variety, and short talks. By 1942 the Forces Programme was attracting more
listeners than the Home Service, which continued to operate under more
Reithian principles.

The true significance of the Forces Programme is that it began the process
of "cultural streaming within the BBC's output."[40] After the war the BBC
reorganized domestic broadcasting into two distinct services: the Light Programme, modeled on the Forces Programme, and the Home Service, designed
to provide the mixed programming characteristic of the pre-war BBC. The
BBC also restored the regional networks, and gave them a greater degree of
independence. The Light Programme was a national network, available to listeners in all but the most remote parts of the British Isles. The post-war Home
Service was "regionalized;" the BBC's regional stations had the right to opt
into the Home Service or broadcast their own material, at their discretion. The
cultural division of the BBC was completed with the introduction of the Third
Programme, meant to cater to cultural elites and minority interests, in 1946.[41]
This division of the BBC into three networks based on the cultural proclivities
of the audience marked the abandonment of Reith's original belief that broadcasting could bring cultural uplift to the masses. But it also, arguably, made the
BBC more connected and responsive to its listeners. The tripartite division of
the BBC after the Second World War remained the model of sound broadcasting until 1970, when the Light Programme became Radio 2, the Third, Radio
3, and the Home Service, Radio 4. However, two important transformations
in post-war broadcasting would fundamentally alter the nature of the BBC: the
spread of television and the breaking of the BBC's monopoly.

The BBC resumed television transmissions in 1946, but the new medium
had a troublesome infancy. William Haley, Director-General of the BBC from
1944 to 1952, disliked television and wished to keep it subordinate to radio.

Various interest groups boycotted the new medium, including West End theater managers and the British film industry. On top of that, it was expensive to make television programs. The service grew slowly but steadily, and by 1950 television seemed ready to replace radio as the dominant electronic mass medium. The north of England began to receive television broadcasts in 1951, Scotland and Wales in 1952. Audience research figures reflected the inexorable spread of television. In 1955 viewing exceeded listening for the first time, and by 1958 the BBC's average evening audience for radio was just over a third of what it was in 1949. In the same year, the government issued 9 million television licenses.[42]

Just as the rise of television augured a new era for the mass media in Britain, so too did the push for commercial broadcasting. Led by Tory backbenchers and the advertising industry, the commercial television lobby faced an uphill battle. After the war the BBC was at the height of its popularity. The Beveridge Committee on Broadcasting, which reported in 1951, recommended that the BBC's monopoly remain intact. The resounding success of the broadcast of the coronation of Elizabeth II in 1953 put the opponents of the BBC's monopoly on their heels. But, in the end, the commercial lobby carried the day, largely because of their ability to frame the question of commercial broadcasting as one of consumer choice. The advocates of commercial broadcasting simply seemed more democratic than the defenders of the monopoly. In 1954, the Television Act, which established the Independent Television Authority, passed Parliament. Because of these fundamental changes in broadcasting, which occurred during the first half of the 1950s, this book concludes in 1953, the year of Queen Elizabeth's coronation.

Synopsis of chapters

This book begins with an evaluation of the BBC's role in constructing discourses of empire. Chapter 1 examines the key role of the BBC in fostering a culture of imperialism from the 1920s to the eve of the Second World War. Chapter 2 focuses on the ways in which the war reshaped the BBC's presentation of empire, as well as post-war programs. These chapters repudiate the long-held, but increasingly challenged, conviction that, after the First World War, Britons turned away, *en masse*, from empire. To judge from the BBC's programs and audience reaction to them, empire remained an important symbol of British prominence and an exemplar of the achievements of the British character. After the Second World War, the BBC continued to champion Britain's imperial heritage, but it also reflected the decline of Britain's imperial power. Some programs on empire sought to ease the inevitable transition from empire to multi-racial Commonwealth, others crudely reinforced stereotypes of colonized peoples as culturally inferior and in need of British guidance.

Chapter 3 argues that the BBC played a pivotal role in helping to remake the monarchy into a symbol of British diversity. The BBC presented the coronations of George VI and Elizabeth II as celebrations of Britain's multi-national make-up. Each of the BBC's regions carried its own special coronation programs, and royal visits to Scotland, Wales, and Northern Ireland were covered extensively by the regional networks. Each region related to the monarchy in its own way, and the BBC persistently pointed out the multi-national nature of the monarchy.

Chapter 4 offers an introduction and reconsideration of regional broadcasting in Britain. Orthodox models that focus on the centralizing and anglicizing tendencies of the BBC do not do justice to the work of the BBC in Scotland, Wales, and Northern Ireland. In terms of both policy—the establishment of BBC stations for each of the minority national groups in Britain—as well as programming, the BBC nurtured national differences in the regions despite its opposition to the Scottish National Party and *Plaid Cymru*, the Welsh nationalist movement. As part of this effort, Chapter 4 examines an important, but overlooked, aspect of broadcasting history: regional broadcasting during the Second World War. For, although the BBC suspended its regional networks during the war, regional programs continued to be made and broadcast on the Home Service and Forces Programme. Rather than yet another example of English disregard for the Scots, Welsh, and Irish, wartime regional broadcasting saw the BBC, for the first time, project a truly multi-national image of Britain as regional productions had to be carried by the one of the two national networks.

Chapters 5, 6, and 7 develop the arguments of Chapter 4 in the context of Scotland, Wales, and Northern Ireland respectively. Scottish broadcasting was the most self-confident and mature. From its inception, BBC Scotland was staffed largely by Scots. By comparison with the other regions, Scottish broadcasting was well funded and effectively led from the mid-1930s by its dynamic Programme Director, Andrew Stewart. Scottish broadcasting also strove to be effectively Scottish in content, although it may have been too middlebrow or too "lowland." Moreover, periodic conflict with London highlights the history of Scottish broadcasting. Although in many ways the most self-confident and accomplished of the BBC regions, Scottish broadcasters were also quick to take offense at perceived slights (a common complaint was the use of "English" when "British" would have been a more accurate adjective).

Chapter 6 considers BBC broadcasting in Wales. The study of broadcasting and national identity in Wales poses several problems unique to the Principality. For one, the Wales region of the BBC was not established until 1937. Until then, an unwieldy "West" region catered to listeners in Wales and the west of England. Further, Wales was divided by language and culture in ways quite different from Scotland. The traditional, rustic way of life of north Wales was quite distinct from the highly industrialized, urban, and Anglophone culture of south Wales. Defining a unitary "Wales" and Welsh identity, while also struggling for autonomy from BBC Head Office, proved to be a challenge for Welsh broadcasters.

Chapter 7 focuses on the BBC in Northern Ireland. Broadcasting in Northern Ireland was quite distinct from broadcasting in Scotland or Wales. The sectarian divide between Catholic and Protestant inevitably dominated BBC policy in Northern Ireland. Yet, despite the neutrality with which Northern Irish broadcasters sought to conduct themselves, the BBC in Northern Ireland strove to forge an "Ulster" identity for the region. "Ulster" represented an organic, primeval community, based on geography and history. Although the whole purpose of "Ulster" identity was to represent the differences between Northern Ireland and the Irish Free State in a way that minimized the role of religion, it was, *de facto*, a Protestant identity. In addition to this state-building function, the BBC in Northern Ireland represented a vital link to the rest of the Britain. Small and peripheral, Northern Ireland needed the BBC to reaffirm its Britishness as well as its regional identity, making the mission of the BBC in the province unique. Indeed, the BBC itself became one of those institutions through which the Northern Irish Protestants could recognize their British national identity.

In his 1949 memoir *Into the Wind*, Reith commented that "if broadcasting had been taken seriously in 1924 subsequent events in India might have been very different."[43] From the inception of the BBC, Reith was convinced that broadcasting could play a vital role in unifying the far-flung British empire through ties of culture and affection. And the BBC complemented broadcasting to the empire by proselytizing empire to the domestic audience and encouraging them to appreciate the contribution of empire to British life. Early broadcasters obsessed over empire, and it is to empire that we now need to turn.

Notes

1   William Haley to Lindsay Wellington, December 31, 1945, BBC Written Archives Centre (hereafter BBC WAC), R34/420.

2   See, for example, Peter Mandler, *The English National Character: The History of an Idea from Edmund Burke to Tony Blair* (New Haven, CT: Yale University Press, 2006). Nationalism and national identity will be discussed in more detail below.

3   See Benedict Anderson, *Imagined Communities: Reflections on the Origin and Spread of Nationalism* (London: Verso, 1986). Anderson's work will be discussed in detail below.

4   Paddy Scannell and David Cardiff, *A Social History of British Broadcasting: 1922–1939*, vol. 1, *Serving the Nation* (Oxford: Blackwell Publishers, 1991), xi.

5   For an account of the early years of audience research at the BBC, see Robert Silvey, *Who's Listening? The Story of BBC Audience Research* (London: George Allen and Unwin, Ltd., 1974).

6   Anderson, *Imagined Communities*; Eric Hobsbawm, *Nations and Nationalism Since 1780: Programme, Myth, Reality* (Cambridge: Cambridge University Press, 1990); Eric Hobsbawm and Terence Ranger, eds, *The Invention of Tradition* (Cambridge: Cambridge University Press, 1983); Ernest Gellner, *Nations and Nationalism* (Ithaca, NY: Cornell University Press, 1983).

7   Anderson, 6.

8   Ibid.

9   Anderson, 62.

10   Rogers Brubaker, *Nationalism Reframed: Nationhood and the National Question in the New Europe* (New York: Cambridge University Press, 1997), 18.

11   Ibid., 23–6.

12   Linda Colley, *Britons: Forging the Nation 1707–1837* (London: Pimlico, 1992), 6.

13   For an application of the core/periphery model to Britain, see Michael Hechter, *Internal Colonialism: The Celtic Fringe in British National Development* (Berkeley, CA: University of California Press, 1975). On blending, see Keith Robbins, *Nineteenth Century Britain, England, Scotland, and Wales: The Making of a Nation* (Oxford: Oxford University Press, 1989). Robbins notes that blending was ultimately impossible in nineteenth-century Britain: "the demographic facts speak for themselves … England had a commanding role within the structure of Britain." Robbins, 5–6.

14   See Colley, *Britons*, and Linda Colley, "Britishness and Otherness: An Argument," *Journal of British Studies*, 31 (1992): 309–29.

15   Select publications include: Brendan Bradshaw and Peter Roberts, eds, *British Consciousness and Identity, 1533–1707* (Cambridge: Cambridge University Press, 1998); Laurence Brockliss and David Eastwood, eds, *A Union of Multiple Identities: The British Isles, 1750–1850* (Manchester: Manchester University Press, 1997); G. H. Murray Pittock, *Inventing and Resisting Britain: Cultural Identities in Britain and Ireland, 1685–1789* (Basingstoke: Palgrave Macmillan, 1996); Brendan Bradshaw and John Morrill, eds, *The British Problem, c. 1534–1707: State Formation in the Atlantic Archipelago* (Basingstoke: Palgrave Macmillan, 1996); Liah Greenfeld,

Nationalism: Five Roads to Modernity (Cambridge, MA: Harvard University Press, 1992).

16 Mandler, *Character*; Paul Ward, *Unionism in the United Kingdom, 1918–1974* (Basingstoke: Palgrave Macmillan, 2005); Wendy Webster, *Englishness and Empire, 1939–1965* (Oxford: Oxford University Press, 2005); Paul Ward, *Britishness Since 1870* (London: Routledge, 2004); Robert Colls, *Identity of England* (Oxford: Oxford University Press, 2004); Sonya Rose, *Which People's War? National Identity and Citizenship in Wartime Britain, 1939–1945* (Oxford: Oxford University Press, 2003); Krishan Kumar, *The Making of English National Identity* (Cambridge: Cambridge University Press, 2003); Richard Weight, *Patriots: National Identity in Britain, 1940–2000* (London: Macmillan, 2002).

17 Ward, *Britishness*, 4–8. Ward's introduction provides an excellent introduction to the historiography of British national identity.

18 Ibid., 5.

19 J. G. A. Pocock, "'British History:' A Plea for a New Subject," *Journal of Modern History,* 47 (1975): 601–28.

20 Ibid., 605.

21 T. W. Heyck and Stanford Lehmberg, *The Peoples of the British Isles: A New History,* 3 vols (Belmont, CA: Wadsworth, 1992); Hugh Kearney, *The British Isles: A History of Four Nations* (Cambridge: Cambridge University Press, 1989). For other examples of this pluralistic approach to British history, see Weight, *Patriots*; Arthur Marwick, *A History of the Modern British Isles, 1914–1999: Circumstances, Events and Outcomes* (Oxford: Blackwell Publishers, 2000); Norman Davies, *The Isles: A History* (New York: Oxford University Press, 1999); Keith Robbins, *Great Britain: Identities, Institutions, and the Idea of Britishness* (London: Longman, 1998). In addition, the twentieth-century volume of the new *Short Oxford History of the British Isles* is explicitly "British" in approach and concerned in large part with the issue of British national identity. See Keith Robbins, ed., *The British Isles* (Oxford: Oxford University Press, 2002). See also Hugh Kearney, "Four Nations History in Perspective," in *History, Nationhood and the Question of Britain*, Helen Brocklehurst and Robert Phillips, eds (Basingstoke: Palgrave Macmillan, 2004), 10–19, and Raphael Samuel, "Four Nations History," in *Island Stories: Unravelling Britain*, vol. 2 *Theatres of Memory* (London: Verso, 1998), 21–40. The New British History has prompted some scholars to narrowly focus on *English* identity. For example, see Mandler, *Character*; Peter Ackroyd, *Albion: The Origins of the English Imagination* (New York: Anchor Books, 2004); Kumar, *English National Identity*.

22 Asa Briggs, *The History of Broadcasting in the United Kingdom*, 5 vols—1. *The Birth of Broadcasting;* 2. *Sound and Vision;* 3. *The War of Words;* 4. *The Golden Age of Wireless;* 5. *Competition*—(Oxford: Oxford University Press, 1961–95). All page numbers in the notes refer to the 1995 reissue.

23 Raphael Samuel, "The Voice of Britain," in *Island Stories*, 188.

24 Asa Briggs, "Problems and Possibilities in the Writing of Broadcast Histories," *Media, Culture, and Society,* 2 (1980): 11–12.

25 See Scannell and Cardiff.

26 Siân Nicholas, *The Echo of War: Home Front Propaganda and the Wartime BBC,*

1939–45 (Manchester: Manchester University Press, 1996).

27 John Davies, *Broadcasting and the BBC in Wales* (Cardiff: University of Wales Press, 1994); Gillian McIntosh, *The Force of Culture: Unionist Identities in Twentieth Century Ireland* (Cork: Cork University Press, 1999), 69–95.

28 W. H. McDowell, *The History of BBC Broadcasting in Scotland, 1923–1983* (Edinburgh: Edinburgh University Press, 1992).

29 Webster, *Englishness*; Rose, *Which People's War?*

30 Ward, *Britishness*; Weight, *Patriots*.

31 For a brief overview of the history of broadcasting in Britain, see James Curran and Jean Seaton, *Power Without Responsibility: The Press, Broadcasting, and the New Media in Britain*, 6th ed. (London: Routledge, 2003), 107–96, and Andrew Crisell, *An Introductory History of British Broadcasting*, 2nd ed. (London: Routledge, 2002). Except where otherwise noted, the following historical sketch of the BBC is taken from these two sources.

32 The BBC fell under the purview of the Postmaster General because it was the Ministry responsible for telegraph and telephone lines. In its infancy, radio was for point to point communication and referred to as "wireless telephony. " "Wireless" became a common term for the radio receivers.

33 Reith has been the subject of numerous biographies, the most recent and comprehensive being Ian McIntyre, *The Expense of Glory: A Life of John Reith* (London: Harper Collins, 1994). See also Andrew Boyle, *Only the Wind Will Listen: Reith of the BBC* (London: Hutchinson, 1972).

34 Briggs, *Sound and Vision*, 221.

35 Briggs, *Golden Age of Wireless*, 235–7.

36 J. C. W. Reith, *Broadcast Over Britain* (London: Hodder and Stoughton, 1924), 34.

37 The classic example was the BBC's pro-government coverage of the General Strike in 1926, and Reith's syllogism that "since the BBC was a national institution and since the Government in this crisis was acting for the people … the BBC was for the Government in the crisis too." Curran and Seaton, 118.

38 Despite its monopoly, the BBC could not prevent stations in Europe from broadcasting English-language programs to Britain. The continental stations Radio Luxembourg and Radio Normandie produced gayer fare than the BBC. They proved especially popular with listeners on Sundays because Reith demanded that the BBC use Sunday exclusively for church services, inspirational talks, and religious music. See Donald R. Browne, "Radio Normandie and the IBC Challenge to the BBC Monopoly," *Historical Journal of Film, Radio and Television*, 5 (1985): 3–18.

39 Scannell and Cardiff, 17.

40 Crisell, 60.

41 On the Third Programme, see Kate Whitehead, *The Third Programme: A Literary History* (Oxford: Clarendon Press, 1989), and Humphrey Carpenter, *The Envy of the World: Fifty Years of the Third Programme and Radio Three* (London: Weidenfeld and Nicolson, 1996).

42 Crisell, 81–2.

43 J. C. W. Reith, *Into the Wind* (London: Hodder & Stoughton, 1949), 133.

"Jolly proud you are a Britisher:" empire and identity, 1923–39

On the evening of December 13, 1939, Val Gielgud, Head of the BBC's Features and Drama Department, listened to the final installment of the Drama Department's serialized adaptation of A. E. W. Mason's imperial adventure story *The Four Feathers*. The following day he wrote to the producer of the series, Peter Creswell, to congratulate him on its success. He noted to Creswell that the Director-General, F. W. Ogilvie, and the Home Service Board praised the program,[1] concluding that "the romantic formula [was] considered acceptable even in wartime."[2] Creswell had earned the praise of Ogilvie and the rest of the Home Service Board, for his version of *The Four Feathers* proved to be a major undertaking. It starred accomplished radio actor Marius Goring as Harry Faversham and Clive Baxter, reprising his role from the Korda film version of *The Four Feathers*, as the young Harry. Serialized into eight installments, Creswell's radio adaptation employed multiple studios and various effects including "recordings of special Arab noises and chatter and desert sounds" from the Korda production.[3] The start of the Second World War and the evacuation of the Drama Department to Evesham disrupted the production of this ambitious series of programs.[4] But, with the start of the war, the BBC hierarchy was less concerned with the move to Evesham than the tone and tenor of *The Four Feathers*. With Britain engaged in a major war for the second time in twenty-five years, the Home Service Board was concerned that the story of Harry Faversham's redemption through imperial combat might strike listeners as inappropriate.

The broadcast of *The Four Feathers* reveals several aspects of the BBC's relationship to empire and imperialism during the period from its inception in the early 1920s to the Second World War. It is but one example of how various BBC departments, especially Drama, Talks, and Features, extensively mined imperial history and literature for program material. *The Four Feathers* represented a fairly common type of BBC program, the dramatized life of the imperial hero. It was also one of a number of successful imperially themed films to be adapted to the radio. In addition to unashamedly representing Britain's imperial past, the BBC became a consistent supporter of the empire during the interwar years. It presented the empire as an environment in which the best aspects of the British character and British institutions were at work; the empire, as reflected by the BBC, both constructed and reinforced British national identity. The BBC actively sought to explain and justify the empire to British listeners. And although the BBC did not suppress criticism of the empire, the dominant message was uncritical acceptance of imperialism as an integral part of British life.[5]

The BBC and the new imperial history

Chapters 1 and 2 together address contentious debates which have arisen from the "New Imperial History," arguably the most important recent development in the field of British history. Proponents of the New Imperial History argue that the empire had a "constitutive" impact on domestic institutions and British culture. The origins of the New Imperial History can be traced back to two different sources. First there is the path-breaking work of John M. MacKenzie and the other contributors to his *Studies in Imperialism Series*.[6] MacKenzie and his collaborators examine how a range of media, institutions, organizations, and cultural forms constructed and propagated an "imperial vision" in the late nineteenth and early twentieth centuries.[7]

In addition to MacKenzie, the genealogy of the New Imperial History goes back to Edward Said's highly influential work *Orientalism*.[8] According to Said, Europeans came to base their own sense of identity on hierarchical racial differences. Modern European identity was the product of the "othering" of colonized peoples and the establishment of binary oppositions between "West" and "East:" white/black, masculine/feminine, rational/irrational. Both *Orientalism* and Said's later *Culture and Imperialism*[9] have had a profound impact on one group of scholars associated with the New Imperial History. In addition to Said, these scholars take their influences from Marxism, feminism, and post-colonial theory. Much, but by no means all, of this scholarship focuses on the intersections of empire, gender, and sexuality.[10] Although there are significant differences, in terms of theory and methodology, between what Catherine Hall calls the "Manchester School" (i.e. MacKenzie) and the more Saidean approaches, both represent a broad body of scholarship that acknowledges the deep and important impact of imperialism of British society, culture, and politics.[11]

Still, the New Imperial History hardly represents an historical orthodoxy or consensus. The extent to which Britain was "imbricated with the culture of empire"[12] remains very much a contested issue. Bernard Porter, in his recent book *The Absent-Minded Imperialists*, argues that only when the scraps of empire are corralled and de-contextualized, or the definition of "imperial" stretched to include a broad range of phenomena, can one find much evidence of the empire in Britain's domestic history.[13] Porter and other scholars would argue that this is particularly true of working-class Britons.[14] In his book, Jonathan Rose writes that "the majority of ... youths were working-class, and they seem to have been strikingly unaware of their empire ... even after a century of unrelenting indoctrination, most working people knew little of the empire and cared less."[15]

This chapter, and the subsequent one, argue that the BBC committed itself to projecting the empire in a broad range of program types—talks, features, plays, outside broadcasts, variety, and music. Given the reach and potential influence of the BBC, this suggests that empire remained important to British national identity into the 1950s, even after the first wave of decolonization. Certainly, to borrow David Cannadine's phrase, what the empire "looked like" changed significantly from 1922 to 1953, but it was almost always in the BBC's schedules.[16]

The BBC produced and broadcast programs about empire for several different reasons. Some of the empire programming on the BBC was more propagandistic in purpose, produced specifically to try to change or reinforce public perceptions about the empire. Other programs were specifically educational because the professional elite that dominated the BBC despaired at the public's lack of knowledge of the empire. This is suggestive; for while it confirms the commitment of the professional class to empire it also suggests that the majority of the country, the working classes, cared little for imperialism. But a considerable amount of empire material made it to the airwaves because it was popular and entertaining, and an integral part of Britain's history and cultural heritage. Of course, the lines between an "organic" program produced largely to entertain or interest listeners, and propaganda or education, were not always so clear cut. Some audience research numbers seem to confirm the broad arguments of Porter and Rose; empire talks might entice only 3 to 5 per cent of the listening audience to tune in. But other imperially themed programs drew audiences of around 20 per cent of listeners. Rose makes a valid point when he notes that "too often, those who examine literature for evidence of imperialism, racism, or male supremacy assume that these values were unproblematically transmitted to its readers."[17] Yet Rose's research is based on working-class autobiographies and memoirs—admittedly not a large or representative sample of working-class readers and listeners. BBC listener research allows us to consider the reaction of a much larger and more representative group to imperial culture. Presumably, if Britons knew little and cared little for their empire, broadcasts about empire would draw few listeners; but this was not always the case. While it may be true that by the middle of the twentieth century, few Britons knew the difference between a Dominion and a colony, millions still consumed empire as entertainment in the form of BBC programs. Of course, whether listeners tuned into the BBC's empire broadcasts or not, empire was certainly "there," on the air and in the pages of the *Radio Times* and any other newspaper that listed radio programs. Even the act of turning off a program on empire could serve as a subtle reminder of the imperial nature of British national identity.

Broadcasting the British empire(s)

How did the BBC validate empire to its domestic audience? How did it construct an empire suitable for a Britain recovering from the First World War and an unprecedented economic downturn? Despite several variables, such as program format, intent, audience, and the inclinations of the individual program producer, speaker, or performer, several important themes emerge. The empire was, above all, united and robust. The BBC asserted this despite, or rather because of, a number of developments in the 1920s and 1930s that suggested that the empire was drifting apart: nationalist agitation in India, Britain's economic weakness, and the push by the white Dominions to assert their own political agendas and sense of national identity, culminating in the Statute of Westminster in 1931.

The BBC at times treated empire as a monolith—"The British Empire"—that included everything from the settler colonies to the recently acquired mandates in Africa and the Middle East. This was a powerful and comforting image of empire, because of the sheer size of the empire, and also because it suggested that only Britain could unite these disparate and dispersed territories. More often, however, the BBC represented the settler colonies quite differently from the rest of empire. It was the Dominions, and their aspirations for self-government, that caused considerable disquiet in imperial circles during the early decades of the twentieth century. But, the Dominions were

"British," enabling the BBC to produce reassuring narratives about kinship and brotherhood and the extension of British values and institutions, such as parliamentary democracy, around the world.

In contrast, the dominant discourse of the BBC's programs about India and Africa remained, in various forms, the "civilizing mission." The mission, as presented by the BBC, was more secular and less militaristic than that of the Victorians, but equally paternalistic and condescending. The BBC reminded its audiences that the British had brought law, order, technology, and the rational use of resources to the colonies, producing a benevolent modernization. And while the image of a munificent empire deflected growing criticism of imperialism as thoroughly exploitative, it also reasserted the moral and cultural superiority of the British, and the power that they wielded over their subject peoples.[18] Overall, the BBC's programs constructed the empire as a progressive entity, acquired by trade or settlement (not conquest), a truly *British* empire.

The Home Service Board's concern over the "romantic" nature of *The Four Feathers* also highlights a central contradiction in the BBC's treatment of the British empire, one that lasted until the process of decolonization was well under way. This contradiction could be characterized as that between "practical" and "romantic" conceptions of empire, and it mirrored the BBC's commitment to both educate and entertain its audience. On the one hand, the empire represented a serious political and economic commitment. In a mass democracy, the BBC's leadership felt obliged to inform the public about imperial issues. On the other hand, the empire still represented a realm of fantasy and adventure, a place utterly unlike Britain, populated with hazardous and humorous natives and exotic flora and fauna. For the BBC, the empire provided an excellent source of interesting and amusing programs, but these did not often reflect the "reality" of the empire that the BBC tried to present in more serious broadcasts. The fact that entertainment tended to be more popular than education exacerbated the problem. In order to fulfill its goal of interesting listeners in imperial matters, the BBC was often forced into producing appealing programs that reproduced the romantic visions of empire that they, at the same time, tried to moderate.

The extent and range of programs that had empire as their subject matter, arranged by all of the BBC's production departments, were considerable. Variety programs such as *Empire Vaudeville* epitomized the notion of a Commonwealth "family" by bringing together entertainers from the Dominions to perform in one program. In the *Radio Times*, a map of the world highlighting the British empire accompanied the program announcement.[19] The BBC's broadcasts for schools made the empire and Commonwealth, whether as history, geography, or current affairs, a regular part of their curriculum. The Talks Department churned out programs on the empire, and the Features and Drama Departments adapted movies and popular fiction such as *The Four Feathers* to radio, produced specials to honor past imperial heroes, and created empire-themed programs for holidays such as Empire Day and Christmas.

The motives behind the BBC's programs on the empire also were exceptionally varied. Some of the BBC's programs were designed to encourage specific behavior. For example, in the early 1930s, the BBC had many contacts with the Empire Marketing Board,[20] and the Corporation agreed to cooperate when the latter initiated its "Buy British" campaign in 1931.[21] The BBC used its morning program *Housewives' News* for Empire Marketing Board material. The message of the program was twofold. Empire was presented as a boon to the British housewife, providing her with an array of nutritious foodstuff. But also, patriotic women were expected to use their domestic power to further the interests of the British empire by purchasing imperial goods.[22] Eventually, the propaganda element of *Housewives' News* became so overbearing that the Assistant Director of Talks had to reprimand the producer of the program.[23]

At the other end of the spectrum one finds a broadcast like *The Four Feathers*. There is no evidence that this production was anything other than an attempt to make a radio version of a popular book and successful film. Of course, *The Four Feathers* and similar creative programming contained their own ideological and symbolic importance. They recreated fantasy worlds in which typically British characteristics such as courage, perseverance, and governing genius were on display for an eager audience. They offered a stark contrast between British "civilization" and the "backwardness" and "barbarity" of the colonized world. These programs affirmed British superiority not only to Africans and Asians but also to other Europeans. Most of the programming examined in this chapter falls somewhere between these two extremes.

Finally, exactly what these broadcasts sounded like when they went out over the air depended in large part on the individual producer or department head. The BBC's Control Board set broad policy regarding empire programs and, before the Second World War, the BBC received occasional guidance from the Colonial, Dominions, and India Offices. But this guidance was rare and restricted to programs that had a direct connection to current politics. For example, in 1931, the BBC colluded with the government to prevent Winston Churchill from giving a talk on current events in India. As will be discussed below, the Colonial Office, in 1938, successfully prevented the broadcast of a series of talks on the colonies, due to Germany's demands for the return of her African territories.[24] But, essentially, the final program that made it onto the air was the product of the producers and BBC contributors.

A brief look at the family, educational, and social background of key BBC personnel helps us understand why the BBC was so sympathetic to the idea of selling the empire to the British public. Reith was thoroughly conventional in his patriotism and reverence for British institutions, notably the monarchy. Under his command the BBC projected the monarch as a symbol of the unity of the entire empire/Commonwealth (see Chapter 3) and he was devoted to the idea of empire. A veteran of the First World War, Reith remembered the conflict as a powerful moment of imperial cooperation. In his memoirs he described the western front as follows:

> Spots of light from fires, hurricane lamps, candles; supremely moving in terms of what they signified. War cabinets, munitions works, patriotic speeches, national efforts of every kind, all the gigantic machinery of the Empire at war.[25]

When Reith became first Managing Director of the BBC in 1922, he worked hard to put such ideals into practice, and the creation of the Empire Service in 1932 represents one of his greatest victories in this regard.[26] Reith had great faith in the power of empire broadcasting to develop imperial unity and act as "a connecting ... link between the scattered parts of the British Empire."[27] He also appreciated the importance of the BBC as a medium by which to bring the empire to the British public. His persistence played a large role in the King's decision to broadcast from the 1924 Empire Exhibition, and Reith consistently supported the cooperation between the BBC and the Empire Day Movement and Empire Marketing Board.

In addition to Reith, men of conservative stripe and imperial sympathies held many key positions at the BBC. Stephen Tallents, who became the BBC's public relations director in 1935, previously worked for the Empire Marketing Board. John Coatman, appointed by Reith to head the News Department in 1937, held a Chair, funded by the Empire Marketing Board, in Imperial Economic Relations at the London School of Economics;[28] R. S. Lambert referred to him as "full of a mystic vision of Empire."[29] Also in 1937, Reith made Sir Richard Maconachie, a former Indian Civil Servant, Director of Talks, in part to take hold of a department that appeared to have too many left-wing inclinations.[30] Described by one Talks producer as "an Indian Civilian out of the world of Kipling," Maconachie became Controller of Home Programmes in 1941, responsible for all domestic spoken-word output, including school broadcasts.[31] George Barnes, who took over the Talks Department after

Maconachie's promotion, had joined the BBC in 1936 after being person-ally recruited by Reith. A graduate of King's College Cambridge, Barnes knew many members of the Bloomsbury circle. Yet he was also the scion of a long line of Indian Civil Servants and a godson of Lord Curzon. John Green, a producer in the Talks Department, recalled that Barnes "was of the Raj ... an establishment figure with a nagging Christian conscience."[32] And even if they lacked the impeccable imperialist credentials of a Coatman or Tallents, most of the creative and administrative staff of the BBC had similar backgrounds to Barnes; they were members of the professional class, and usually educated at public schools and Oxbridge. The empire had long served as an outlet for such professional men, where they found enormous opportunity to engage in pater-nalistic service, the central plank of their ideological platform.[33] Under the direction of such men the BBC frequently represented empire as an expansive arena for the conduct of selfless public service.

From its inception the BBC acted as an agent to promote the empire among its audience. Empire Day and Christmas Day afforded the BBC opportuni-ties to put on popular empire programs.[34] In 1925, J. C. Stobart, the BBC's Director of Education, contacted the Empire Day Movement about doing a broadcast. He also canvassed the Earl of Meath, founder of the movement, to give a talk to the schools. It marked the beginning of a thirty-year relationship between the Empire Day Movement and the BBC, which often resulted in the latter consenting to the demands of the former.[35] The Corporation's treatment of Empire Day varied from year to year, though it usually included a broadcast to the schools by a representative of the Empire Day Movement, the relay of a speech by some dignitary, and a special program about the empire. The day also received considerable coverage in both the *Radio Times* and the *Listener*.[36]

The main evening program for Empire Day and Christmas Day usually consisted of a feature, about one hour in length, which consisted of a series of linked vignettes from or about various parts of the empire. In the first ever Christmas Day program, "the British announcer was transmuted into an 'aerial postman' who ... intoned his greetings to each dominion and colony to the sound of a striking clock."[37] These Empire Day and Christmas Day programs emphasized the loyalty of the empire and its size, reach, and power. They also importantly reflected the *Britishness* of the Empire, that it was the common accomplishment and responsibility of all the peoples of the British Isles, and the symbol of a shared destiny. The Empire Day edition of the 1924 *Radio Times* noted, "The Spirit of England rises from the waves. She summons the spirits of Scotland, Ireland, and Wales. The four sisters ... storm across the world to found new nations and colonies."[38] The 1939 Empire Day feature, another radio tour of the empire broadcast from Canada, concluded with a representation of the United Kingdom:

> SECOND ANNOUNCER: (*quietly*) now, in the last of this chain of greeting, Canada calls the people of the Homeland. It was their vigour that created the Empire; it was their vision that made it free. From these islands grew the British Family of Nations and with it the principles of individual liberty, of justice, of tolerance, of good government, of fairness, of a world at peace …
>
> FIRST ANNOUNCER: Canada is proud to call across the Atlantic Ocean to the people of Scotland, Ireland, Wales and England![39]

Stereotypical representatives of Scotland (a schoolmaster), Northern Ireland (a linen weaver), Wales (a miner), and England (a boy from Manchester), were brought to the microphone to discuss the links between Canada and each nation of the British Isles. The broadcast concluded with a speech by the King from Winnipeg.[40] For listeners, this reaffirmed the importance of the British world and made the empire the common accomplishment and the common destiny of all the peoples of Britain.

By the late 1920s, Reith and other officials at the BBC had become fully committed to using radio to promote the empire to British listeners. The Corporation became increasingly engaged with the Empire Marketing Board and launched a major series of talks on India in 1929. In March of the same year Reith notified the Assistant Controller of Programmes, "we should boost Empire Day."[41] At a meeting on June 3, 1930, the BBC's Control Board, the highest of the BBC's decision-making bodies besides the Board of Governors, considered whether "further talks should be given to stimulate interest in the Empire." Two weeks later the Control Board resolved "that the Corporation should identify itself closely with Empire consolidation, and that more time in the programmes should in the future be given to Empire matters."[42] The Control Board's decision marks an important point of departure for the BBC. For while the BBC had, as a matter of course, employed the empire as a theme in its programs, the Control Board's decision marks the point at which promoting the British empire became enshrined as Corporation policy.

Talking about the empire

As the Control Board suggested, talks were one way to teach the public about the empire and stimulate interest in imperial matters. And over the next six years, the Talks Department made a concerted effort to fulfill the Control

Board's policy by launching series after series of talks about the empire. The autumn of 1930 saw the debut of three talks series—*Edges of the World*, *Strange Peoples and Places*, and a major series of evening talks on Africa, *Dark Continent*. In the winter of 1931 the BBC debuted *Contact Between Peoples Today*, which, while not dedicated wholly to imperial matters, began with two talks on "relations between ourselves in Europe and the primitive peoples of the tropics."[43] The year 1932 saw four major series on imperial matters: *Other People's Lives*, *Life Among the Native Tribes*, which focused largely on pre-modern African communities, a series of four talks by Kenneth Bell on the Imperial Conference at Ottawa, and a series of morning talks on India which began in the autumn. Following on the heels of these efforts was a major series of evening (6:50 p.m.) talks on the British empire from the autumn of 1933 to the summer of 1934. Anticipating a "maximum" audience for this program, the *Radio Times* boasted that the first talk in the run, by S. M. Bruce, was "an event that [would] arouse widespread interest among British listeners."[44] Also in 1933, travel writer and regular broadcaster Clifford Collinson gave a series of talks entitled *Pioneers in World Exploration*.[45] Though not exclusively imperial, many of the talks focused on the founding fathers of the British empire—James Cook and the Scots David Livingstone and Mungo Park. A series entitled *Travellers' Tales* replaced it in the autumn.[46] In 1935 the BBC broadcast an important series of controversial political talks on India, "undoubtedly the outstanding [talks] series of the year."[47] Broadcast twice weekly on Tuesdays and Fridays, it boasted Samuel Hoare, Clement Attlee, Stanley Baldwin, and Winston Churchill, among others, as contributors. Finally, in 1936, the BBC broadcast two monthly series, *Empire at Work* and *From the Four Corners*, and a weekly series for discussion groups, *The British Commonwealth and Colonial Empire*.

Talks on the empire consisted of three kinds: those that provided an opportunity for debate over imperial policy but limited largely to politicians or experts, such as the 1935 series on India, didactic talks to educate the public about the empire (including talks for schools and adult discussion groups), and light talks, often based on the personal experience of the speaker, designed to entertain.

From 1930 to 1936, the BBC broadcast four major series of evening talks on the empire that were mainly educational: *Africa: The Dark Continent* in 1930, *Life Among the Native Tribes* in 1932, and two series of talks on the British empire and Commonwealth as a whole in 1932–33 and 1936. Additionally, the BBC consistently included programs on the history, geography, and peoples of the empire in its broadcasts to schools.

By and large these programs were informative, didactic, and sometimes quite frank. Problems such as the relationship between settler and colonized in South Africa were at least acknowledged, if not satisfactorily analyzed. In *Dark Continent*, Roy Campbell, a South African poet contributing to the series, told British listeners "colour hatred is rife on all sides … it dates from a century of mutual bloodshed," while actually criticizing whites for the "native problem" in South Africa.[48] In contrast, Reginald Coupland was considerably less forthcoming in his 1936 talk "Nations of the Commonwealth," in which he defended the actions of South African whites: "blacks [are not] accepted on an equal footing with the whites … but remember … how difficult it is for an outsider, six thousand miles away, to see all sides of the problem."[49] The BBC found it particularly problematic to confront the issue of South African discrimination because it contradicted the primary message of these didactic programs. For although the talks covered a range of topics and featured dozens of different speakers, several common themes ran through them: the empire was acquired not by conquest but exploration and trade; the empire and Commonwealth represented a happy union of British peoples and colonized peoples; the empire stood for freedom, justice and individual liberty; the empire benefited the colonized by exposing them to Western science; and the empire paid, although it became increasingly important to demonstrate that both Britain and the colonies derived economic benefits from the imperial relationship. The idea of the British exploiting indigenes was not acceptable. Finally, many of these talks emphasized that the British ought to be proud of their empire. The empire was a grand accomplishment. It represented British power and the British genius for government and administration. It spread British values and institutions throughout the world

For example, in 1928, Collinson gave a series of broadcast talks for schools on empire geography. They are notable for their bombast and national self-satisfaction. In his fifth talk, Collinson discussed the "Keynotes of Empire."[50] "First of all," Collinson began:

> let me remind you that the British Empire was not won by fighting. Australia is ours purely by settlement. New Zealand was handed over to us, of their own free will, by the Maoris. South Africa was bought from the Dutch and in Canada the only part that was conquered was Quebec.

In addition to denying the role of violence in the acquisition of empire, the quote is telling because of Collinson's use of "ours" and "us," especially as he is referencing the Dominions. Some parts of the empire, he conceded, were subjected by force, but where this was the case, Collinson justified conquest through progress. Referring to an Empire Marketing Board poster, Collinson noted that the Gold Coast produced half the world's cocoa, "where it is grown by men who, when I was a boy at school, were bloodthirsty savages."[51] "This," he concluded with a note of pride, "is the kind of thing the British Empire does." And in referencing cocoa, Collinson was not merely emphasizing the "civilizing" aspects of empire, he was reminding his young listeners that their consumption of a favorite product—chocolate—depended in part on empire. He based his second keynote, "freedom, liberty, justice" on the fact that the empire represents "a big family that helps to keep the peace of the world and give liberty and justice to all within its borders." Collinson went on to discuss two more "keynotes." "Self-government" was, he argued, evident from the development of the Dominions and India. The fourth he called "Past and Present," a reminder to his young audience that they would determine the future of the empire: "what may happen in the future will depend on *what you are* and do today [emphasis mine]." In short, the empire depended on the *character* of the British, especially the youth of Britain. Like his Victorian forebears, Collinson regarded education as character development for the next generation of imperialists.[52]

Above all, Collinson argued that a young "Britisher" should be proud of the empire, not merely because of its altruistic ideals, but also because of its size, might, and grandeur. In his final geography lesson "All Aboard the Southern Cross," Collinson took his listeners on an imaginary journey throughout the empire. "People here at home seem to think of the British Empire in vague and muddled terms," exclaimed Collinson,

> but, when you actually see with your own eyes these hot and dusty Islands and ports, with the good old Union Jack waving in the wind from the top of the flagstaffs, you simply can't help feeling a thrill go right through you, and it makes you jolly proud you are a Britisher.[53]

Completing his tour of the world, he concluded this talk, and the entire series on imperial geography in similar language, noting "whichever way you go … you will see the British flag floating in the wind and begin to realise, with a thrill of pride, that you are a citizen of the Empire 'on which the sun never sets.'"[54]

Similar, if more muted, sentiments characterize the 1936 series *Commonwealth and Colonial Empire*. These talks were designed for an adult audience, and presented by a considerably more academic personality, Reginald Coupland, holder of the Beit Chair of Colonial History at Oxford. Coupland never encouraged his audience to be "jolly proud" of the empire, but he and

H. V. Hodson, who gave half of the talks in the series, presented an empire not unlike that of Clifford Collinson. In his first talk, "Bird's-eye View of the British Empire," Coupland explained the acquisition of the empire in exactly the same terms as Collinson: emigration and settlement, trade, and finally, reluctant conquest. "A country was subjected to British rule," Coupland noted, "because it was so lawless and ill-governed that trading could not prosper."[55] Not quite as colorful as Collinson's cannibals transformed into laborers for global capitalism, but a similar sentiment. Coupland also added in the factor of international competition at the end of the nineteenth century, not to explain British motives, but rather to imply that British rule was preferable to domination by another European country.

> Not an acre of the British Empire in the tropics would at this moment be free and independent if it were not British; it would be under some other European rule. One last point. Often, but not always, annexation meant force; but the fighting was generally clean and quickly over. At no time or place was there anything like what is happening in Abyssinia today.[56]

Like Collinson, Coupland and Hodson's broadcasts also emphasized the massive size of the empire. Subtlety and reflection replaced the bombast of Collinson, but the effect was similar. Coupland explicitly stated that he would not "boast" about the size of the empire, but he began his first talk with a sort of grand tour, beginning, of course, in Britain, "the centre of the Empire." He continued until "the circle is completed … the Empire straddles the world … in each of the five continents and in every ocean."[57] Here too was an empire on which the sun never set.

Finally, these broadcasts above all stressed imperial unity, particularly within the "family" of the Commonwealth. In his second talk, "The Nations of the Commonwealth," Coupland noted the legal independence of the Dominions, but he also claimed that "nationalism does not mean separatism, republicanism or a series of new-style of American Revolutions."[58] Of course, Coupland and his listeners took for granted the continued loyalty of the Dominions because of their whiteness. Unlike India or Africa, the white Dominions could handle responsible government; and Britons could be confident of their commitment to the empire because of bonds of kinship and culture. Hodson developed this latter notion further in his talk the following week, "The Nature of the Commonwealth." Here he talked of the Commonwealth as a super-nation, composed largely of British peoples sharing "a common blood and history … and common destiny."[59] His talk focused on the common bonds of language, traditions, and crown that made the Commonwealth a "wider nation [which] has itself a set of fundamental opinions and beliefs that … make up the real glue that holds it together."[60] Hodson, a Canadian, discussed his own sense of Britishness. During one talk he claimed that he felt "two kinds" of patriotism, "patriotism towards Canada and patriotism towards the British Empire."[61]

In addition to didactic lectures, the BBC produced a number of talks that took a lighter approach to the empire. One of these was *Edges of the World*, the first full series of programs to be broadcast after Control Board's decision to align the BBC with the empire. Taking a "human interest" approach, the series consisted of broadcasts by "men whose job it is to work in the out-of-the-way corners of the empire [who] will tell simply and straightforwardly the story of their daily lives."[62] *Edges* tried to present the "reality" of working in the Empire, and attacked romantic versions of British imperialism, especially as portrayed in popular fiction. The "heroic male" and "damsel in distress" conventions of such work were particularly ridiculed. In an article publicizing the series, J. B. Harker savaged the writers of this type of popular fiction and its audience:

> The thought that men, when banished to the South Seas or the Belgian Congo became Men, was very consoling to the sort of lady who goes to the lending library and, beaming at the librarian asks 'Have you anything *nice* in at the moment?' These subscribers don't want men to be Men too near home. The disclosure that men are not 'Men' at the Edges of the World, but merely 'men' may have fatal effect upon the popularity of the writers who cater for them.[63]

According to popular fiction, Harker continued, the typical day for the "lean-jawed, clean limbed, well-tubbed *pukka sahib*" included flogging a native, rescuing a "beautiful but foolish" English girl, twice, and "a long interval … for gritting your teeth and refusing to make love to … [the] English girl." In contrast, the life of "real Empire Builders," to be presented in *Edges*, included meals of "potted meat," "water strongly flavoured with disinfectant," and evenings "alone in a corrugated-iron house."[64] In addition to poking fun at some of the conventions of imperial fiction, *Edges* contained a clear message: life in the empire was not a holiday or an adventure fantasy, but a form of disinterested service.

A similar tone can be found in the series *The Empire at Work*. The BBC broadcast *Empire at Work* monthly on Sunday evenings from January to October 1935, and occasionally thereafter. John Green produced the program, which, like *Edges of the World*, consisted of "vignettes of Dominion and colonial life for the listeners in this country [through] personal experience."[65] Green and his assistants continually stressed the lighter feel and "human interest" angle of the series to potential participants. "It is essential that they should be real travel talks," wrote the Talks Executive to one contributor, "and not ... - geography lessons."[66] Green regarded the program as an antidote to the Corporation's somewhat academic treatment of the empire, and one that could attract a wide audience. The BBC attested to the popularity of the show, although before the advent of listener research it is impossible to know how many people listened to the program, or how exactly the BBC arrived at this conclusion.[67] As in *Edges of the World*, *The Empire at Work* attempted to depict "real life" in the colonies for British listeners, "emphasizing the ordinary as opposed to the romantic aspects" of the empire.[68]

The BBC's decision to try and cure the excesses of fiction and film found its way into numerous programs. While the Talks Department tried to remedy it by presenting the hard life of an empire builder, Variety Department simply ridiculed popular images of empire. In 1932 the BBC broadcast *Africa Shrieks*, a "burlesque of the jungle talkie ... crammed full of tigers, pythons, Masai, crocodiles, pygmies and so on, with maybe a native being eaten by lions." The writers of *Africa Shrieks* included John Watt, future director of the Variety Department, comedian Harry Pepper, and Roger Eckersley, the BBC's Head of Programmes. One can find similar themes in Ernest Longstaffe's broadcast revue, *Ninety Days Leave*. Longstaffe's show was based in part on a location called "Dhustipore," "one of those hill stations on the fringes of fiction—all full of sahibs, punkah wallahs, chotah pegs, tiffin and brave little women."[69]

Like George Orwell's anti-imperialist classic, *Burmese Days*, the BBC attempted to disparage romantic narratives of empire.[70] Of course, unlike *Burmese Days*, which exposed the hypocrisy and rot behind the rhetoric of empire, these shows meant to inspire admiration for those doing the hard work of managing Britain's overseas possessions. Looking back, Green described himself as "very right wing" in the 1930s; he had an ideological, as well as professional interest in a series like *Empire at Work*.[71] "It is very important to interest people in this country in Imperial life," he wrote to one *Empire at Work* contributor, "and I am particularly anxious that we should lose no opportunity in this respect."[72] Yet *Empire at Work* embodied the contradiction between the "practical" and the "romantic" empire that characterized the BBC's images of the empire, a contradiction which derived from the Corporation's dual mission to both educate and entertain. Although the BBC tried to emphasize the simple and ordinary aspects of life in the empire, they often presented the bizarre and the exceptional. Indeed, the subject matter of the talks, and the desire to attract audiences determined that this be so. The first episode of *Empire at Work* opened with a talk "by that *romantic* figure the Bishop of the Arctic, who will say something of his *stirring* [emphasis mine] life in North Canada."[73] This was not an untypical program. Most of the speakers for the series lived under conditions far removed from the experience of the average listener. Green himself preferred shows based on occupations "typical of each part of the world, as opposed to those which … do not vary with the differences of climate and conditions."[74] Each program required a certain amount of escapade or just plain weirdness for *The Empire at Work* to be successful.

Edges of the World exhibits similar tensions, and another comparison with *Burmese Days* is instructive. In the novel, Orwell portrays the loneliness, languor, and enervating effects of life in the empire. But his characters endure their isolation to get rich or to enjoy the prerogatives of rule; there is no higher purpose to British imperialism.[75] The tone of *Edges of the World* is quite different. That life is rough out in the empire makes the sacrifice of the empire builders that much greater. They are admirable, even heroic, *because* they are ordinary men laboring under extraordinary conditions. As Harker notes in his article, they are "the quiet, unemotional, Edgar Wallace-reading men who carry on our Empire."[76] They engage in selfless service; they possess "character," and are exemplary representations of the professional ideal that dominated the BBC.

Two tales regarding the peculiar use of a glass eye offers another vivid example of the tension between the "practical" and the "romantic" in the BBC's empire programming. In 1932, the *Radio Times* reprinted "a good story" from the Talks series *Other People's Lives*. Like *Edges* and *The Empire at Work*, *Other People's Lives* brought to the microphone men and women with odd or amusing tales about their experiences in the empire. This particular tale involved a West African planter:

> The owner of a plantation, finding that his natives worked well when he was watching, less well in his absence, removed his artificial eye and perched it on a rock. He told the men that, even thought he might be far away, the eye would be watching them … This ingenious idea did wonders—until after a week or so work began to fall off again. The planter set himself to find an explanation. Hidden behind a tree, he saw a native wriggle through the grass towards the watching eye, then spring up and clap his hat over it. Work was immediately abandoned.[77]

Clearly, the BBC considered *Other People's Lives* "entertainment." This particular story provided little information about the empire to the audience, but rather confirmed stereotypes that legitimated Britain's domination of African territory (Africans are gullible yet crafty; naturally lazy and therefore in need of the strong hand of Britain to guide them towards progress). A year later, the BBC began one of its educational series on the state of the empire. One of the talks, on government in Africa by the scholar Margery Perham, received extra promotion in the *Radio Times*. Particularly relevant to this discussion was the way the BBC chose to publicize this talk.

> This talk … will deal with the machinery of government in the African colonies. Our own ideas on this subject are derived from novels, and we feel they need bringing up to date. We doubt, for instance, whether the two staple methods are still predicting eclipses *and taking out your glass eye* [emphasis mine]. We are not even certain that all government is carried on by men in sun-helmets sitting in cane chairs on verandas, drinking whisky and quinine, saying, "The Palaver is finished" to a lot of heavily armed chieftains.[78]

In the context of a "serious" talk, the BBC could ridicule the representations of empire they themselves were projecting. What was amusing in one context is suddenly derided in another. The problem for the BBC hierarchy was that the amusing and anecdotal programs attracted larger audiences than the serious didactic programs. In trying to expose the maximum number of listeners to empire material, the BBC undermined its own attempt to educate and reveal what it regarded as the real purpose and challenges of empire. This division between the meticulously constructed but lightly listened to educational program, and the entertaining and popular but hardly edifying program, suggests how empire could still matter, culturally, and to British identity, even though most Britons could only name a handful of colonies when asked by pollsters.

Imperial heroes: history

Of course, the BBC did not merely try to inform British listeners about the facts of empire through a range of talks. Imperial national history formed a cultural milieu from which the BBC drew stories, characters, and locations for broadcasts. In turning to imperial history for program material the BBC continually reproduced an "imperial myth." By the interwar period the myth lost some of its militaristic edge, but it remained central to the British worldview. This myth, like any myths, required heroes. Imperial heroes embodied the myths of empire and served as an archetype of national virtue.[79]

The reproduction of imperial myths and the celebration of imperial heroes during the interwar years were never unproblematic. Some "heroes" of the past, such as Robert Clive or Henry Havelock, received little or no recognition because they were too obviously involved in territorial conquest or motivated by avarice.[80] A program on Cecil Rhodes in the radio series *Short Lives of Great Men*, broadcast right at the beginning of the Second World War, shows the discomfort of the BBC when confronting the militaristic aspects of Britain's imperial heritage. The *Radio Times,* noting that "imperialism has gone out of fashion now, to be replaced by internationalism," claimed that Rhodes's greatest legacy "was his belief in the future of the Anglo-Saxon race, and the friendship of England and the United States."[81] Only a few weeks after commemorating the death of Charles Gordon at Khartoum with a special feature program, the BBC also broadcast a sardonic version of the Victorian melodrama *The Relief of Lucknow.*[82] Yet, even after the First World War, the imperial hero could still play a role not unlike his (the imperial hero was always male, and usually overly masculine) late-Victorian and Edwardian counterparts. He epitomized the best aspects of the national character while his heroic actions explained the acquisition of empire and justified British domination overseas.

To take one example, in 1935, the BBC marked the fiftieth anniversary of the death of Charles "Chinese" Gordon with two programs. In one program, a survivor of the Gordon relief mission came to the microphone to discuss the campaign and his reaction to the news of Gordon's death. The other program was a ninety-minute dramatization of Gordon's last stand at Khartoum. It was no small affair, and the program required numerous actors, the simultaneous use of several studios, and an array of special effects. It portrayed Gordon as a stoic imperial hero, beloved by the "good" natives, and prepared to strike at the "bad" natives.

Gordon of Khartoum aired on January 26, 1935. Peter Creswell, producer of *The Four Feathers* and another feature titled *Fashoda*, wrote and produced the program. Like any special program, it received considerable publicity in the *Radio Times* during the weeks leading up to the broadcast. The promotion in the *Radio Times* established the central themes of the coming feature— Gordon's heroic stature, the righteousness of his mission, and the mutual affection between Gordon and the Sudanese. The *Radio Times* noted: "Gordon was already a national hero … [when he] was slain … a national outcry went up such as the loss of no other British general has ever provoked."[83] The promotion for the program included an illustration of Milton Prior's sketch of the relief of Khartoum, "drawn on the spot." The *Radio Times* also published a portion of the script, depicting Gordon's initial arrival in the Sudan.

4TH VOICE:—As he walks to the Governor General's Palace they press forwards from all sides.

3RD VOICE:—Calling him Sultan and Father, they kiss his hands and feet, and even the ground as he passes.

4TH VOICE:—The tax-collectors' books are burnt before the palace doors.

3RD VOICE:—The instruments of torture, the kourbash—a whip of raw rhinoceros hide—the flogging benches, the branding irons, are broken to pieces in the public square and on the burning pile.[84]

Here, Gordon represents the physical embodiment of the imperial ideal of the 1930s. Gordon's empire is characterized by progress and paternal affection; the British rule in the interests of their subjects. Yet the program maintains a strict racial division between white and black, superior and inferior, civilized and barbaric. The white Gordon brings justice and order to chaotic Africa, defending those who cannot defend themselves. In return the Sudanese accept and love Gordon.

The broadcast opens with Gordon steaming up the Nile River and quickly uses Gordon's physical attributes to establish his status as an imperial hero. The program describes Gordon as "smoking furiously … a small slight man of forty," eerily resembling such fictional imperial adventurers as Cutcliffe Hyne's Captain Kettle, or Edgar Wallace's Commissioner Sanders.[85] Sanders, for example, smokes, is about forty, of average stature and "has 'cold, unwavering eyes' (grey, but which often seem blue)," a physical indicator of his masculinity and steadfastness.[86] Creswell similarly highlights Gordon's eyes as the feature begins. As he chugs upstream, Gordon surveys the Nile landscape with "his light blue eyes, eyes lit with a steadfast purpose. Eyes like blue diamonds."[87] And to confirm Gordon's celibate masculinity, Creswell opens the program with Gordon writing feverishly to a woman in Britain—his sister Augusta, the only woman mentioned in the feature.[88] Similarly, Creswell quickly demonstrates that Gordon is motivated by service, not greed or glory. The program opens in 1874, and Gordon is heading not yet for Khartoum, but to "Gondokoro, to strike a blow at … the slave trade." Approximately ten minutes into the program listeners heard a graphic description of a slave raid.[89]

The performance repeatedly emphasizes Gordon's heroism and integrity, often in contrast to the foolishness and wavering of Gordon's superiors, especially William Gladstone and his cabinet. Gordon represents steadfastness and acceptance of Britain's responsibility to the colonies; the anti-imperial Gladstone represents vacillation and weakness. At Gladstone's first announcement that Khartoum is to be "evacuated and abandoned" Creswell faded in the sounds of an angry crowd.[90] Later, when Gladstone asserts that England is not responsible for the safety of Khartoum, he gets "a storm of booing and hissing" in reply.[91]

Gordon, in contrast, possesses ability and character in superhuman abundance. Like his distant fictional relation Commissioner Sanders, Creswell's Gordon possesses such strength that he can accomplish great feats of organization and governance with almost no assistance. Throughout the broadcast characters repeatedly assert Gordon's greatness: "If the Mahdi is a prophet, Gordon in the Sudan is greater;" "We cannot send a regiment to Khartoum, but we can send a man who on more than one occasion has proved himself more valuable than an entire army. Why not send Chinese Gordon." Upon arriving in Khartoum, Gordon "orders the lives" of its inhabitants, "and never lets them see him other than calm, confident and serene," while "his raw troops draw their only virtue from his courage."[92] The most obvious contrast between Gordon's heroic virtues and the wavering of Gladstone comes when the latter makes his final announcement that the British army cannot relieve Khartoum. Not only does this engender "boos, hisses and cheers—a tumult," but Gladstone receives the following rebuke from a fellow MP, W. E. Forster:

> General Gordon will not desert those who have trusted him. The wonderful resources of that wonderful man may come out when he is left by himself, as they did in China, as they also did in the Sudan when he was there before. He may be found a match for all his enemies; and although he is not supported by English power or the English government, he may yet assert the grandeur of the English character and the heroism of a brave and devoted Englishman ... (fade out on tremendous applause).[93]

Unlike Gladstone, Forster recognizes the inherent courage and leadership qualities of the English, and understands Britain's imperial responsibilities. Gordon represents the best of English manhood and derives his strength and resolve from his Englishness (though many listeners would have known that the part-Scottish Gordon was British).[94]

The historical Gordon succumbed to the army of the Mahdi, and his death was memorialized countless times in print, film, painting, and in wax at Madame Tussaud's museum. Accounts and representations of his death are similar, although they vary in important details. Gordon is usually represented at the top of a staircase, with a revolver, or a sword, or both, facing a horde of Mahdist soldiers. Sometimes he appears poised to draw his weapons; others show or tell of him carrying a Bible. All of them emphasize Gordon's sacrifice, for the empire, for Christianity, and for civilization. He enjoys the fate of imperial martyrdom. In the BBC's *Gordon of Khartoum*, the listener heard that Gordon walked to the head of a staircase wearing "a white uniform with a sword at his belt and a revolver in his right hand." The whiteness of Gordon symbolizes his preparation for a martyr's death,[95] but also racial difference, which is invoked twice more in the short scene dealing with Gordon's death. The forces of the Mahdi wait for Gordon "at the foot of the stairs – dark faces and bright spears;" then one Mahdist "hacks off his [Gordon's] white head." The broadcast notes that Gordon "does not defend himself," but records the brutality of Gordon's death, emphasizing his moral and racial superiority.[96]

A year after the BBC aired *Gordon of Khartoum* it broadcast a similar appreciation of Kitchener. Like Gordon, Kitchener made his reputation as a defender of British imperial interests who died in the service of his country and empire. Further, their lives were linked in heroic action. Kitchener won the decisive battle over the Mahdi and took back Khartoum, thereby avenging Gordon's death. Like Gordon, Kitchener was idolized during his lifetime and after his untimely death.[97] The fact that Kitchener died at sea, when his ship the HMS *Hampshire* struck a mine off the Orkney Islands, only added to his mystique. After Kitchener's death, some claimed that he had not been on the *Hampshire*; others hoped that he had miraculously survived the sinking of the ship and was in hiding, waiting to return when the nation was in dire need; still others asserted that his body was found and buried in Norway. If few believed such fanciful claims, many felt that Kitchener had not been properly honored. A false claim that Kitchener's body had been found caused a major scandal in 1926. To the public, Kitchener represented "Britain's last national hero—the defender of the Empire, the Lion of the Seas, the man who was trusted when he cried 'Your Country Needs YOU.'"[98]

On June 2, 1936, the BBC broadcast *Kitchener*, an hour-long feature program. The program was written by Harold Temperley and produced by Laurence Gilliam. Like *Gordon of Khartoum*, the BBC regarded *Kitchener* as a fitting tribute to a fallen imperial hero and it received considerable publicity. Temperley wrote an article for the *Radio Times*, and the script of the program was reprinted in the *Listener*.[99] Gilliam regarded *Kitchener* as "one of the most important feature programmes in the year," and requested that it be performed twice to "give it greater weight."[100]

The program presented Kitchener above all as an *imperial* hero. Nearly four-fifths of the broadcast was devoted to Kitchener's work in the empire. As in the program honoring Gordon, *Kitchener* quickly established the justness of imperialism and the heroic physical bearing of the man. Kitchener "stands several inches over six feet, straight as a lance and looks out imperiously above most men's heads, slender but firmly knit, he seems built for tireless steel-wire endurance."[101] Also of note is Kitchener's superhuman strength of character. He "fashioned men to his will" and it was "by his dominating will" that the British retook Khartoum.[102] The broadcast created a narrative link between Kitchener and Gordon by opening with the former receiving the news of the fall of Khartoum. "Kitchener," the narrator exclaimed in a statement that smacked of Edwardian jingoism, "lived with but one object—to avenge Gordon; to recapture Khartoum and to reconquer the Sudan for the Empire."[103] Of course, the program also stressed Kitchener's paternalistic concern for the colonized. After his conquest of the Sudan, accomplished "with so much blood and slaughter," the audience heard that Kitchener "thought not of victory, but of peace; not of conquest but of education." To this end he established Gordon Memorial College in Khartoum. In Egypt, "Kitchener's chief [concern] … was for the patient *fellahin* … these men, hard working masses of people, Kitchener lived and worked for."[104] The feature concluded with the organization of "Kitchener's Army" during the First World War, and Kitchener's untimely death in 1916. The final lines of the program reiterated his importance as an empire builder. "He lives in our history as … a conqueror in the Sudan, a peacemaker in South Africa, a statesman in India, the whole Empire's shield in Armageddon."[105]

David Livingstone was perhaps the imperial hero memorialized most frequently by the BBC. He was the subject of at least two full-length feature programs before 1942 and frequent talks on both the National Programme and the Scottish Regional Programme.[106] Better even than Kitchener and Gordon, Livingstone represented the ideal imperial hero for the interwar period—paternalistic, progressive, and without the taint of militarism. Even more than Gordon, Livingstone was a "British" imperial hero, and the BBC's Scottish region handled the major broadcasts about his life. When the Home Service broadcast a feature on the famous meeting of Livingstone and Stanley in 1942, Moultrie Kelsall, from Scotland, produced the program.[107] The region also broadcast its own program, *The Man Livingstone*.[108] And Livingstone, having grown up working-class in Glasgow, was a hero with cross-class appeal.[109]

As with the Gordon and the Kitchener programs, *The Man Livingstone* opened with a testament to the righteousness of the man and his cause. The broadcast, quoting Curzon, praised Livingstone as "a servant of God … [an] indefatigable servant of science, [and] as a denouncer of the slave trade he was the fiery servant of humanity."[110] The abolition of the slave trade was repeatedly emphasized in the program, as in *Gordon of Khartoum*. In the 1942 production, it is Livingstone's desire to stamp out the slave trade that drives him to discover the source of the Nile:

> If I go back to England as the discoverer of the true source of the Nile, I shall be able to influence our government to put down forever the abominable slave trade that darkens God's light here. The Nile sources are valuable to me *only* as a means of opening my mouth with power ... I must never go home till I am able to heal this – this open sore in the civilised world [emphasis text].[111]

Though not a military man, Livingstone possesses, like Gordon and Kitchener, the physical traits of the imperial hero. He was a missionary, but, according to *The Man Livingstone*, not the "dumpy sort of man with a Bible under his arm." On the contrary, his appearance is jarringly like that of Gordon. *The Man Livingstone* describes him as "not taller than five feet eight and a half inches. His shoulders are not broad but he is very firmly set. His chest is full and he stands perfectly erect ... The most striking feature of his face is his piercing eyes."[112] In appearance and in deeds, Livingstone is the personification of the imperial ideals of the 1930s: economic and scientific development, interdependence, and mutual affection between colonizer and colonized.

Imperial heroes: fiction and film

In addition to commemorating imperial heroes drawn from history, the BBC also adopted fictional heroes and adventurers, particularly from the late-Victorian and Edwardian era. The BBC regularly adapted fiction with imperial settings into broadcast plays or serials. These included William Archer's *The Green Goddess* in 1932 and Wilson Collison's *Congo Landing*, the story of a dissolute woman who finds her calling working in Africa at the side of a selfless doctor, in 1935.[113] In 1933, the BBC's *Children's Hour* serialized *The Poisoned Arrow* by Sir George Dunbar, a story set on "the edge of the Empire."[114] With its "lean hard men up on the frontier, and ... tribe of savages called the Kombongs," *The Poisoned Arrow* was a juvenile escapade straight out of the nineteenth century. The *Radio Times* compared the serial to such periodicals as *Boy's Own Paper* and *The Captain*.[115]

Feature films inspired similar ventures. The BBC asserted that such adaptations were based on the novels, and were, indeed, more genuine interpretations of the original books than the films. "With all due respect to Messrs. Korda, Banks and Robeson," noted the *Radio Times* on the film version of *Sanders of the River*, "that film was not exactly our Sanders dream come true."[116] Similarly, before the first broadcast of *The Four Feathers*, the *Radio Times* stated, "for the sake of readers who have seen the film, we may add that Peter Creswell (who has made the radio adaptation) is quite convinced that radio will bring out an entirely different aspect of the book."[117] Gielgud himself wrote to Creswell, "I was particularly pleased by the way in which the original spirit of the book was preserved—a thing which the film so signally failed to accomplish."[118] Yet, the BBC was clearly trying to capitalize on the success of Korda's films. As noted above, the radio adaptation of *The Four Feathers* was based on the 1939 film. In the fall of 1936 the BBC launched a series of short plays based on Edgar Wallace's *Sanders* novels, also in reaction to the popularity of Korda's film *Sanders of the River*.[119] Broadcast every Saturday night, the BBC titled the series *The Palaver Is Finished*. This was an evocative choice, for in the film, it is with these words that Sanders summarily dismisses the native chiefs, thereby asserting his own (and British) superiority.[120] An illustration promoting the series in the *Radio Times* effectively captures the theme of both the film and the BBC serial: a stern, square-jawed Sanders points a pistol into the mouth of a hapless-looking African. A Union Jack is pictured in the background.[121]

Promoting empire in the late 1930s

As the political situation in Europe became increasingly tense in the late 1930s, the BBC re-emphasized its policy of projecting the empire and produced more and more empire programs. In 1937 the BBC broadcast another important series of talks titled *The Responsibilities of Empire*.[122] Later that year Basil Nicolls, the head of program output, decided to include "weekly items about the empire in the Home programmes during the first three months of 1938."[123] These included a dramatization of the Fashoda crisis, special broadcasts from the Empire Exhibition in Glasgow, and a new series of features, *Lines on the Map*. The intention of the *Lines on the Map* series was "to persuade English listeners to take an interest in imperial geography." Though the program was not to consist of "the usual clichés or jingoistic stuff," any late-Victorian Briton would have recognized its themes of empire as a progressive force. A synopsis for the first episode, on transportation, reads:

> Roads have always been as much a cause as a consequence of civilization; they both precede and follow it …
>
> General shape of programme:
>
> I.   Dramatic representation of the frustration and hopelessness of a country without transport—still more of an Empire without transport, then:–
>
> II. Specimen dramatisation of heroic buildings of roads or railways.

III. Bring in cars, motors, etc., in a survey with documentation and realism, noises OB's, etc., of exactly contemporary transport conditions.[124]

Although western technology has replaced Christianity and commerce as marks of "civilization," the story outlined above is a familiar one. Britons bestow the fruits of modernity to grateful natives living in "frustration" and "hopelessness;" engineers have become, quite literally, "heroic" empire builders; imperialism, in this benevolent form, still provides the British with worthy global responsibilities.

In 1938 Nicolls ordered his program departments to maintain the empire's prominent place in the BBC's schedules. He suggested a monthly series from empire locations on the lines of the series *America Speaks*, and the use of recorded programs, "as a means of increasing the representation of the Empire."[125] In response to these requests, the Talks Department proposed a series of evening programs on the empire in 1938, but the Colonial Office demurred because of Germany's recent demands for the return of her former colonies in Africa; the Colonial Office maintained that a series of BBC talks might run the risk of offending German opinion, thereby undermining their efforts to find a settlement on the issue. In deference, the BBC limited itself to one talk concerning the return of mandated territories to Germany, but it also began to prepare for a major series of empire talks to begin in the autumn of 1939.[126] Vincent Harlow, Professor of Modern History at Southampton University, and Vincent Alford, a Talks producer, developed a series of thirteen talks on colonial problems, including contributions from Philip Noel-Baker, Margery Perham, and Leo Amery. But the series was cancelled due to the outbreak of the Second World War.[127]

Several factors account for the BBC's efforts to increase broadcast material from and about the empire in the years immediately preceding the Second World War. As diplomacy broke down in Europe, it seemed only natural that Britain would need the support of her empire in the case of war. Programs that reflected a progressive, just, and united empire would demonstrate to the British public exactly what Hitler would face in time of war, and, hopefully, boost morale. Another concern expressed at Programme Board was "broadcast propaganda adverse to British imperial interests."[128] While it is not exactly clear what worried the Programme Board in this instance, the statement most likely referred to German shortwave stations broadcasting to Britain and the empire. Finally, the BBC may have been trying to defend the empire from potential critics in Britain. In a time of crisis, the empire needed to appear as a source of strength, not weakness.

Therefore, it is not surprising that when war came in 1939, the empire figured prominently in the BBC's programming. Government officials rushed to the microphone to praise the loyalty of the empire and to insure the British people of the empire's support for the war effort. Before the end of October, Anthony Eden, then Secretary of Commonwealth Affairs, made three broadcasts, each time emphasizing the unity of the British people and the British empire in the face of the Nazi threat.[129] As the war progressed the BBC devoted a remarkable amount of time in its schedules to promoting the empire. However, the needs of war and the increasing use of audience research would cause considerable changes in the ways in which the BBC handled the empire for the domestic listener. These developments, and post-war broadcasting on the empire, will be examined in Chapter 3.

Notes

1 Val Gielgud to Peter Creswell, December 14, 1939, BBC WAC, R19/392.
2 Home Service Board, December 1, 1939, BBC WAC, R3/16/1; Briggs, *War of Words*, 104.
3 Creswell to F. D. Executive, October 24, 1939, R19/392.
4 Briggs, *War of Words*, 103–4.
5 For example, in the series *Some Political Ideas of Today*, Kingsley Martin, then editor of the *New Statesman*, debated imperial administration with Sir Edward Grigg. *Radio Times*, March 31, 1933, 828. (Note that the *Radio Times* was paginated quarterly until 1934 when it changed to weekly pagination.)
6 John M. MacKenzie, ed., *Popular Imperialism and the Military, 1850–1950* (Manchester: Manchester University Press, 1992); John M. MacKenzie, ed., *Imperialism and the Natural World* (Manchester: Manchester University Press, 1990); John M. MacKenzie, ed., *Imperialism and Popular Culture* (Manchester: Manchester University Press, 1986); John M. MacKenzie, *Propaganda and Empire* (Manchester: Manchester University Press, 1984).
7 Mackenzie, ed., *Popular Culture*, 9.
8 Edward Said, *Orientalism* (New York: Vintage Books, 1979).
9 Edward Said, *Culture and Imperialism* (New York: Knopf, 1993).
10 See Philippa Levine, *Prostitution, Race and Politics: Policing Venereal Disease in the British Empire* (London: Routledge, 2003); Catherine Hall, *Civilising Subjects: Metropole and Colony in the English Imagination, 1830–1867* (Chicago: University of Chicago Press, 2002); Kathleen Wilson, *Island Race: Englishness, Empire and Gender in the Eighteenth Century* (London: Routledge, 2002); Angela Woolacott, *To Try Her Fortune in London: Australian Women, Colonialism, and Modernity* (Oxford: Oxford University Press, 2001); Clare Midgley, ed., *Gender and Imperialism* (Manchester: Manchester University Press, 1998); Antoinette Burton, *At the Heart of Empire: Indians and the Colonial Encounter in Late Victorian Britain* (Berkeley,

CA: University of California Press, 1998); Mrinalina Sinha, *Colonial Masculinity: The "Manly Englishman" and the "Effeminate Bengali" in the Late Nineteenth Century* (Manchester: Manchester University Press, 1995); Anne McClintock, *Imperial Leather: Race, Gender, and Sexuality in the Colonial Contest* (London: Routledge, 1995); Antoinette Burton, *Burdens of History: British Feminists, Indian Women, and Imperial Culture, 1865–1915* (Chapel Hill, NC: University of North Carolina Press, 1994); Catherine Hall, *"White, Male, and Middle Class:" Explorations in Feminism and History* (London: Routledge, 1992).

11 For example, Catherine Hall finds the "Manchester School" bound by "the traditions of British social history" and "sceptical of new theoretical approaches." Catherine Hall, *Cultures of Empire: A Reader* (New York: Routledge, 2000), 21. MacKenzie critiqued some of the excesses of Saidean approaches to imperialism in his *Orientalism: History, Theory and the Arts* (Manchester: Manchester University Press, 1995).

12 Hall, *Civilising*, 12.

13 Bernard Porter, *The Absent-Minded Imperialists: Empire, Society, and Culture in Britain* (Oxford: Oxford University Press, 2004), 7–13; see also Philip Harling, "The Centrality of Locality: The Local State, Local Democracy, and Local Consciousness in Late-Victorian and Edwardian Britain," *Journal of Victorian Culture*, 9 (Autumn 2004): 227–9.

14 Porter, 177–80, 194–226; Richard Price, "One Big Thing: Britain, Its Empire, and Their Imperial Culture," *Journal of British Studies*, 45 (July 2006): 609; Richard Price, *An Imperial War and the British Working Class: Working-Class Attitudes and Reactions to the Boer War, 1899–1902* (London: Routledge and Keegan Paul, 1972).

15 Jonathan Rose, *The Intellectual Life of the British Working Class* (New Haven, CT: Yale University Press, 2001), 321–2.

16 David Cannadine, *Ornamentalism: How the British Saw Their Empire* (Oxford: Oxford University Press, 2001), xvii.

17 Rose, 322.

18 Said, *Culture*, xvii.

19 *Radio Times*, September 6, 1929, 504.

20 Stephen Constantine, "'Bringing the Empire Alive:' The Empire Marketing Board and Imperial Propaganda, 1926–1933," in *Popular Culture*, Mackenzie, ed., 207–8.

21 Control Board, October 27, 1931, R3/3/7.

22 For an interesting take on how the consumption of imperial products constituted good citizenship, see Keith McClelland and Sonya Rose, "Citizenship and Empire," in *At Home with the Empire: Metropolitan Culture and the Imperial World*, Catherine Hall and Sonya Rose, eds. (Cambridge: Cambridge University Press, 2006), 275–97.

23 J. M. Rose-Troup to Miss Wace, May 2, 1932, BBC WAC, R51/241. "The 'Buy Empire Produce' propaganda material supplied," Rose-Troup complained, "is much too blatant and should be toned down."

24 On Churchill and India, see Scannell and Cardiff, 54. On the cancelled series of

empire talks, see BBC WAC, R51/89.

25 Reith, *Into the Wind*, 27.

26 On the origins of the Empire service, see Gerard Mansell, *Let the Truth Be Told, 50 Years of BBC External Broadcasting* (London: Weidenfeld and Nicolson, 1982), 1–19; Briggs, *Golden Age of Wireless*, 342–62.

27 The above quote is from Reith's address to the empire during the BBC's first empire transmission, December 19, 1932. See Mansell, 2, 7.

28 Constantine, 207–8. During the war, Coatman spent some of his free time lecturing on India to American servicemen. John Coatman to A. H. Joyce, June 18, 1944, British Library, A.P.A.C., India Office Records (hereafter IO), L/I/1/671.

29 R. S. Lambert, *Ariel and All His Quality* (London: Victor Gollancz, 1940), 84.

30 Scannell and Cardiff, 160–1.

31 John Green to Anthony Barnes, July 21, 1988, File Misc. 72/6, Barnes Papers, Archive Centre, King's College Cambridge.

32 Ibid.

33 Harold Perkin, *The Rise of Professional Society: England Since 1880* (New York: Routledge, 1989).

34 For Empire Day broadcasting, see John M. MacKenzie, "'In Touch with the Infinite:' The BBC and the Empire, 1923–53," in *Popular Culture*, MacKenzie, ed., 169–81, and Scannell and Cardiff, 286.

35 See MacKenzie, "Infinite."

36 The School Broadcasting Department tried to dissociate itself from the Empire Day Movement. See Programme Board, 7 February 1936, BBC WAC, R34/600/8. Mary Sommerville, the Director of School Broadcasting, reported to the Programme Board that "School Department were not anxious to associate their broadcasts with the official outlook of the [Empire Day] Movement."

37 Scannell and Cardiff, 287.

38 Quoted in MacKenzie, "Infinite," 169.

39 *Empire Day Broadcast, 1939*, BBC WAC, Script Library.

40 Ibid.

41 J. C. W. Reith to Assistant Controller (Programmes), March 15, 1929, BBC WAC, R34/213/1.

42 Control Board, June 3, 1930, June 17, 1930, BBC WAC, R3/3/6.

43 *Radio Times*, January 2, 1931, 4.

44 *Radio Times*, September 22, 1933, 653.

45 *Radio Times*, September 22, 1933, 655. Among Collinson's many publications were *Life and Laughter 'Midst the Cannibals* (New York: E. P. Dutton and Company, 1926) and *Cannibals and Coconuts* (London: George Philip and Son, 1929).

46 *Radio Times*, October 20, 1933, 191; *Radio Times* November 17, 1933, 503.

47 *Radio Times*, December 14, 1934, 900.

48 "It will be a long while before backward white intelligence can be brought to regard them as a necessary and important factor is South African life." *Radio Times*, October 24, 1930, 241.

49 *Listener*, May 6, 1936, 882.

50 The following based on "Keynotes of Empire," BBC WAC, Scripts, School Broadcasting Scripts, Reel 1/2.

51 "Yet I expect that, not far from your school, you may have seen, in the last month, a poster showing the people of the Gold Coast, where Ashanti is situated, peacefully gathering the cocoa bean." Ibid.

52 On the inculcation of imperial values in Victorian schools, see J. A. Mangan, ed., *"Benefits Bestowed?" Education and British Imperialism* (Manchester: Manchester University Press, 1988), and J. A. Mangan, ed., *The Imperial Curriculum: Racial Images and Education in the British Colonial Experience* (London: Routledge, 1993).

53 "All Aboard the Southern Cross," BBC WAC, School Broadcasting Scripts, Reel 1/2.

54 Ibid.

55 *Listener*, April 29, 1936, 802.

56 Ibid., 802–3.

57 Ibid., 802.

58 *Listener*, May 6, 1936, 883.

59 *Listener*, May 13, 1936, 910. The quote is in reference to a potential war: "If any of them have to make up their minds whether they will fight in support of other members of the Commonwealth who have been drawn into war, their remembrance of common blood and history, and their recognition of a common destiny, will sway them powerfully over and above all other considerations."

60 Ibid., 910.

61 Ibid., 908.

62 *Radio Times*, August 22, 1930, 373.

63 Ibid., 375.

64 Ibid.

65 John Green to Colonel Vanier, December 10, 1934, BBC WAC, R51/133.

66 S. J. de Lotbinière to C. H. Dale, November 23, 1934, Ibid.

67 "Listeners seem to be unanimous in their opinion that this series … is the very thing that was needed on Sunday nights." *Radio Times*, April 26, 1935, 18. See also *Radio Times*, September 6, 1935, 18.

68 Green to Mr James, n.d., BBC WAC, R51/133.

69 *Radio Times*, October 7, 1932, 11.

70 Take, for example, when John Flory "rescues" Elizabeth Lackersteen from a Burmese water buffalo. George Orwell, *Burmese Days* (San Diego: Harcourt Brace and Company, 1962), 79–81. See also Daniel Bivona, *British Imperial Literature: Writing and the Administration of Empire* (Cambridge: Cambridge University Press, 1998).

71 Green to Anthony Barnes, July 21, 1988, File Misc. 72/6, Barnes Papers, Archive Centre, King's College Cambridge.

72 Green to Vanier, December 10, 1934, BBC WAC, R51/133.

73 *Radio Times*, January 4, 1935, 18.

74 Green to James, n.d., BBC WAC, R51/133. The occupations featured in *The Empire at Work* included: fur trapper, lumberjack, magistrate from the Solomon

Islands, schoolteacher in Nigeria, and Rhodesian tobacco farmer, among others. *Radio Times*, February 7, 1935, 20; *Radio Times*, March 1, 1935, 19; *Radio Times*, September 6, 1935, 18.

75 As Flory exclaims to Dr Veraswami, "I'm here to make money, like everyone else." Orwell, 39.

76 *Radio Times*, August 22, 1930, 375. Similarly, whereas Harker describes the "real," decent empire-builders as "Edgar Wallace-reading," Orwell singles out Wallace for abuse in *Burmese Days*. Flory, in contrasting Burma to Paris for the benefit of the recently arrived Elizabeth Lackersteen, notes: "It's not white wine and Marcel Proust here. Whisky and Edgar Wallace more likely. But if you ever want books, you might find something you like among mine. There's nothing but tripe in the Club library." In addition to popular thrillers, Wallace authored *Sanders of the River* and its sequels. Orwell, 85.

77 *Radio Times*, September 9, 1932, 602.

78 *Radio Times*, February 9, 1934, 309. When the BBC broadcast a serial based on *Sanders of the River* in 1936, they titled it, of course, *The Palaver is Finished!* The phrase "predicting eclipses and taking out your glass eye" is also a reference to H. Rider Haggard's novel *King Solomon's Mines*, which the BBC adapted for radio. See below.

79 Robert H. MacDonald, *The Language of Empire* (Manchester: Manchester University Press, 1994), 81–108; John M. MacKenzie, "Heroic Myths of Empire," in *Popular Imperialism and the Military*, MacKenzie, ed. See also Kathryn Tidrick, *Empire and the English Character* (London: I. B. Tauris, 1990), 6–47.

80 For example, in November 1940, the BBC cancelled a proposed Clive program because of "possible topical implications," probably because it might prove offensive to Indian opinion. On Henry Havelock as an "imperial hero," see MacKenzie, "Myths," 116–21.

81 *Radio Times*, December 7, 1939, 670.

82 *Radio Times*, February 15, 1935, 4. The fact that the BBC broadcast *The Relief of Lucknow* at all was very likely due to the satirical nature of the program. For example, a film version of *The Relief of Lucknow* was banned by the British Board of Film Censors in 1938 over concern that it would "revive memories of the days of conflict in India which it has been the earnest endeavour of both countries to obliterate." See Jeffrey Richards, *The Age of the Dream Palace: Cinema and Society in Britain, 1930–1939* (London: Routledge and Kegan Paul, 1984), 104, 144–5. The BBC was similarly sensitive to Indian opinion. See note 80, above.

83 *Radio Times*, January 4, 1935, 4.

84 *Radio Times*, January 18, 1935, 11.

85 *Gordon of Khartoum*, BBC WAC, Script Library, 1.

86 MacDonald, 224.

87 *Gordon of Khartoum*, BBC WAC, Script Library, 1.

88 In the script, Queen Victoria is simply referred to as "woman's voice." She has a few lines, but is never named in the broadcast. Ibid.

89 Ibid., 2, 4–5. "The assault! Huts burning! The very old and very young murdered

as being useless! Women and men, the young, the able bodied torn away! Marching now across the desert with the yoke on their backs. Skeletons lying bleached in the track of the raiders."

90 Ibid., 12.

91 Ibid., 21–2.

92 Ibid., 10, 14, 39.

93 Ibid., 37.

94 Herbert Wilcox's film *Sixty Glorious Years* uses the episode of the death of Gordon to critique the government's policy of appeasement. Although *Gordon of Khartoum* presents Gladstone as a cautious and weak politician, it does not make an explicit critique of British foreign policy. On *Sixty Glorious Years,* see Richards, *Dream Palace,* 265–8.

95 MacDonald, 98.

96 "Men are slashing at him with their swords. A dozen spears are in his body. As he falls one hacks off his white head." Seconds later listeners heard the Mahdists gloating over the decapitated head, now "stained and fouled." *Gordon of Khartoum,* 47, 49–50.

97 The following is from Joanna Bourke, "Heroes and Hoaxes: The Unknown Warrior, Kitchener and 'Missing Men' in the 1920s," *War and Society* 13 (October 1995): 41–62.

98 Ibid., 49.

99 *Listener,* June 3, 1936, 1048–9.

100 Laurence Gilliam to Director of Programme Planning, November 11, 1935, BBC WAC, R19/609.

101 *Kitchener,* BBC WAC, Script Library, 2.

102 Ibid., 4, 3.

103 Ibid., 1.

104 Ibid., 7, 9–10, 22. Likewise, in an increasingly democratic Britain, it did not hurt to show Kitchener as the champion of the Egyptian working class.

105 Ibid., 31.

106 *Radio Times,* April 24, 1925, 216; *Radio Times,* May 12, 1933, 354; *Radio Times,* October 20, 1933, 191; *Radio Times,* March 18, 1938, 45.

107 *Stanley and Livingstone,* BBC WAC, Scripts, Scottish Regional Scripts, Reel 132.

108 Although produced in Scotland, the BBC broadcast the program to all the regions. They also repeated the broadcast on the Scottish network. *The Man Livingstone,* BBC WAC, Script Library.

109 *The Man Livingstone* emphasized Livingstone's humble origins, mostly to identify him with the Scottish, working-class listeners who made up a majority of the Scottish regional station's audience. Ibid., 4–6.

110 Ibid., 1.

111 *Stanley and Livingstone,* 16.

112 *The Man Livingstone,* 23.

113 See the *Radio Times,* December 23, 1932, 939; *Radio Times,* October 18, 1935.

114 *Radio Times,* September 29, 1933, 4.

115 Ibid. For the role of juvenile fiction in transmitting imperial ideals, see Kathryn Castle, *Britannia's Children: Reading Colonialism Through Children's Books and Magazines* (Manchester: Manchester University Press, 1996); Jeffrey Richards, ed., *Imperialism and Juvenile Literature* (Manchester: Manchester University Press, 1989); J. S. Bratton, "Of England, Home, and Duty: The Image of England in Victorian and Edwardian Juvenile Fiction," in *Popular Culture*, MacKenzie, ed., 73–93.
116 *Radio Times*, September 25, 1936, 5.
117 *Radio Times*, August 18, 1939, 4.
118 Gielgud to Creswell, December 14, 1939, BBC WAC, R19/392.
119 For an analysis of the film versions of *The Four Feathers* and *Sanders of the River,* see Jeffrey Richards, *Films and British National Identity: From Dickens to Dad's Army* (Manchester: Manchester University Press, 1997), 34–40.
120 Ibid., 34.
121 Unfortunately, there is no script for this 1936 adaptation at the BBC Written Archive Centre. A script for the 1946 serialized adaptation of *Sanders of the River* has survived. I will discuss this adaptation of *Sanders* in Chapter 2.
122 Control Board, March 2, 1937, BBC WAC, R3/3/12.
123 Programme Board, August 19, 1937, BBC WAC, R34/600/9.
124 Leslie Stokes to Northern Regional Director, December 3, 1937, BBC WAC, R19/304.
125 Programme Board, June 23, 1938, BBC WAC, R34/600/10.
126 Richard Maconachie, "Record of Interview at the Colonial Office," October 21, 1938; Maconachie to Nicolls, November 22, 1938; Barnes to Maconachie, n.d., BBC WAC, R51/89.
127 See BBC WAC, R51/90.
128 Programme Board, June 30, 1938, BBC WAC R34/600/10.
129 *Listener*, September 14, 1939, 503; October 12, 1939, 702; November 2, 1939, 843.

2

From the war to Westminster Abbey: the BBC and the empire, 1939–53

For the historian, examining the BBC's representation of empire during the Second World War is both challenging and particularly revealing. Consistent with its policies from the 1930s, the BBC broadcast a considerable number of empire programs. As Chapter 1 made clear, these pre-war programs carried a significant amount of ideological content. But during the war, the empire and Commonwealth had to be constructed with even greater deliberation and precision. Although the BBC had resolved, as early as 1930, to make more room in its schedules for programs about the empire, it was only during the Second World War that the BBC established detailed guidelines as to how this was to be done. Ambiguous information, programs potentially offensive to an ally, or material that could be used against the British in enemy broadcasts had to be avoided at all costs. The BBC did curtail certain images of imperialism, but it did not play down the empire.[1] With the conclusion of the Second World War, empire ceased to be a pressing propaganda problem, but the BBC did not radically reduce the representation of empire in its schedules. Instead the Corporation reiterated its general commitment to doing imperial-themed programs. Indeed, imperial culture, at least in broadcasting, enjoyed a revival after the war as the BBC rediscovered that the empire could provide an appealing backdrop for light, entertaining programs as well as material for more didactic broadcasts.

This chapter takes up many of the arguments established in Chapter 1. The sheer quantity of empire programs generated during the war is impressive, given the myriad demands made on the BBC by the government. The BBC continued to employ the empire as a symbol of *British* unity and common effort. The themes of the benevolence of British rule and imperial unity, well established in the programs of the 1930s, continued during the war. And the tension within the BBC between education, and entertainment, discussed in

Chapter 1, took on a new urgency during the war. As the conflict dragged on, the BBC became increasingly committed to the idea that the British public, particularly the working class, needed to learn about and appreciate the importance of the empire. To this end, the BBC experimented with new forms of programming to attract this audience and, they hoped, make them interested in imperial matters. When the Corporation's first efforts, interview programs such as *Dominion Commentary* and *Palm and Pine*, attracted disappointing audiences, it quickly developed methods to make empire more appealing. This included program "infiltration," the insertion of Empire material into popular broadcasts such as *Brains Trust* or *Postscripts*, and the use of different program formats more amenable to listeners such as discussions, quiz shows, and variety.

The post-war structure of the BBC encouraged the continuation of the BBC's janus-faced policy towards the empire as either a serious political matter or a source of entertainment. With the division of the BBC after the war into the Home Service, Light Programme, and Third Programme, serious discussion about imperial issues could be safely quarantined on the Third, which attracted few listeners. Lighter but still informative fare appeared on the Home Service with mixed success. Popular imperial adventure stories, like H. Rider Haggard's *King Solomon's Mines* and A. E. W. Mason's *The Four Feathers* drew large audiences when carried by the Light Programme.

Despite the continuities with the 1930s, the war inevitably conditioned the BBC's representation of empire. The Corporation scotched bombast and programs that invoked past militarism. Further, empire and imperial-themed programs were used to make general propaganda points about British values and Britain's role in the war. Three aspects of the BBC's projection of empire during the period 1939–53 especially stand out. First, empire programs during and after the war emphasized the full equality of the Commonwealth members and the cultural bonds that tied it to Britain. The Commonwealth nations supported Britain in her time of greatest need not because they had to, but because they wanted to. From the middle of the war, this Commonwealth ideal came to be applied to India, and to some extent other parts of the empire, as well as the white Dominions.

Second, the BBC promoted an image of empire that could accommodate itself to declared war aims and the social and cultural conditions of the "people's war."[2] In *Ornamentalism*, David Cannadine argues that the British projected their own highly stratified class system onto the societies they colonized. P. J. Marshall makes a similar argument, suggesting that British imperial identity is best thought of as a mirror in which Britain saw its best, idealized self.[3] While *Ornamentalism* has been criticized for asserting too strongly the primacy of class over race, its central thesis that ideas about social class conditioned British perceptions of empire is borne out by the actions of the BBC during the war. As the war transformed traditional, hierarchical views of British society into hopes for a more egalitarian Britain, images of empire required a similar over-haul. Wendy Webster coined the term "people's empire" to describe this recon-figuration and has examined its deployment in film and other media during the war.[4] The discourse of the "people's war" forced the professional elites who managed the BBC to remake the empire into something more suitable for a social democracy. The pivotal year was 1942, when the public, and to a lesser extent, the official mind, became fervent about the issue of reconstruction after the physical destruction caused by the Blitz and the publication of the Beveridge Report. The BBC embraced the idea of the "people's empire" but constructed a similar yet alternative vision. The BBC framed the empire as a "state socialist empire," or perhaps a "professional's empire" where the ideal of service by government experts seamlessly replaced the *noblesse oblige* that characterized the imperial vocation during the previous one hundred years.

Third, progressive themes such as the Commonwealth ideal of brotherhood and the "professional empire" continued after war, but the mid-1940s also saw a revival, in broadcasting, of rousing and racist juvenile imperial fiction. From 1946 to 1949, the BBC's Drama Department produced several serial-ized adaptations of imperial fiction: *King Solomon's Mines, Allan Quatermain, Sanders of the River, Captain Kettle, The Four Feathers*, and *No Other Tiger*. After the 1939 Drama production of *The Four Feathers*, the BBC largely ignored the imperial adventure story. The predominant themes of imperial propaganda during the war were tolerance, cooperation, and mutual respect within the empire. Dramas and Features on empire focused on the work of education, or the eradication of pests like locusts and the tsetse fly—what John MacKenzie has called "the empire of peace and economic regeneration."[5] Faversham, Sanders, and Quatermain represent the empire of conquest, rule, and eco-nomic exploitation. These were novels written during the heyday of empire, when one-quarter of the globe was red and Britannia ruled the waves. The BBC produced extraordinarily faithful adaptations, reproducing the casual racism and hierarchy of racial difference characteristic of the Victorian and Edwardian periods. Yet the BBC did not seem to recognize the contradiction between the "professional empire" or the idea of a multi-racial Commonwealth, and these rather different representations of empire; nor did they find it problematic that these adaptations drew huge audiences by comparison with programs that reflected the "professional empire."

Based on the work of the BBC, it seems clear that an imperial popular culture persisted in Britain well after the end of the Second World War. William Haley, the Director-General from 1944 to 1952, reaffirmed the BBC's commitment to projecting empire and during this time the BBC produced a remarkable amount of programs on the topic. More importantly, some of these programs garnered large audiences. The BBC did not succeed in fully educating Britons about their empire, but it insured that empire remained an important part of the cultural baggage of Britons into the second half of the twentieth century.

The first war-time empire broadcasts

Following policies laid down before the war, the BBC did its best to make sure that the British public was well aware of the importance of the empire's war effort. For example, the cover of the September 28 issue of the *Listener* depicted "India at War," and included a reprint of a talk delivered by Lord Hailey, former Governor of the Punjab and the United Provinces, assuring the loyalty of India, praising the efforts of the Indian Princes, and claiming that the Congress Party stood against the Nazis.[6]

More important than the ministerial speeches was the creative programming produced by the BBC in the first year and a half of the war. This included a series on the *Makers of Empire*[7] and *The Empire Answers*, "a dramatic chronicle of the entry of the nations of the British Commonwealth into the war," broadcast on October 6.[8] Produced by Laurence Gilliam, it, like his earlier Empire Day and Christmas Day broadcasts, took the listener to various outposts of the empire to hear about war preparations and declarations of loyalty from the colonies. The heavy-handed manner in which the Viceroy brought India into the war did not feature in the program; nor did the demands of Congress for an independent India. Looking back, Gilliam assessed the importance of the program, and the empire, to Britain's psyche at the beginning of the war. *The Empire Answers*, he wrote, "reassured us of the strength of the ties of kinship. We were 'not alone' and were immensely comforted."[9] The reassurance provided by programs like *The Empire Answers* was badly needed in the first weeks of the war, for the immediate response of the empire was not so enthusiastic as portrayed by the BBC. Eire quickly declared neutrality; South Africa nearly did the same. Indian opinion about the war was split, and even anti-Nazi Indians remained suspicious of British intentions.

The BBC's first regular empire program for its domestic audience, *Dominion Commentary*, began in November 1939, and was broadcast fortnightly on Saturday (later Tuesday) nights at 9:20. Modeled after Raymond Gram Swing's highly successful talks from America, *Dominion Commentary* employed a variety of speakers from Australia, New Zealand, Canada, and South Africa to discuss politics and the war effort of the Commonwealth. The talks were placed so as to attract a large audience—right after the news at 9:00 p.m. In the autumn of 1940, The BBC added two new programs, *Palm and Pine*, and *In It Together*: the latter referencing the war effort, the former Kipling's poem *Recessional*. Their format was similar to *Dominion Commentary*; representatives from the Commonwealth speak directly to British listeners in their own words. But the subjects of *Palm and Pine* and *In It Together* turned from politics and the war to everyday life, "the trade they followed and the land they lived in, which may be commonplace to them but will be romantic to the people of Great Britain." Vincent Alford, the producer of *Palm and Pine*, characterized it as "definitely not propaganda, just good tough guy stuff."[10] Both programs attempted to create an air of friendly conversation and informality, in contrast to the pomp associated with empire. Guests referred to the British host, Dr Thomas Wood, as "Doc," and to themselves by a nickname—"Tony" or "Ribs." These programs were designed to demonstrate the loyalty of the Dominions to the war effort, but avoided outright patriotism. One episode of *In It Together* opened with an *homage* by Wood to the empire troops that arrived in 1914, to the somewhat affected embarrassment of his Australian guest.[11] The program tried to convey the message that the Commonwealth troops were not "heroes," but merely average men who, like the Tommies, were willing to take on the tough job ahead of them.

These initial attempts by the BBC to reflect the empire in the Home Service met with mixed success. During its fourteen months on the air, *Dominion Commentary* attracted an average weekly audience of 14.5 per cent of all potential radio listeners. This represented a considerable number of people tuning in—over 4 million. Yet it proved disappointing compared to the number of listeners who tuned in to *American Commentary* each fortnight. The Raymond Gram Swing talks had an average audience of 5,800,000 in October 1940.[12] "The problem is not easy," the Director of Talks reported to the Controller of Home Programmes:

> The main subject of the commentaries was inevitably the Dominions' war effort and it was difficult to make this [as] interesting to the Home audience as, for instance, the American commentaries, which were not confined to that subject. The South African Commentary tended to be an embarrassment politically.[13]

Palm and Pine also produced mixed results. Maconachie praised the show for being "as good as anything we have ever had from the empire," and considered that one or two of the episodes had been "remarkable." Yet, *Palm and Pine* proved even less appealing than *Dominion Commentary*, attracting only 10 per cent of the listening audience. Alford felt the departure of the ANZAC troops, who were featured in the show, hurt its ratings. Others suggested that the title deterred listeners. For Maconachie, a consistent pessimist when it came to public interest in imperial matters, the problem was simply "resistance to talks about Empire."[14]

Although *Palm and Pine* was cancelled in April 1940 to make room for *The Week in Westminster*, the BBC continued to design and prepare a variety of empire programs. The BBC celebrated relevant Dominion holidays[15] and marked Empire Day in 1941 with a feature, *Brothers in Arms*, "which focused in a forty-five minute programme the unbreakable unity of the Empire."[16] As with previous Empire Day programming, care was taken to ensure that the empire was represented as a British achievement. The Director of Programme Planning rejected the proposal to include a performance of "Merrie England," in the program because "it would raise a storm from our friends across the Scottish and Welsh borders."[17] Instead, the BBC substituted a new Dyson song, "The Motherland."

Pepper-pots and program infiltration

Complaints from the Dominions Office about the presentation of the empire in domestic broadcasts,[18] and the apparent lack of popular interest in such programs, seemingly confirmed by Listener Research numbers, forced the BBC, not for the last time, to rethink its method and message in regard to empire programs. In August 1941, Maconachie met with E. Rawdon-Smith and Noel Sabine, Publicity Officers for the Dominions and Colonial Offices respectively, to discuss empire representation in the domestic services. They also enquired about the possibility of using features, Sabine writing directly to Laurence Gilliam about the matter.[19] Their discussion reflected on the shortcomings of *Dominion Commentary* and *Palm and Pine*. Maconachie agreed with Rawdon-Smith and Sabine that "Empire subjects and Empire characters should find a regular space throughout the year in our talks." But he felt the need to try something other than a new series of interviews.

Two strategies emerged out of this meeting between the Talks Department and the Dominions and Colonial Offices. Instead of starting a new series on the empire it was decided that individual empire talks should be sprinkled throughout the schedule. Talks Department referred to this as the "pepper-pot" method and found it convenient for several reasons. With domestic output limited to just the Home Service and the Forces Programme, broadcast time was precious, and there was little room for a new series of talks. The extraordinary demands of wartime broadcasting—programs to support government campaigns, information bulletins, regional programs, and special programs for wartime allies (e.g. *News in Norwegian*) further exacerbated the situation. Pepper-potting also helped insure the quality of the talk and kept a poor talk from ruining a series that the department had spent considerable time and effort preparing. The BBC also began to disseminate empire propaganda by way of program infiltration. Program infiltration was an early form of product placement, the insertion of empire-related material into popular programs. Maconachie explained this new approach to the Regional Programme Directors in September 1941:

> We have been asked by the Dominions Office whether we can include in our programmes more talks on this subject [Empire]. It seems to me that the object of such talks, to make the Home listener aware of the Empire … is best achieved not by a series labeled "Empire" or "Dominions" but by the infiltration into our general programmes of speakers from the Dominions. I should be grateful therefore if … you would bear in mind the desirability of including material of this kind. "At Home Today" is an obvious place for descriptive talks of the travelogue kind.

On the same day, Maconachie released a memo suggesting that empire speakers be considered for the BBC's popular magazine program *The World Goes By*. [20]

This new thrust satisfied the Dominions and Colonial Offices. Rawdon-Smith and Sabine seemed to concur with the policy that "quality rather than quantity" should be the standard by which empire talks were broadcast. Nevertheless, the Dominions Office began to request regular updates on the number of empire talks in the Home Service. In the fifteen weeks between August 31 and December 13, 1941, the BBC broadcast seven weekday evening talks on some aspect of the empire. This figure, though it might seem unimpressive, represented nearly one-quarter of the weekday evening talks given during this period. [21] The Talks Department also inserted Dominion speakers to deliver the popular Sunday night *Postscripts* after the 9:00 news. Of the thirteen *Postscripts* given during this period, four were by Dominion speakers. [22] One of these proved highly successful, and confirmed for the Talks Department the effectiveness of the "pepper-pot" method. Listener Research reported a 74 per cent favorable rating for the talk. "The report" George Barnes wrote Rawdon-Smith, "stated … that Baume [the post-scripter] was … compared to his advantage with the American post-scripters … that it was good to hear a representative of Dominion opinion."[23] Barnes's reference to American speakers is significant. It reflects not only the department's disappointment that *Dominion Commentary* failed to deliver the same number of listeners as the American version of the program, but also a certain anxiety regarding the interest showed by the British public in American politics and popular culture. The entry of the United States into the war on December 7, 1941, amplified these concerns.

Re-tooling empire for the "people's war"

Events from December 1941 to March 1942 again forced the BBC to reconsider its policy towards the empire. The entry of America, and American men, money, and arms into the war ensured an ultimate British victory. Churchill was euphoric: "So we have won after all! … England would live; Britain would live; the Commonwealth of Nations and the Empire would live."[24] Yet, the American alliance was problematic. Many within the United States government, and a large section of American public opinion, regarded the British empire as an anachronism, a source of British weakness, and contrary to positive war aims. After 1941 the empire needed to be defended against both Hitler's propaganda and Britain's newest and most powerful ally. And while America's entry into the war aroused neither popular celebration nor affection, American culture appeared to be more popular than ever and renewed fears of "Americanization."[25] Thus, the BBC was required to both foster Anglo-American understanding and encourage the British public to take more interest in imperial, as opposed to American, affairs. The BBC often contrasted empire programs to programs about America, at times almost regarded as a defense against American cultural penetration. To many at the Corporation, the empire could still represent the best aspects of the British character.[26]

Churchill's elation at America's declaration of war did not last long. To use Lawrence James's terse phrase, "1942 was a bleak year for the British Empire."[27] Britain experienced a number of humiliating military setbacks in Asia after the Japanese attack on Pearl Harbor. Hong Kong fell to Japanese forces on Christmas Day. The Japanese navy quickly sank the *Prince of Wales* and the *Repulse*, the only ships that could be spared for action in Asia. The fall of Singapore in February was perhaps the hardest blow. British prestige in the Far East was ruined; notions of racial superiority that had helped to sustain the empire had been severely undermined, and the nature and method of British rule came to be publicly questioned. The capitulation of Burma in March similarly exploded common assumptions about the empire. Not only were the Japanese now poised to invade India, but reports of Burmese collaboration with the Japanese exposed the myth of empire loyalty that justified British rule and had informed so much propaganda from the beginning of the war.

The BBC also needed to take into account the growing concern with post-war reconstruction. A topic of interest since the beginning of the Blitz, the setbacks and low morale of 1942 stimulated more discussion of post-war planning, reaching a high point with the publication of the Beveridge Report in November. Although Churchill discouraged public debate of specific peacetime policies, the BBC tried to reflect the change in the public mood from 1942 and began to allow open discussion of reconstruction in the autumn of 1943.[28] This was, after all, the "people's war," and the consent of the people was maintained, in part, by promises of a more egalitarian Britain after the war.

The new and improved Britain required a new and improved empire, and the BBC had to reconsider the number, method, and message of its empire programs. In early 1942, the BBC held an "Empire project meeting" that focused on ways to make the empire more interesting to the working classes.[29] The preparations for Empire Day in 1942 demonstrate the concern of many within the BBC after the recent military setbacks. Christopher Salmon, a young producer, talked in quasi-religious terms as he proposed a program for Empire Day. "I should like to suggest," he wrote to Barnes, "a discussion designed to inspire us, particularly the working men and women of this country, to a faith in our Empire."[30] The Assistant Director of Programme Planning reported that Basil Nicolls was "anxious" that references to Empire Day should be included the Forces Programme and requested "suitable representation" in a range of programs including *Reveille*, *Maple Leaf Matinee*, and *Women and the Call-Up*.[31] Empire Day was extensively observed in both networks. Home Service programs included a concert, a postscript by Duff Cooper, and a special feature, *Lest We Forget*.[32] This represented, with the exception of the news and a period from 7:15 to 8:45, an entire evening of listening from 6:45 to 10:30 p.m.

By June of 1942, the Dominions and Colonial Offices and the Ministry of Information were again canvassing the BBC for more representation of the empire in the Home Service. Vincent Harlow, now at the Ministry of Information (MOI), wrote to Barnes proposing a series on "everyday life in the Dominions and Colonies."[33] More importantly, the Directors-General, Robert Foot and Cecil Graves, requested that all departments should examine their proposed Autumn schedules "with reflection of the Empire in mind." Their memorandum indicated a certain anxiety towards the public interest in American culture and politics, though the BBC itself catered to the British appetite for programs by or about Americans. "It was important," they wrote, "that with increasing contributions from the United States, listeners' interest in the Empire should be similarly stimulated."[34] The juxtaposition of America and empire by the Directors-General is significant. Though America may have been a close and vital ally, it was still foreign. Empire, in contrast, was implicitly British—part of the shared past of the British Isles and a guarantor of British security and independence after the war.

Barnes, who had been putting considerable effort into getting empire material into the output of the Talks Department, responded defensively, admitting that there were no current plans for a new series on the empire, and emphasizing the work of his department along the lines agreed to in 1941. An increasing number of Dominion and colonial speakers were asked to give talks, and the department continued its policy of program infiltration. Noting that the department was "in close touch with the MOI and with the Dominions and Colonial Offices," Barnes assured his superiors that it was Talks Department "policy to include as many Dominion and Colonial speakers in our Home Programme as possible."[35]

At about the same time, however, Barnes and Laurence Gilliam, who was also asked to provide more empire material from the Features Department, approached R. A. Rendall, the Assistant Controller for the Overseas Service, for assistance in constructing appropriate programs about the empire. Together they met with S. J. de Lotbinière, Director of Empire Programmes, and Michael Barkway of the North American Service. The group decided that broadcasting of empire matters depended on a positive statement of guidelines from the highest levels of the Corporation. To that end, Rendall drafted a memorandum to serve as a declaration of BBC policy in regards to empire programming. A blueprint for the BBC's empire programs until after the end of the war, Rendall's memorandum deserves to be considered at some length.

It is clear that Rendall was thinking in terms of both wartime and post-war objectives in drafting the memorandum. The purpose of the BBC, he said, should not be merely to justify the empire against Axis propaganda or internal criticism, but to foster in the British public the will to maintain Britain as an imperial power: "The main objectives must … be to stimulate interest, dispel ignorance and foster a responsible and intelligent attitude towards imperial problems." Only through such an educative effort, Rendall continued, would there be popular support for a "constructive imperial policy, which cannot succeed without cost to the taxpayer and demand for service from many individuals."[36] These "many individuals" included not only the Oxbridge bureaucrat who would engage in active service in the empire but also the broader national community. It was only during the war that the BBC fully recognized "the importance of the working class ... as a major component of the national audience."[37] In an age of mass democracy and total war, imperial policy was going to depend on the willingness of the working class to embrace Britain's imperial responsibilities. British imperialism had to accommodate itself to British socialism. From 1942 on, concern with the apathy of the working classes informed much of the BBC's activities in developing empire programs. "Ignorance [of the Empire] is widespread among the working classes," wrote Rendall, "in parallel ... there is a tendency on the part of the working classes to feel that the Empire is the concern of the bosses ... there is also a belief among the uninformed that the Empire is somehow operated by the ruling classes ... to the detriment ... of the British worker.[38] The working class, then, became the primary target of empire programs. When proposing how to appeal to the interest of workers, Rendall began with "the appeal to material advantage," but quickly added "the appeal to idealism." Rendall believed that a special appeal could be made to the British worker's sense of disenfranchisement by arguing that they, as victims of an unjust system, had a special responsibility to see the empire run honorably.

Most of Rendall's other suggestions replicated older, more commonplace British attitudes towards their empire and Commonwealth—the empire as a place of adventure and encounter with the unknown, the sentimental union between the Dominions and Britain, the importance of the empire to Britain's status as a world power. The empire, Rendall concluded, could also be a source of "patriotic pride where it can be shown that our imperial responsibilities present a challenge to us as a nation to show the same vigour and enterprise in dealing with this problem today as was shown by our ancestors who first built the Empire."[39] These challenges were quite different from those of a Clive or a Kitchener. They were the challenges of administration, economic development, and political stewardship. But that did not mean they could not be a source of British self-satisfaction.

Rendall ended his memorandum by examining the methods by which the BBC should present the empire. He recommended more discussion-type programs for talks, and more representation of the empire in the news. Features and Drama could best handle "emotional appeals," but he warned that "patriotic pride" should be stimulated as much by future plans as past imperial glories. Program infiltration, "one of the most effective ways of introducing such themes," was to continue, and Rendall targeted some of the BBC's most listened to programs, such as *Radio Reconnaissance, The World Goes By, In Town Tonight* and *Brains Trust*, for the placement of empire material.[40] At a Programme Policy Meeting on October 23, Rendall's blueprint was "approved in principle ... [and] circulate[d] to staff concerned."[41]

One of the first empire programs conceived and produced after the implementation of Rendall's memorandum was a series of discussions titled *Red on the Map*. First proposed at a meeting that included Rendall, Barnes, W. M. Macmillan and Tahu Hole, *Red on the Map* clearly reflected several of Rendall's suggestions. The program emphasized colonial development and the future role of the empire in guaranteeing world peace. *Red on the Map* accommodated empire to other wartime propaganda, particularly the fight for freedom ("British" freedom) against Nazi tyranny. The format of the program was a round-table discussion, where the informed could instruct the ignorant, and "attitudes and phrases" could be "set against the facts."[42] However, broadcasting ignorance proved to be problematic. The Talks Department worried that casting "an Englishman for the role of ignoramus" might confirm for many listeners the belief that Britons knew little about their empire. In the end they settled on an American. "There is no better way of getting an audience to sympathise with a point of view," Barnes reasoned, "than by allowing a friendly foreigner to criticise a British institution."[43] Not only did the Talks Department hope to inspire a defensive patriotism for a "British institution," but employing an American would help deflect criticism of British imperialism emanating from the United States. Frederick Kuh, London correspondent for the *Chicago Sun-Times*, played the role of the American "ignoramus."

Like other highly scripted "discussion" programs, *Red on the Map* served a dual purpose. On the one hand, it kept attention focused on imperial issues and provided a justification for the maintenance of Britain's overseas commitments. On the other hand, it demonstrated the openness of British society as compared to Nazi Germany. In Germany dissent was not tolerated; in Britain it was broadcast over the public airwaves. The program derived significant propaganda value out of what appeared to be a free exchange of ideas. The Talks Department allowed Kuh to be critical and confrontational, but only so that other members of the panel could remedy his misconceptions. For example, Kuh, representing "American opinion," claimed that the term "empire" brought up connotations of "conquest by force; subjugation of populations; exploitation of peoples and resources and not necessarily entirely for their own good." The other panel members politely corrected him.

W. K. HANCOCK: My father used to say, "I consider myself am good imperialist."

FREDERICK KUH: What did he mean by that Hancock?

HANCOCK: Well, I think he meant that he wanted to keep unity with Great Britain and with the other communities too, and that he wanted this unity in the basis of freedom.

KUH: Freedom?

HANCOCK: Yes, certainly …

KUH: Would he have felt that same way, do you think, if he had [been] … an Indian?

HANCOCK: Well quite possibly he would. My father believes in unity. He thinks that every bit of unity we have in this war-divided world we should try and hang on to.[44]

The dialogue between Hancock and Kuh embodied most of the themes of the series. The empire is and ought to remain united. Since this unity is based in freedom, it must be consensual, emphasized by Hancock's claim that his father would been an imperialist even "if he had been an Indian." Finally, common institutions and values, like "freedom," give the empire its unity. And Hancock's reference to imperial unity in a war-torn world is not merely a reference to the empire's support of Britain's conflict with Germany. It suggests that the empire and Commonwealth be regarded as a model of international cooperation. Later episodes of the series more fully developed this theme, and in a subsequent episode of *Red on the Map* Hancock concluded, "The map of war strategy is the map of peace strategy, and without the British Empire that map doesn't make sense."[45] Like many of the BBC's empire programs in the latter half of the war, *Red on the Map* defended Britain's imperial past and emphasized the potential of the empire to play a leading role in international affairs after the war.

From the autumn of 1942 the BBC significantly increased the number of empire broadcasts to the domestic audience and began to monitor the number of empire programs produced by select departments such as the School Broadcasting Department. In the first two months of 1943, for example, the School Broadcasting Department produced twelve programs on the empire.[46] The Corporation also began to explore the suitability of more popular forms of programming for empire propaganda. In September 1942, the Variety Department introduced a new, empire-themed series of the popular program *Everybody's Scrapbook*, produced by Leslie Baily. This latest version of *Scrapbook* "was deliberately designed 'to act as a real Empire link.'"[47] It proved to be a popular series and the BBC broadcast it in Canada and Australia, as well as

Britain. Following the success of *Scrapbook*, Baily wrote to Nicolls, "the ignorance and indifference about the Commonwealth is an evil that broadcasting
should tackle," and he proposed a more comprehensive version of *Scrapbook*
to promote the empire on the "common man's level."[48] The result was the
weekly series *Travellers' Tales*, which appeared in 1943. It combined first-hand
accounts, music, and colorful vignettes in order to appeal to wide range of
listeners. The BBC also did an empire session of *Brains Trust*, in which Lord
Hailey, Professor Reginald Coupland and Learie Constantine joined series
regulars Julian Huxley and Malcolm Sargeant.[49]

The Features Department also became more active, producing in 1943
three programs, *War Against Locusts*, *War Against Superstition*, and *Life of a District Commissioner*. As these titles suggested, the BBC prominently displayed
new, progressive visions of empire, an empire of service, where Western science
finally triumphs over nature. The hopes for a new Britain became increasingly
projected onto the empire—the empire, it seemed, was to undergo a post-war
reconstruction of its own. In March 1943 the cover of the *Listener* was dedicated to a talk on *Health in the Colonies*, while in May the BBC broadcast talks
in the Forces Programme on *New Homes in Old Africa* and *West Africa's Industrial Revolution*.[50] Margaret Read discussed mass education in Africa on *Red on
the Map*, striking all the appropriate notes: "This young member of the family,
the 'black British' … needs our aid in personnel, in money, in modern science
and learning."[51] At about the same time, J. Grenfell Williams, the African
Service Director, proposed a series of programs for the Home and Empire
Service titled *Experiment in Freedom,* "to demonstrate the achievement of those
who helped to create the Empire and to show how … the Empire [would] continue to be a very real progress towards freedom."[52] The show would combine
talks and discussions with dramatized biographies of important "empire builders;" Williams's suggestions reflected the changing perception of empire as well
as popular hopes for post-war Britain. His list of "empire builders" included
"the unknowns, [the] Medical Officer, District Officer, District Nurse, Public
Officer, Schoolmaster, Missionary." Clive, Gordon, and Rhodes did not make
it on to Williams's list.[53]

Brush Up Your Empire

No series of programs better exemplifies the concerns, strategies, and message of
the BBC's empire propaganda during the second half of the war than *Brush Up
Your Empire*. The program was the brainchild of Maconachie, and represented

the first attempt by the Talks Department to boost consciousness of the empire by employing a popular program format—the audience participation show. In that a "serious" subject like empire was to be treated in a "light" manner, *Brush Up Your Empire* marked something of departure for the Talks Department, and demonstrates how concerned some of the BBC's staff had become with the perceived apathy and ignorance of the listening audience. And although the strategy changed, the overall message of *Brush Up* was similar to all other empire programs: "brotherhood" with the Dominions and "stewardship" of the Colonies.

The impetus for *Brush Up* came from a memorandum circulated by Maconachie to Barnes, Rendall, and Hilton Brown, the producer who ultimately took charge of the series. Concerned about the "apathy as well as ignorance about the Empire among the Home radio audience," and frustrated at the failure of previous empire series, Maconachie proposed an "Empire Quiz." Maconachie argued that the Talks Department had been successful at educating already interested listeners, but felt a quiz-type program, "on cheaper and 'brighter' lines," would attract a mass (i.e. working-class) audience. The BBC should "not disdain … to appeal to the 'believe it or not' sort of interest," Maconachie continued, and he encouraged his staff to devise a way for the show to contain some element of listener participation. "Educational circles would probably sniff," he concluded, "but that would not worry me if the series achieved its unpretentious but useful purpose."[54]

Rendall replied enthusiastically, and Barnes and Brown immediately went to work on the program, enlisting the assistance of members of the BBC's Listener Research Department, and eventually the Colonial, India, and Dominions Offices. They debated the format of the show, the extent of the audience's participation, and whether the quiz should stand alone or be introduced as a segment in an already popular show such as *Monday Night at Eight*. In the end, the Talks Department decided on a format where the show's host interviewed a representative of the Dominions or Colonies. In this sense it was similar to the Talks Department's earlier efforts, *Dominion Commentary* and *Palm and Pine*. There were, however, two key differences that accounted for the popularity of *Brush Up*. First, instead of the show being hosted by a university professor, the popular announcer Lionel Gamlin played the role of questioner. Gamlin possessed a good-natured style and avoided condescending to his audience.[55] Second, the listening audience proposed the questions for *Brush Up*, a formula that in part explains the popularity of similar programs such as *Brains Trust*.

The questions were not asked in real time by a live audience, nor did the

BBC solicit questions for *Brush Up* on air. Rather, the Listener Research Department collected questions from their contacts "and these would be put and answered as actual questions sent in by listeners, the listeners' name being quoted."[56] The following, from an episode of *Brush Up* on India, was typical:

> Gamlin: The other Indian feature that interests most people in Europe is the Taj Majal. Mrs. Sanders of Bedworth asks this—how old is the Taj Mahal? ... [answer provided by guest] ... Gamlin: And what about Parsees? Mr. Rhodes of Guiseley asks who Parsees are exactly. [57]

Convenience, more than deception, was the original reason why the BBC used this process to get questions for the show. Brown worried that by the time listener questions were solicited, sorted, and checked for suitability, *Brush Up Your Empire* would be off the air.

Besides the participatory element, the BBC took great care with the content of the show. After reviewing a program outline by Brown, which included the question "How many Indians can read a newspaper?" (the answer stressing Britain's contribution to Indian education), Maconachie warned against making *Brush Up* a vehicle for obvious self-congratulation; "propaganda should be as unobtrusive as possible ... I feel that detectable propaganda would sink the programme."[58] Though Maconachie's use of the word "detectable" is not unimportant, he conceived of *Brush Up* first and foremost as education, then entertainment, then finally propaganda.

Perhaps the most revealing debate in the development of the show concerned its name, and it demonstrates the considerable care the BBC took in representing the empire as a dynamic entity devoted to democracy and equality. In October of 1943, Brown circulated a "very urgent" memorandum to the Talks Department staff requesting suggestions for a title for the program. These ranged from the basic "Empire Enquires" and "Why and Where," to titles that were suggestive of the traditional links between Crown and empire—"How is the Empire?" for example, the legendary last words of George V. Others, such as "What's a Kangaroo Daddy?" reflected an attempt to use the more curious aspects of the empire to create listener interest.[59] Brown thought the matter settled with "Brush Up Your Empire," but Kenneth Adam, head of the BBC's publicity department, demurred. In a memorandum to Barnes, Christopher Salmon, now Assistant Director of Talks, noted that Adam was "seriously worried" about the title, feeling that it would "strike Dominions people and Empire citizens generally as very condescending." Adam was particularly concerned with the word "your," which denoted British ownership or control of the empire. An exasperated Barnes noted in the memo "I will be amazed if this programme ever gets on the air!"[60] And though the title was retained, the publicity for *Brush Up* reveals the disquiet over the title and reflects the extent to which the BBC was reformulating its representation of the empire and what it meant to the British. Brown suggested the following promotion to *Programme Parade*, the BBC's weekly publicity show:

> Many of you will remember a series of little books which appeared before the war—Brush up your French, Brush up your German, and so on. At 9:25 in the Forces Programme, we are presenting the first of a new series called, similarly, *Brush Up Your Empire*. In the same way as the little books set out to refresh one's knowledge of French and German and so on, the new series sets out to refresh our knowledge of various parts of the Empire … And by the way, when we say "your" Empire we mean everybody in the Empire. A Canadian may brush up his knowledge of India—a South African may get some new tips about Australia and our own people at home may learn something new about all these places."[61]

Despite Barnes's concern, the program finally debuted on November 24, 1943.

Listener research for *Brush Up* confirmed Maconachie's belief that in order to attract an audience, empire material required "light" treatment. It also demonstrates that programs about the empire did not turn off listeners, so long as they were quick-paced and undemanding. When asked to name nine new series they heard, Listener Research contacts most frequently cited *Brush Up Your Empire,* just ahead of *Vaudeville of 1943*, an all-star variety show starring Beatrice Lillie, Fay Compton, the Western Brothers, and Gillie Potter. "Generally referred to as interesting and instructive," concluded Listener Research, "the *Brush Up Your Empire* series was frequently mentioned by listeners, nearly always favorably."[62] Reaction within the BBC was similar. Barnes reported to Brown that the series was "highly commended" and that an "extension of it was urged." In a memorandum to the Director General, Maconachie singled out *Brush Up* as "the most successful" empire program the Talks Department had done, suggesting "that the listener will not stand for a very formal or 'studied' approach."[63]

The success of the first run of *Brush Up Your Empire* convinced the Corporation to broadcast six additional episodes in 1944. But with the transformation of the Forces Programme into the General Forces Programme (which could not be heard in Britain), *Brush Up* moved to the Home Service. The new installment was to include episodes on New Zealand, the Pacific Islands, East Africa, the West Indies and significantly, the United Kingdom, reinforcing the image of a shared and consensual empire; Britain was presented as just another part of the empire, the political equal of the Dominions. During the preparations for the new series Barnes scotched a suggestion by Brown to include an episode on Eire, which had declared its neutrality at the outset of the war. He earlier had given assurances to the Programme Director in Northern Ireland that Eire would not be included in the series.[64] Instead of Eire, the BBC chose to broadcast on Burma. It was a broadcast in which the India Office was to play a major role.

Barnes had considered including Burma in *Brush Up Your Empire* during the early stages of planning for the second run of the series in December 1943.[65] Similarly, the India Office had been concerned about the lack of representation of Burma in the Home Service and Forces Programme, and was eager for the BBC to do a broadcast.[66] By February 1944, the India Office had contacted the BBC in regard to a Burma program and they received an encouraging reply. The India Office desired to use the Burma program for a specific propaganda purpose, to combat accounts of low morale and Burmese collaboration during the Japanese invasion. Because of the format of the program, Alec Morley noted to his colleagues at the India Office, "it is possible to rig, and select from, the questions sent in," though admitting "we should ... be prepared for pressure to allow one or two awkward political questions to be asked."[67] While both before and during the war the BBC cooperated with the Colonial, Dominion, and India Offices, often seeking guidance on questions of fact, conditions in the empire, or official policy, these offices did not dictate program content. This proved not to be the case with the Burma installment of *Brush Up Your Empire*.

As the date for the new series of *Brush Up* approached, Brown contacted the India Office, notifying them of the impending program and requesting advice. When Alec Morley of the India Office replied, he included a list of questions that the India Office wanted to be covered on the show. Further, he requested that the BBC indicate which questions would likely be used for the program, so that it could be arranged for them to be asked by "suitable sounding persons." The India Office was especially keen to divert criticism of the response of the civil service during the Japanese invasion.

> The question to which I think the Burma Office would attach particular interest in is number 1 ... they are very anxious to give a "puff" to the work of the civil administration during the 1942 retreat.

Question number 1 read: "Is it true that the Civil Service in Burma suffered from what the Americans call "Singapore Mentality? Were there any Burmese in it?"[68] Brown responded politely and not once objected to the intrusion of the India Office. He incorporated seven India Office questions, "asked" by the "people" put forward by Morley. Brown included the "puff" question, which a certain "Miss Clarke of Gerrards Cross" had the honor of posing.[69] Gamlin's guest that evening assured the listening public that "both Burmese and Englishmen were keen on their work and good at it" and not "to blame for anything that happened in Burma."[70]

The end of the war and post-war broadcasting on empire

After the second run of *Brush Up Your Empire*, the BBC began to curtail the number of its empire broadcasts, in part because significant time was going to be devoted to covering the invasion of Europe and combat on the western front. *Brush Up Your Empire,* despite its success, did not return for a third installment. The lack of new empire programs distressed Rendall, who fired off a memorandum to the Director-General stressing the importance of continuing the work of reflecting the empire in the Home Service, and praising the BBC's efforts in 1943. "We decided without reference to the views of the government departments that we had a responsibility [to the empire]," he wrote, and "we have shown that it is possible to fulfill that responsibility and to do so in programmes that have programme value in their own right."[71] Foot tried to assuage Rendall's concerns, though his response was something less than full endorsement of current policy. "The principle of using broadcasting as an important link in the British Commonwealth chain," wrote Foot, "remains completely valid."[72] He suggested that, with the reorganization of broadcasting after the war, ample opportunity would be provided for empire programs.[73] Foot's lukewarm response may have been due in part to his decision to resign as Director-General.

Although there necessarily was a reduction in empire programs during the last year of the war, the BBC continued to pepper the schedule with empire-themed talks and other broadcasts. *Travellers' Tales* remained in the schedule, and there is no evidence that the BBC discontinued program infiltration. The contributions of the empire to the war effort were prominent in V E Day programs, which included a "*Tribute to the King* from around the Empire."[74] And Rendall need not have been too concerned about the BBC's commitment to the empire after the war. Foot's replacement as Director-General, William Haley, was to be as committed to the empire as Rendall himself.

William Haley, a newspaperman all his life, came to the Corporation in 1943 to be the BBC's first ever "Editor-in-Chief." He became Director-General in April 1944 and was to serve in that post until 1952. Although he took the reins of the BBC during a time of tremendous change, he remained committed to the public service ideals that had animated the BBC since the days of Reith. In a press release on the nature of the post-war BBC, Haley claimed "we shall safeguard broadcasting from becoming a glorified jukebox ... [rather] we shall play our part in making this country the best-informed democracy in the world."[75] In internal correspondence, he reminded his staff that "the aim of the BBC must be to conserve and strengthen serious listening ... [we] must never lose sight of its cultural mission."[76] And like Reith, Haley was committed to using the BBC to foster interest in imperial matters. In December of 1945, in a memorandum to Lindsay Wellington, Haley encouraged the "constant" projection of empire as "a great heritage, responsibility, and opportunity."[77] He quite explicitly tied empire to British national identity—the island story (which was also a world story)—as well as British prestige.[78]

Haley's attitude towards the empire was no more evident than during the British withdrawal from India in 1947. He directed the BBC to develop programs commemorating the Transfer of Power and the British legacy in India, including a series of documentary programs that would focus on British achievements.[79] Despite objections from his producers and words of caution from the historian Reginald Coupland, Haley insisted on maintaining the theme of national accomplishment.[80] Even the India Office, which had serious misgivings about Haley's plans, could not dissuade him from using the BBC to justify and celebrate British imperialism in India.[81]

All of the program departments were responsible for implementing Haley's policy of promoting the empire. In May 1946, the acting Controller of the Entertainment division reported: "it is likely as a matter of policy that we shall endeavour to introduce Commonwealth programmes regularly into our Home Services, both as a service to listeners, and as an overall Commonwealth job."[82] The Variety Department resurrected *Travellers' Tales* in the autumn of 1945.[83] And the Talks Department continued its yeoman's work on behalf of empire after 1945, including the long-running series, *Commonwealth and Empire*.

Commonwealth and Empire was the longest-running series the BBC produced on the empire after the war. The debates surrounding the development and course of the series provide an excellent window through which to view some of the problems the BBC faced in continuing its efforts on behalf of the empire after 1945. Broadcast on Sunday evenings at 7:15, the series revived the format of earlier programs such as *Palm and Pine* and *Empire at Work*. Like these, *Commonwealth and Empire* consisted of talks by speakers with first-hand experience, although it occasionally delved into the realm of colonial policy.

The program focused on the white Dominions and Africa.[84] India and Pakistan were initially excluded because of the political situation in south Asia from 1946–47. Like its wartime predecessors, *Commonwealth and Empire* tried to interest the British listener on the personal and "common man's" level, while also providing educational information. According to producer Donald Boyd, the series aimed "to illustrate the lives of the people of the Commonwealth and Empire with … human material," as well as provide "lofty political comment … on the Lord Hailey level."[85] As with *Travellers' Tales*, the BBC stressed actuality to stimulate listener interest. The BBC built *Commonwealth and Empire* around "first hand observation and experience accurately and vividly described," and "never second hand [material]."[86] The dual role of the program is perhaps best reflected in the Talks Department's suggestion to promote it in both the "serious press" and the "light and comic papers."[87]

During the war, the BBC made important strides towards presenting the Commonwealth and empire as more of a family of equals, even if some members of the family were more equal than others. As noted above, benevolence, progress, and partnership became dominant program themes, and the BBC allowed more and more colonized peoples as contributors in talks. In two poignant broadcasts, Learie Constantine and a representative of the Indian community in Britain talked about their experiences of prejudice and racial intolerance. "Learie Constantine," wrote W. E. Williams, "did more to shame us out of racial prejudice than anyone else is ever likely to do."[88] Of course, with so many West Indians in Britain engaged in vital war work, these talks had a practical, propagandist purpose. Yet, they also represent an explicit rejection of the crude racial stereotyping the BBC not infrequently engaged in before the war, and mark a shift in the BBC's official attitude towards the empire.[89]

This trend quickened after the war. The transfer of power to India and Pakistan, which included their membership in the Commonwealth, provided a powerful image of the development of the British empire into a multi-racial community of free nations. The producers of *Commonwealth and Empire* reacted accordingly. After its first year on the air, the program was put on hiatus and retooled. The producers of the show came to regard the white Dominions as less important than Africa and Asia. The white Dominions already had their own separate series, *Outward Bound*, based on the experiences of newly arrived immigrants to Australia, New Zealand, and Canada.[90] The focus of *Commonwealth and Empire* shifted to India, Pakistan, "tropical Africa and the Crown Colonies," and Eire.[91] As the 1940s wore on, the BBC struggled to find a common ground on which to construct an imperial vision appropriate to new political and economic realities. The old ties of affection, and race, between the Dominions and Britain did not cease to exist, but they were undermined by the closer alignment of Canada and Australia with the United States. Nor did the settler colonies represent the new Commonwealth. "If we desire to create a sentiment which will assist in keeping the new Dominions within the Commonwealth," wrote Neville Barbour of the Eastern Service, "we should avoid the atmosphere of an Anglo-Saxon club ... we should initiate a discussion with the oriental Dominions (as well as the Southern Irish and the non-Anglo-Saxon peoples of the Empire)."[92]

However, if the BBC worked to promote the new, multi-racial Commonwealth in its talks and news programs, its entertainment programs reproduced the "romantic" empire of adventure, exoticism, power, and racism. From 1946 to 1949, the Drama Department adapted several Victorian and Edwardian imperial novels into serialized radio plays. These included: H. Rider Haggard's *King Solomon's Mines* and Edgar Wallace's *Sanders of the River* in 1946, Cutcliffe Hyne's *Captain Kettle* in 1947, A. E. W. Mason's *The Four Feathers* and Rider Haggard's *Allan Quatermain*, in 1948, and Mason's *No Other Tiger*, set in Burma, in 1949. In addition, when the popular detective serial *Dick Barton* took its regular hiatus in 1948 the BBC replaced it with *Adventure Unlimited*, which was "set against a background of tom-toms, pidgin English, flashing knives, and poisoned darts." The *Radio Times* described the hero of the new serial as "tall, red-haired, deep-voiced—an Englishman every bit as fearless as his predecessor [Barton]."[93] The BBC even invented its own imperial hero, District Commissioner Bellamy. In yet another example of the confluence of radio and film, the BBC's *Remember Bellamy?*, the "story of the early adventurous days in Nigeria and the work of an unconventional District Commissioner," starred the accomplished film actor Leslie Banks, who had portrayed Sanders in the film version of *Sanders of the River*. To promote the program, the BBC used a photograph of Banks from the *Sanders* film.[94] The "imperial heroes" of these adventure stories represent the opportunities provided by empire and reveal different aspects of the national character.[95] District Commissioner Sanders is a man of singular purpose and unparalleled leadership capabilities who has devoted his life to the empire. In *King Solomon's Mines*, Allan Quatermain demonstrates the economic opportunities of empire, where an Englishman with a little pluck and derring-do could make his fortune. Harry Faversham, the central character of the *Four Feathers*, represents Britain's military tradition, loyalty, and the redemptive power of empire.

These programs, above all, were exercises in nostalgia for a simpler time.

Writing about *King Solomon's Mines* in the *Radio Times*, Val Gielgud admitted that Haggard was "a little out of fashion," but he could not resist "drawing to this story the attention of all listeners who share [his] own weakness for yarns which gave them, or should have given them, extreme pleasure when they were schoolboys."[96] Two years later, Gielgud encouraged younger listeners to tune into *Allan Quatermain* "if only to realise what used to keep their fathers from their homework!"[97] Likewise, the BBC emphasized the authenticity of these programs and the Drama Department stayed true to the original sources. Take, for example, the introduction to the first episode of *Sanders of the River*:

> We are in a primitive land; a strip of British West Africa … inhabited by a million black folk whose minds are as the minds of children … here dwelt Mr. Commissioner Sanders – Sanders of the River – a man who understood the minds of his people, and knowing them, loved them.[98]

This is a far cry from Learie Constantine's wartime broadcast on the racial intolerance he experienced in Britain. Compared to the rest of the BBC's programming on empire, which emphasized progress, benefice, and a better understanding of the non-white Commonwealth, these sentiments are wholly out of place; but they are loyal to Wallace's *Sanders* novels. The *Radio Times* was similarly unabashed in promoting Wallace, noting that he took his inspiration from "the primitive tribes, with … their childish logic and forest superstitions."[99] The BBC revealed a similar desire for authenticity with their *Captain Kettle* broadcasts, assuring listeners: "we shall hear the real Kettle … and only when it is absolutely essential will the little fire-eater be 'brought up to date.'"[100] The Drama Department regarded these broadcasts as harmless fun, or a return, if only for an hour a week, to a simpler time. But these programs also reproduced the imperial world-view of racial hierarchy and British domination. Unfortunately they undermined the very ideal of Commonwealth that the BBC was trying to foster in its talks and other empire programs.

Some evidence suggests that the BBC's promotion of the empire waned by the late 1940s. Without the war, it became less necessary for the BBC to regard empire as a propaganda problem or a propaganda opportunity. The influence of outside organizations that had successfully lobbied the BBC in the past, such as the Empire Day Movement and the Empire Youth Movement, decreased after the war. Publicity for Empire Day and related programs graced the cover of the *Radio Times* for the last time in 1948, and by 1952, recognition of Empire Day on the radio was reduced to a feature in the variety program *Welsh Rarebit*.[101] It is telling that the BBC broadcast *Commonwealth and Empire* at 7:15 p.m.

on Sundays, as opposed to the peak weekday evening hours that similar programs enjoyed before and during the war. But in other ways the BBC's commitment to the empire reached full blossom after 1945. In addition to a solid
helping of talks, features, and variety programs, the BBC broadcast numerous
special programs for King George VI's tour of Africa, the Transfer of Power to
India and Pakistan in 1947, and "Colonial Month" in 1949.[102] In 1950 Haley
assured the Commonwealth Relations Office that the BBC would continue to
do its part to represent the empire in its schedules.[103] His successor, Ian Jacob,
saw that the coronation of Elizabeth II was "foremost ... a Commonwealth
affair."[104] Special broadcasts on the empire/Commonwealth were arranged for
the weeks leading up to the coronation, and the ceremony itself was broadcast
across the globe "so that listeners in far distant lands could feel they were part
of the bigger whole."[105] During the Suez crisis, when Britain's imperial impo-
tence in the face of American opposition became manifest, the BBC favored
the government's pro-intervention position.[106]

The BBC's empire programs: an assessment

What influence, if any, did the BBC make in shaping British attitudes
towards the empire? It is difficult to determine to what extent these broadcasts impacted British listeners. High-ranking members of the BBC themselves disagreed as to the effectiveness of empire broadcasts. Maconachie, who
attributed the failure of early efforts such as *Dominion Commentary* to "audience resistance," remained pessimistic, writing to the Director-General that
even after the Corporation's efforts, there was still "a deplorable apathy in the
adult Home audience regarding the Empire."[107] J. B. Clark, Controller of the
Overseas Service during the war, offered a different opinion. Underlining the
importance of stimulating interest in the empire among the domestic audience, Clark maintained that "experience has ... proved that broadcasting can
make a really substantial contribution in this field."[108]

The fact that the BBC hierarchy felt that it had to do a "selling job" on behalf
of the empire suggests that it appeared, to them, to be far removed from the
lives of most Britons, particularly the working class. A Listener Research report
on India concluded, "on the whole India is looked on as a foreign country."[109]
The historian W. M. Macmillan, working in the Empire Intelligence section
of the BBC, put it succinctly: "we need to be aware of public boredom with
'problems' that are remote from themselves. Can we make them theirs?"[110] The
"public" Macmillan refers to can be more precisely identified as the working

class, and as the war progressed the BBC became more and more concerned that the working class simply did not know enough about their empire. Since, in a mass democracy, the continued existence of the empire would depend on the cooperation, or at least the tolerance, of the working class, this was cause for concern in many quarters of the BBC. Listener Research reports seem to confirm the opinion of Maconachie and Macmillan. *Dominion Commentary* and *Palm and Pine* were ratings disappointments. *Red on the Map* proved to be a critical success, but it too drew relatively few listeners.[111]

It would be a mistake to conclude from these numbers that the empire simply did not interest, or turned off, British listeners. *Dominion Commentary*, *Palm and Pine*, and *Red on the Map* all shared something in common: they were straightforward interview/discussion-type programs produced by the Talks Department. Talks in general, not just talks about the empire, drew smaller audiences. When empire appeared in other program formats it attracted large audiences. For example, *Brush Up Your Empire*, as noted above, was a popular program. Despite strong competition from the Home Service, the first five episodes of *Brush Up Your Empire*, broadcast on the Forces Programme, averaged an audience of 12.7 per cent. The sixth, on Malaya, pulled in an audience of 16.4 per cent and rated 88 on the appreciation index, "an extremely good figure."[112] When the BBC introduced the Variety program *Travellers' Tales* it set new records for its 6:30 Sunday evening time slot, drawing over 14 per cent of the listening audience.[113] At times attracting up to 6 million listeners, *Travellers' Tales* was considered by some in the Corporation "the most popular and effective programme about the Commonwealth" that the BBC ever produced.[114]

These audience numbers do not suggest that Britons, by 1945, were hostile or indifferent to the empire. Rather, empire, as culture and entertainment, continued to be consumed in large quantities. This trend of empire talks attracting small audiences, but empire in other types of programs getting larger audiences, continued after the war. *Commonwealth and Empire* delivered mixed results, attracting a small but appreciative audience that hovered between 2 per cent and 5 per cent of the listening audience. Though the former appears quite low, Boyd regarded the latter number, registered for talks on Canada and Australia, as "very high" for the time period. Also, *Commonwealth and Empire*, like most of the BBC's programs on the empire, registered high scores on the Listener Research appreciation index.[115] In contrast to the meager audience for *Commonwealth and Empire*, the audience numbers for the post-war adaptations of Victorian imperial fiction were impressive. In 1946, 1.75 million Britons listened to the final episode of the *Sanders of the River* serial. The number would have been larger, but only the London and Midland regional stations carried *Sanders*. Significantly, the serial that followed *Sanders* in the same time slot, *Shorty and Goliath*, drew only 700,000 listeners.[116] Seven million people listened to the first episode of *King Solomon's Mines*, which was carried in the Light Programme, also in 1946. Although there was some fluctuation, the serial more or less held its audience for all eight of its installments.[117] *The Four Feathers*, broadcast in the Light Programme in 1948, drew an audience of nearly 9 million for its first installment, and drubbed its competition on the Home Service, the venerable comedy program *Monday Night at Eight*. At no time during its eight-week run did the *Four Feathers* attract less than 20 per cent of the available audience, or 7,200,000 listeners.[118] These are not audience numbers that suggest that Britons, even by the late 1940s, were indifferent or unaware of their empire.

Rather than ignoring or playing down the empire, the BBC engaged in a long and deliberate effort to promote an awareness of the empire among its audience. What began as a tribute to the unity of the empire and its importance to the war effort evolved into a sizeable campaign to project the empire to British listeners in a wide range of programs. During the Second World War, the BBC constructed this empire with great care, making sure that it accorded with official and unofficial war aims. It was often presented as a working example of international cooperation, and necessary to maintaining international stability after the war. The BBC's empire was egalitarian, and committed to stewarding the dependent colonies towards self-rule. The BBC also accommodated the empire to the emerging welfare state, presenting it as a mirror to working-class desires for social improvements at home. This new British empire demonstrated the power of the modern state when it committed itself to social improvement and development, and bestowed the blessings of modern science and organization on her colonies. Finally, the empire emerged as a counterpoise to American might. The Corporation deflected American criticism of the empire, often portraying it as ignorance or lack of appreciation for British accomplishments or for the bonds of affection and culture that held the empire together.

Certainly, Britain's imperial identity remained essential for the Oxbridge professional class that ran the empire, and the BBC, though perhaps less so for the bulk of British population. Whether or not the BBC actually educated Britons about the empire is impossible to know. Maconachie did not think so, although as a former member of the Indian Civil Service his expectations of what the average Briton knew about the empire may be been too high. Statistical data from the 1940s have often been cited as proof that Britons knew little, and therefore cared little, about the empire. But, as Andrew Thompson has argued, historians have only selectively used such evidence, particularly a 1948 Colonial Office survey which showed, for example, that only half of those surveyed could name a single colony. Yet, the same survey also noted that 44 per cent of respondents could name a recent event in the colonies, 67 per cent were familiar with the Tanganyika groundnuts scheme, and 59 per cent knew that Britain provided financial support to the colonies. "These were not," concludes Thompson, "the response rates of an imperially illiterate population."[119] It is impossible to know if respondents learned their information from radio or other sources, but it is not unreasonable to think that the BBC played some role in their familiarity with the empire. Further, while an empire enthusiast might have a considerable amount of factual knowledge about the empire, such surveys cannot tell us much about how Britons understood the empire or its impact on their sense of Britishness. Lack of factual knowledge should not be taken as an indication that the empire had no impact on the metropole. Indeed, such ignorance "could be understood as a manifestation of an imperial mentality, and the power relations that shaped the direction in which knowledge flowed."[120] People from the colonies and Dominions knew quite a lot about Britain, but Britons, at the center of a far-flung empire, enjoyed the luxury of ignorance.

Listener research figures for empire programs suggest that even by 1950, Britons were hardly turning their backs on their empire. Talks attracted small audiences; therefore talks about the empire attracted small audiences too. But when the empire inspired more populist programs like Variety shows and serials, audiences responded. *King Solomon's Mines* and similar programs did not teach Britons anything about the empire; but they powerfully reinforced common representations of empire as a site of adventure, sexual and racial domination, and economic exploitation.

Empire, according to the BBC, maintained Britain as a great power and insured British political influence on a worldwide scale. It facilitated the spread of British parliamentary democracy and cultural values. And it was an arena where the best aspects of the British character—in the form of leadership skills or devotion to public service—could be fulfilled. After the war, many at the BBC would continue to lament public ignorance of imperial affairs. But what the BBC did, like film and popular fiction, was to privilege the dominant discourse of Britishness and Britain's place in the world, which depended in part on the empire. For those who listened in, and there were millions of them, the

BBC offered a rosy vision of empire that implicitly confirmed British superiority to their subject peoples and to other European powers, and Great Power equality with the United States.

Notes

1 This view is expressed by Siân Nicholas in her *Echo of War*, 235. Nicholas has since revised her view. See Siân Nicholas, "'Brushing Up Your Empire:' Dominion and Colonial Propaganda on the BBC's Home Services, 1939–45," *Journal of Imperial and Commonwealth History*, 31 (May 2003): 207–30.
2 Angus Calder, *The People's War* (London: Jonathan Cape, 1969).
3 Cannadine, *Ornamentalism*; P. J. Marshall, "Imperial Britain," *Journal of Imperial and Commonwealth History*, 23 (1995): 389–90.
4 Webster, 19–22.
5 MacKenzie, "Infinite," in *Popular Culture*, MacKenzie, ed., 183.
6 *Listener*, September 28, 1939, 601–3.
7 Home Service Board, January 3, 1941, BBC WAC, R3/16/2.
8 *Radio Times*, September 29, 1939, 3. The script of the program was published in the October 12, 1939 edition of the *Listener*, complete with a cover photo of Australian troops.
9 Laurence Gilliam, "The Radio Documentary in Wartime," *BBC Yearbook 1945*, 56.
10 Vincent Alford to Dunnett, December 19, 1940, BBC WAC, R51/678.
11 *In It Together*, BBC WAC, Talks Scripts, Reel 663/664. The show opened with: "DR WOOD: Twenty-five years ago there was another war on … [and] the Strand was … a regular parade ground for all the uniforms of the Empire. There I saw some men of a type quite new to me … they all looked seven feet high. They walked with a slow, magnificent, careless stride … MURRAY ['RIBS']: Break it down a bit doc, break it down. DR WOOD: It's true …"
12 *BBC Handbook 1941*, 79.
13 George Barnes to Richard Maconachie, August 6, 1941, BBC WAC, R51/91/1.
14 Maconachie to Alford, May 6, 1941, BBC WAC, R51/678.
15 By 1943 it was "compulsory" to mark, among others, the following anniversaries: January 26, Australia Day, May 24, Empire Day, May 31, Union of South Africa, July 1, Dominion Day, and September 25, New Zealand Day. Basil Nicolls, circulating memorandum, n.d., BBC WAC, R34/190/3.
16 *BBC Handbook 1942*, 13.
17 Director of Programme Planning to Music Programme Director, March 8, 1941, BBC WAC, R34/213/2.
18 E. Rawdon-Smith to Maconachie, August 2, 1941, BBC WAC, R51/91/1.
19 Noel Sabine to Gilliam, September 13, 1941, Ibid.
20 Maconachie to Regional Programme Directors, September 22, 1941, Ibid.
21 Barnes to Rawdon-Smith, December 13, 1941, BBC WAC, R34/350/1. Barnes was quick to explain that the BBC broadcast only two evening talks per week, and

that his numbers represented only the programs done by the Talks Department, and excluded news talks and school broadcasts as well.

22 Ibid.

23 Barnes to R. B. Pugh, October 4, 1941, BBC WAC, R51/91/1. Some unfavorable comments included: "A piece of imperialist propaganda; Ordinary; Propaganda of the most blatant type."

24 Churchill, quoted in Calder, *People's War*, 264.

25 Nicholas, *Echo*, 177.

26 For more on the relationship between American culture and imperial culture at the BBC, see Thomas Hajkowski, "*Red on the Map*: Empire and Americanization at the BBC, 1942–1950," in *Anglo-American Media Interactions*, Joel Wiener and Mark Hampton, eds (Basingstoke: Palgrave, 2007).

27 Lawrence James, *The Rise and Fall of the British Empire* (New York: St Martin's Press, 1996), 496.

28 Nicholas, *Echo*, 240–50, 253.

29 Ivan Smith to R. A. Rendall, April 3, 1942, R34/350/1.

30 Christopher Salmon to Barnes, April 16, 1942, BBC WAC, R51/91/1.

31 Assistant Director of Programme Planning to Leslie Perowne, Gerry Wilmot, H. R. Pelletier, and Archie Campbell, May 22, 1942, BBC WAC, R34/350/1.

32 J. B. Clark, Controller (Overseas), responding to an enquiry about the BBC's preparations for Empire Day from Leo Amery, May 21, 1942, BBC WAC, R19/305.

33 Vincent Harlow to Barnes, June 19, 1942, BBC WAC, R51/91/1.

34 Extract from Programme Policy Meeting, July 10, 1942, Ibid. See also Assistant Controller (Home) to Barnes and Mary Sommerville, July 15, 1942, BBC WAC, R34/350/1.

35 Barnes to Assistant Controller (Home), July 15, 1942, BBC WAC, R51/91/1; Barnes to Assistant Controller (Home) July 16, 1942, BBC WAC, R34/350/1.

36 Rendall to Barnes, Gilliam, S. J. de Lotbinière, and Michael Barkway, September 5, 1942, BBC WAC, R34/350/1.

37 David Cardiff and Paddy Scannell, "Radio in World War II" *U203 Popular Culture*, Block 2 Unit 8 (Milton Keynes: The Open University Press, 1981), 40–1.

38 Rendall memorandum, September 5, 1942, BBC WAC, R34/350/1.

39 Ibid. "We must show that we still mean to be Empire *builders* (in a new sense), that we know what sort of Empire we want in relation to the part we want to play in the post-War world [emphasis text]."

40 Ibid.

41 Minutes, Programme Policy Meeting, October 23, 1942, Ibid.

42 Notes of a Meeting on Empire Discussion, December 8, 1942, Ibid.

43 Barnes to Maconachie, February 15, 1943, Ibid.

44 *Red on the Map*, BBC WAC, Talks Scripts, Reel 197.

45 *Red on the Map*, Ibid.

46 Assistant Director of School Broadcasting to Barnes, March 1, 1943, BBC WAC, R34/350/1.

47 Briggs, *War of Words*, 514.

48 Leslie Baily to Nicolls and Kenneth Adam, February 16, 1943, BBC WAC, R34/350/1.

49 Alec Morley memorandum, May 17, 1943, IO, L/I/1/948.

50 *Listener*, March 4, 1943, 261; *Listener*, May 27, 1943, 622; *Listener*, June 3, 1943, 647.

51 *Listener*, December 23, 1943, 714.

52 J. Grenfell Williams to Rendall and Empire Service Directors, March 26, 1943, BBC WAC, R/350/1.

53 Ibid.

54 Maconachie to Barnes, Rendall, and Hilton Brown, April 29, 1943, BBC WAC, R51/60.

55 Lionel Gamlin, *You're on the Air: A Book about Broadcasting* (London: Chapman and Hall, Ltd, 1947), 40–3. W. E. Williams gave *Brush Up Your Empire* a positive review in the *Listener*, but criticized Gamlin for his "brittle facetiousness." *Listener*, December 2, 1943, 648.

56 Brown to Adam, November 5, 1943, BBC WAC, R51/60.

57 *Brush Up Your Empire: India*, BBC WAC, Talks Scripts, Reel 177.

58 Maconachie to Barnes, June 23, 1943, BBC WAC, R51/60.

59 Brown to Talks Producers, October 21, 1943, Ibid.

60 Salmon to Barnes, November 6, 1943, Ibid.

61 Brown to Peter Bax, May 31, 1944, Ibid.

62 Listener Research Report 2278, December 28, 1943, BBC WAC, R9/9/7.

63 Maconachie to Robert Foot, March 5, 1944, BBC WAC, R 34/350/1.

64 Barnes to Ursula Eason, October 30, 1943, BBC WAC, R51/60. Brown noted on the memo, "Curious how one *does* forget about Eire being in the Empire."

65 Barnes to Brown, December 11, 1943, BBC WAC, Ibid.

66 Morley to Sir John Walton, January 16, 1944, IO, L/I/1/949.

67 Morley to Walton, March 3, 1944, Ibid.

68 Morley to Brown, June 22, 1944, Ibid.

69 Brown to Morley, June 27 1944; Morley to Brown, June 29, 1944, Ibid.

70 *Brush Up Your Empire: Burma*, BBC WAC, Talks Scripts, Reel 177.

71 Rendall to Foot, February 28, 1944, BBC WAC, R34/350/1.

72 Foot to Rendall, March 9, 1944, Ibid.

73 Ibid.

74 Nicholas, *Echo*, 269. Nicholas notes that some listeners criticized this program for its "egotistical 'line-shooting.'"

75 Briggs, *War of Words*, 652.

76 William Haley, Memorandum on Home Programme Policy, n.d. BBC WAC, SC5/32.

77 Ibid.

78 See Introduction.

79 Haley, Diary, June 9, 1947, File Haley 13/34, Churchill College Archives, Cambridge.

80 Gilliam, Meeting on India, Notes given by Professor Sir Reginald Coupland, July

16, 1947; Wellington to Haley, October 16, 1947, BBC WAC R34/432.

81 On the India Office's objections to Haley's programs for the transfer of power, see IO, L/I/1/965.

82 Acting Controller (Entertainment) to PCD, May 30, 1946, BBC WAC, R34/350/1.

83 *Radio Times*, September 21, 1945, 5.

84 Donald Boyd to Assistant Controller (Overseas), July 15, 1947, BBC WAC, R51/93.

85 Boyd to Assistant Controller (Overseas), February 21, 1947, Ibid.

86 Ibid.

87 Boyd press release, Ibid.

88 *Listener*, September 9, 1943, 304.

89 There were limits to how far the BBC would go in this regard. For example, in *Brush Up Your Empire*, Gamlin interviewed an Indian and a Burmese when these colonies were featured. But when the program covered West Africa and East Africa the show used white speakers. The reasons for this are not revealed in the memoranda for *Brush Up*, but it certainly suggests ideas of racial hierarchy. Indians, who were on the cusp of self-government, could speak for themselves. Africans, in contrast, had no "voice" on the radio. Instead, British experts spoke for them.

90 Boyd to Wellington, June 9, 1948, BBC WAC, R51/93.

91 Ibid. The fact that Eire was classified in the empire with Southeast Asia and Africa says much about the low regard the British continued to have for the Irish.

92 Neville Barbour to Controller, Overseas Service, September 13, 1948, Ibid.

93 *Radio Times*, April 2, 1948, 5.

94 *Radio Times*, September, 20, 1946, 6.

95 MacDonald, 81–108.

96 *Radio Times*, September 20, 1946, 3.

97 *Radio Times*, January 23, 1948, 7.

98 *Sanders of the River,* BBC WAC, Script Library, 1.

99 *Radio Times*, September 20, 1946, 4.

100 *Radio Times*, August 29, 1947, 5.

101 Ibid., 176–9.

102 On the King's tour, see Programme Policy Meeting, July 18, 1946, BBC WAC, R34/615/5; *Radio Times*, January 24, 1947, 3; *Radio Times*, March 14, 1947, 4. On "Colonial Month," see *Radio Times*, June 17, 1949, 1, 5, 14.

103 Record of a conversation between Gordon-Walker and Haley, May 3, 1950, The National Archives: Public Records Office (hereafter TNA: PRO) DO35/3847.

104 *Radio Times*, May 5, 1953, 5.

105 Briggs, *Sound and Vision*, 428. I will discuss the BBC's obsequious relationship with the monarchy in more detail in Chapter 3.

106 Tony Shaw, *Eden, Suez and the Mass Media: Propaganda and Persuasion During the Suez Crisis* (London, I. B. Tauris, 1995).

107 Maconachie to Foot, March 5, 1944, BBC WAC, R34/350/1.

108 Clark to Foot, February 29, 1944, Ibid.

109 Listener Research Report LR/382, "India," BBC WAC, R9/9/5.

110 W. M. Macmillan to Rendall, November 10, 1942, BBC WAC, R34/350/1.

111 Listener Research Report LR/1706, April 30, 1943, BBC WAC, R9/68/2; *Listener*, May 20, 1943, 612.

112 Listener Research Report LR/2316, BBC WAC, R9/68/3.

113 Baily to James Watt, December 8, 1943, BBC WAC, R19/1331/1.

114 Notes of a Meeting, September 27, 1948, BBC WAC, R51/93.

115 Boyd to Assistant Controller (Overseas), April 2, 1947; Boyd to Assistant Controller (Overseas), July 15, 1947, Ibid.

116 Listener Research estimated that there were 16,300,000 potential listeners in the London and Midland Regions, combined, compared with 35,000,000 for the United Kingdom as a whole. Had *Sanders* been carried by all the regional stations or the Light Programme, its audience would have probably doubled. "Listener Research for Serials," BBC WAC, R9/12/2.

117 Ibid.

118 BBC WAC, R9/12/3.

119 Andrew Thompson, *The Empire Strikes Back? The Impact of Imperialism on Britain from the Mid-Nineteenth Century* (Harlow: Pearson Longman, 2005), 207–9.

120 Webster, 4–5.

3

The BBC and the making of a multi-national monarchy

In addition to the imperial project, the BBC vigorously promoted the monarchy as a symbol of British national identity. Beginning with the first monarchical broadcast in 1924, the BBC slowly but surely convinced the reigning monarch, King George V, to exploit the possibilities of the new medium of radio. Future monarchs would have little choice but to follow George's lead. The monarchy and the BBC found their relationship mutually beneficial. George V and other royal broadcasters gave radio a legitimacy it was lacking in the early years of broadcasting. The BBC, in turn, helped maintain the popularity of the monarchy by providing it with a powerful new means of communication. Not unlike cinema during the same era, radio "replaced … the magic of distance with … the magic of familiarity" by bringing the voice of the King directly into the homes of his subjects.[1] More importantly, the BBC projected the monarchy as an apt representation of the diversity of Great Britain and the British empire. The BBC framed monarchy as an ideal that united Britons under the umbrella of Britishness, but also respected other national, regional, and local identities.

The monarchy and national identity in Britain

The monarchy has been central to British national identity since the last quarter of the eighteenth century.[2] And, although there is some disagreement as to exactly how and why, it is clear that, beginning in the latter years of Victoria's reign, the monarchy increasingly presented itself in lavish public ceremonies as a symbol of national unity.[3] In 1872 Gladstone effectively ended Victoria's retirement when he orchestrated a public procession and mass at St Paul's cathedral after the recovery of the Prince of Wales from serious illness. This was followed by extravagant pageants that placed the monarchy at the center of British nationalism: the coronation of Victoria as "Empress of India"

(1876), the golden and diamond jubilee celebrations (1887 and 1897), and the coronation of Edward VII as King, Emperor of India, and "ruler 'of the British Dominions beyond the seas'".[4]

David Cannadine has suggested several reasons for this refashioning of the British monarchy as a symbol of national unity during the late-Victorian period: the decline in the effective political power of the monarchy, Victoria's longevity, the weakening of provincial identities, and the "conservative, vulgar, strident, and working-class" mass-circulation press.[5] Most important, for Cannadine, was the rapid social change and social strife that characterized the late nineteenth century. "In an age of change, crisis and dislocation," he argues, "the 'preservation of anachronism,' the deliberate, ceremonial presentation of an impotent but venerated monarch as a unifying symbol of permanence and national community became both possible and necessary."[6]

Like the late nineteenth century, the inter-war years were characterized by social and international tension, culminating in the General Strike and the outbreak of the Second World War, respectively. Although fascist and communist political parties enjoyed little popularity, economic depression, mass unemployment, and the apparent success of authoritarian regimes in Europe undermined the liberalism that formed the essence of Britishness. Further, a bloody and unpopular war with the Irish Republican Army, which resulted in, at best, a draw for the British empire, brought about the most profound constitutional change in the United Kingdom in over a century, the partition of Ireland and creation of the Irish Free State and Northern Ireland. As much, if not more than the late-Victorian period, Britons needed a monarchy that could represent tradition, stability, liberal democracy, and social and national cohesion. The ability of the two Georges to embody these "public values" accounts for the popularity of the monarchy during the inter-war period.[7]

Arguably the most vital function of the British monarchy was to serve as a symbol of an inclusive British identity, one that united the four nations of the United Kingdom. Parliament, although a "British" institution, badly underrepresented Scotland and faced vigorous opposition in the form of Home Rule movements in Scotland and Ireland. Empire was always suspect among certain sections of the political left. The monarchy, in contrast, excepting a minuscule republican movement, was an unproblematic, apolitical, and popular representation of Britain's diversity and unity. On the integrating powers of the monarchy Paul Ward writes: "The celebration of monarchy ... and the link implied to Britain was compatible with the display of a sense of Scottishness, Welshness, and some forms of Irishness. Monarchy ... provided opportunities for establishing the compatibility between the distinctive national identities of the United Kingdom."[8] To this we can add Tom Nairn's far more cynical evaluation: "It is easy to see why this [monarchy] suited a … multi-national state. Defining its peoples in terms of allegiance to a single symbolic family restrained them from too openly resenting one another, and so resorting to separate mobilisations of identity."[9] When necessary, the Windsors could trace their royal lineage back to Scotland and Wales, as well as Germany. In Ireland, the republicanism of the nationalist movement made loyalty to the monarchy the principal measure of Britishness for the Protestant community. In the case of Scotland, Wales, and Ireland, royal unification had preceded formal legislative union. British monarchs had long cultivated their image as Head of State and pinnacle of the social order in the "Celtic fringe" as well as in England. Comical as it may seem now, with the obese King squeezed into a kilt and purple tights, the visit of George IV to Edinburgh in 1822 was a public relations success that confirmed the King's Scottish credentials.[10] Similarly, Victoria spent a considerable part of her reign at Balmoral, in Scotland, although she made few visits to Wales or Ireland.[11]

By the early twentieth century, the monarchy more deliberately cultivated its image as a symbol representing all the peoples of a diverse British Isles and British empire.[12] George V began his coronation procession in Ireland and received an enthusiastic response from Dubliners amid shamrocks, Union Jacks, and banners carrying the slogan *Cead Mile Failte* (a hundred thousand welcomes). The King followed this appeal to the British patriotism of his Irish subjects with a tour of Wales culminating in the investiture of Edward VIII as the Prince of Wales at an elaborate ceremony in remote Caernarfon Castle. The ceremony was conducted in both Welsh and English, and included traditional Welsh poetry and song. The castle and grounds were decorated with images of dragons, daffodils and leeks. Non-conformist ministers played a prominent role in the ceremonies. The Investiture climaxed with the singing of *Hen Wlad Fy Nhadua*, the Welsh national anthem.[13]

At this time the symbolic role of the King as the monarch of a culturally diverse British community stretched to include the empire with George V's visit to India, culminating with the Imperial Durbar at Delhi.[14] The monarchy, then, became an institution to which multi-national British subjects throughout the empire could proudly and safely profess their loyalty as an expression of their British nationality without compromising their Scottish, Welsh, or Irish identities, or their Australian or Canadian ones. Even an Irish nationalist such as Arthur Griffith could argue for the full independence of a united

Ireland with the Windsor monarch as head of state.[15] Britain's imperial subjects also could use loyalty to the monarch as the centerpiece of their own British identities which did not replace, but rather complemented, their identities as Jamaicans or Asians or Africans.[16]

King George V at the microphone

Given the proclivity of the twentieth-century monarchy to put its symbolic power on display it is surprising that George V and his ministers were slow to exploit the new medium of radio. Rather, the BBC, specifically Reith, reached out to persuade members of the royal family to broadcast. For Reith, royal broadcasts represented a natural extension of the role of radio as a public service and a means by which to unite dispersed listeners into a national audience. Further, royal broadcasts would enhance interest in radio (at this time the BBC's first priority was still to sell receiving sets) and give instant credibility to the new medium. Finally, Reith personally held the institution of the monarchy in high esteem, his faith affirmed by his experiences during the First World War. During the conflict, George V visited Reith's unit; Reith described the brief meeting in his autobiography: "I may have imagined a lot, but the look he gave as we shook hands seemed to convey this: 'I can't find words to say what I feel. You may be killed … I represent what you're fighting for. Good luck and safe return home.'"[17] Reith, like many other Britons, internalized the image of the monarchy as it wished to be seen, as the embodiment of the nation and its values.

Reith first broached the idea of a royal broadcast in October 1923. Writing to Lord Stamfordham, the King's private secretary, Reith noted:

> No doubt you are aware of the great progress made by broadcasting in this country in the past nine months. It has developed into a national service, the potentialities of which is difficult accurately to foreshadow … It is our earnest desire that His Majesty the King, should honor us by broadcasting a special message on Christmas or New Year's Day … Such a personal message from His Majesty to all sorts and conditions of people in town and country districts alike would make, in these difficult and anxious times, a national moral impression, the effect of which could hardly be estimated.[18]

Although Buckingham Palace rebuffed the idea of a Christmas broadcast by the King, both George V and the Prince of Wales assented to the BBC carrying their speeches at the opening of the Wembley Empire Exhibition in 1924, the first time the voice of a British monarch was heard over the radio.

The Empire Exhibition broadcast was a smashing success for the BBC. The *Daily Mail* gave it heavy publicity and made special arrangements for massed crowds in Manchester, Leeds, and Glasgow to hear the King. The *Oxford Times* and Oxford Wireless Telephony Company made similar arrangements in Oxford. Police Court proceedings were adjourned at Gateshead during the broadcast. In a year when the BBC issued a little over 1.1 million licenses, an estimated 10 million people heard the broadcast.[19] The *Oxford Times*, in addition to publicizing its own efforts to bring the King's speech to the public, understood radio's ability to bind the nation together by allowing all listeners to participate in public ceremony.

> Many people have realised the wonders of wireless in their own home if they have taken the full opportunity made possible by broadcasting, but it was not until some great national function took place like the State opening of the British Empire Exhibition at Wembley, and the *Oxford Times* and the Oxford Wireless Telephony Company arranged to give citizens the chance to hear the King's speech in St. Giles', that the full force of the miracle of science was realized. For the uninitiated to imagine that broadcasting gives them the opportunity to hear spirited music and the spoken word is a very different thing to realising for the first time that it enables them to take part in some ceremony sixty, one hundred miles, or even greater distances away. It gave the sense of unity with a mighty people, the sense of participation in an unseen event.[20]

The broadcast was a triumph for Reith and the fledgling BBC. In his diary Reith called it "the biggest thing we have done yet."[21]

Despite the success of the broadcast, and the obvious potential of broadcasting to popularize the monarchy, the King remained reluctant to be heard on the radio. The BBC broadcast members of the royal family in the early 1920s, but George V continued to shy away from the microphone, especially for ceremonial occasions. He did not participate in programs in honor of his beloved empire on May 24; listeners had to be satisfied with the Prime Minister instead of the King-Emperor. When Reith broached the topic of a possible Christmas broadcast again in 1927, he was rebuffed by Buckingham palace. Another attempt in 1928, to get the King or Queen to broadcast on the tenth anniversary of Armistice Day, also ended in failure. Instead, Stamfordham read over the air a message "of love and sympathy" from the Queen. A frustrated Reith noted in his diary, "it is extraordinary how conservative they are."[22] Reith's persistence finally paid off and in October 1932 George V agreed to broadcast a speech to mark the official opening of the BBC Empire Service. But, with the Empire Service scheduled to begin on December 19,

Reith again put forward the idea of a Christmas broadcast to Britain and the empire. Encouraged by his Prime Minister, George V finally relented, and the first of the "traditional" Christmas broadcasts by the British monarch took place on December 25, 1932.[23]

The year 1932 was something of a watershed for royal broadcasts, as George V increasingly came to appreciate the power of broadcasting. Between opening the Wembley Exhibition in 1924 and his Christmas broadcast in 1932, George V gave twelve broadcasts in eight years. In the last three years of his life after Christmas 1932, he gave ten broadcasts.[24] The BBC reciprocated the King's newfound attention to radio. His Christmas addresses were duly printed in the *BBC Yearbook*. The BBC made extensive preparations for his twenty-fifth jubilee in 1935, broadcasting the processions, celebrations, and, of course, the King's jubilee speech. Upon the death of George V in 1936 the BBC solemnly broadcast his funeral procession without commentary, "one of the finest sound portraits ever achieved by radio."[25]

Abdication and the coronation of the new King

The death of George V and the accession of his eldest son Edward led to perhaps the most dramatic royal broadcast in history. By late 1936 Reith was deeply concerned about the state of the monarchy and his diary for December was "dominated by the events leading up to the abdication of Edward."[26] Reith strongly disapproved of Edward's behavior and found his abdication incomprehensible. During the crisis Reith gave strict orders that the King was not to broadcast without the permission of the Prime Minister.[27] In his diary he expressed his fears that Edward's abdication might mean "the end of monarchy; or we might have the King as a sort of dictator, or with Churchill as PM."[28] Two days after the abdication Reith passed judgment on the old and new Kings, explicitly linking the institution of monarchy and the nation: "Poor Edward. But thank God he and his ways have passed and there is a new King and Queen. The effect was quite extraordinary. It seemed as if the old England was back."[29]

Perhaps Reith's disappointment in Edward and approval of George VI played a role in the scale and complexity of the broadcasts that would accompany the coronation of George VI in 1937. Almost as if he wanted to expunge the memory of Edward VIII, Reith planned for the BBC to offer a wide-ranging slate of programs to honor the new King. George VI's coronation was the first to be broadcast. It was carried on all of the BBC's domestic radio services, and the Empire Service. It was also relayed to fourteen other countries. In addition, the BBC broadcast the procession from Westminster Abbey on television. Fifty-eight microphones were used for the coronation broadcast, including thirty-two in the Abbey, concealed beneath chairs or in chandeliers and lecterns. Along with microphones, the BBC placed commentators all along the route from Buckingham Palace to the Abbey, all connected to the main control room by nearly five hundred miles of wire.[30]

Even more impressive than the logistical and technical accomplishments of the coronation broadcast itself was the array of programs the BBC put out between Sunday May 9 and Friday May 14, "Coronation Week." A short list of just the most noteworthy programs would include: a special concert of British music, including the first performance of William Walton's Coronation March; a feature program, *The King's Anointing*; a performance of Edward German's *Merrie England*, and Barrie's *Dear Brutus*; an all-star radio "Coronation Revue;" *The Empire's Homage*, a special feature broadcast; a "Coronation Party" from St George's Hall; another concert of British music, including the first performance of John Ireland's "These Things Shall Be;" *The Clyde*, a feature program from Scotland; and *Coronation Carnival*, a program of highlights from the previous week of coronation programs.[31]

As noted above, the investiture of the Prince of Wales in 1911 and the royal tours through Scotland, Wales, Ireland, and the empire following the coronations of Edward VII and George V demonstrated the commitment of the Windsor monarchy to projecting themselves as the head of a united, but admittedly diverse, nation and empire. By the time of George VI's coronation, the BBC was a key component of this process, using its programs to represent both the Britishness of the monarchy and the diversity of Britishness. Many of the BBC's coronation week broadcasts contained regional elements. All of the BBC regional stations, including Scotland, Wales, and Northern Ireland, placed in their own schedules an extensive amount of coronation programming. Northern Ireland broadcast an "all British variety programme" from the Empire Theatre in Belfast. BBC Scotland's programs included an informal coronation celebration from Deeside and an episode of *People and Places in the Scottish Scene*, in which "Mrs. McHaggis and wee Mickie come to London for the coronation."[32] The region also broadcast a special program to Scottish schools, a talk by historian J. D. Mackie on the Scottish origins of the new Queen. "During Coronation Week," the *Radio Times* proudly reported, "the Scottish programme, like programmes from the other Regions, will express the unity of the British people."[33] In Wales, Alun Oldfield Davies broadcast a special coronation lesson to the schools, in Welsh. His talk told the story of Bendigeidvran, a Welsh hero who, in a war with Ireland, made a bridge of his body so that his men could ford a river. Davies then compared Bendigeidvran to George VI, "pointing out that a King is a bridge between the present and the past and between this country and the Dominions."[34] While Davies's lesson contains a certain ambiguity—is "this county" Wales or the United Kingdom?—in the context of a talk on the monarchy it scarcely mattered. For Davies, the monarchy was a symbol of tradition, order, national unity, and imperial cohesion.

In addition to each region's activities, the BBC took pains to include regional contributions for its national and main regional services during the coronation celebrations. "Coronation week tends to focus interest on London," noted an article in the *Radio Times*, "but the week's broadcasts will include several important contributions from the Regions." On May 10 the BBC included a "big Welsh concert" in the main Regional Programme and the West region contributed a feature program on the Duchy of Cornwall.[35] Scotland contributed two noteworthy programs for the main Regional broadcast, *The River Clyde*, written by George Blake, and *Rhymes Royal*, "a programme of songs and stories about Scottish queens of long ago."[36]

The BBC extended the theme of British unity and diversity in the main evening program on the day of the coronation, *The Empire's Homage*. Produced by Laurence Gilliam, it immediately preceded the coronation broadcast by the King himself. Like Gilliam's Christmas Day features, *The Empire's Homage* brought representative speakers from around the globe to pay tribute to the new King. The Prime Ministers of all of the Dominions took part in the broadcast, including Stanley Baldwin. Also like Gilliam's Christmas programs, *The Empire's Homage* represented the King as the head of a global, diverse, and unified empire/Commonwealth. The program began with "a reminder of the central act of the Coronation Service, the alteration of the Oath to include the name of each Dominion."[37] Imperial unity and diversity were represented in the program by the obligatory Catholic French-Canadian, a young woman from Montreal who ended her contribution with a prayer for Princesses Elizabeth and Margaret,[38] and by the inclusion of "two representatives of the King's people" in South Africa, a Transvaal miner and a Natal sugar-planter. The awkward phrasing used to describe the latter contribution, "two representatives of the Kings' people" as opposed to "two Britons" or "two Britishers," reveals that Afrikaners were still marginal and suspect relations in the King's family. *The Empire's Homage* also included a contribution from the Viceroy of

India, who, speaking for India, assured listeners of the loyalty and allegiance of the colony to the new King. The program highlighted not only the diversity of the King's vast empire but also the diversity of the United Kingdom. *The Empire's Homage* opened with the following:

> The King's people are speaking. Not as they spoke in their cheering thousands along the route of the procession earlier in the day, but through the voices of isolated representatives. First the people of England, and as is apt, through the voice of a Londoner. For it has been London's day ... Next, westward to Wales, and the deep, rich voice of a collier from the Rhondda Valley hails the King in the name of the Principality. Then to Northern Ireland for an old and honoured citizen of Belfast re-affirming an ancient and deep-rooted loyalty. Last in the Home Country, to Scotland, whence come heart-felt greetings to the King and the Scots-born Queen in the soft, homely tones of a country woman.[39]

By beginning with this concoction of Britons, stereotypical representatives of the four nations, the program emphasized the Britishness of both the monarchy and the empire.

The BBC also played a central role in the coronation celebrations and their emphasis on the Britishness of the monarchy by providing extensive coverage of the new King's travels throughout Britain. Like his immediate predecessors, George VI visited the four nations of his United Kingdom to reaffirm monarchy's role as a symbol uniting English, Welsh, Irish, and Scots. And the BBC was with the Windsors every step of the way, relaying important moments during the royal family's tours of Scotland, Wales, and Northern Ireland, and producing special programs to complement their visits.

The royal family's first stop was Edinburgh. In an article in the *Radio Times*, Melville Dinwiddie, the BBC's Scottish Director, wrote "the visit of the King and Queen to Scotland next week is their natural recognition of the place of the Scottish nation in the United Kingdom." He described in detail the measures taken by BBC Scotland for the royal stopover. BBC Scotland broadcast the presentation of the King and Queen with the keys to the city of Edinburgh, and set up numerous commentators along Prince's Street to cover the procession to Holyroodhouse. Other events covered by BBC Scotland's Outside Broadcasts unit included a "Rally of Youth" and a commentary of an unveiling ceremony by George VI at Bellahouston Park, future site of the Glasgow Empire Exhibition. At Dumbarton Castle, which guarded the Clyde estuary, BBC Scotland covered the ceremonial handing over of the castle keys to the King, "a sign of [Scotland's] loyalty."[40] Special programs in honor of the coronation visit to Scotland included a service from St Giles' Cathedral, a performance of the Bridie play *Storm in a Teacup*, a "Royal Serenade of special music," a repeat performance of *Rhymes Royal*, and the obligatory program at week's end consisting of highlights of the royal visit. BBC Scotland also produced a special program, *Line of Kings*, which emphasized the Scottishness of the new royal family and the role of the monarchy as a symbol of tradition and stability. According to the *Radio Times* the purpose of the program, broadcast the evening before the King arrived in Edinburgh, was "to show, with the authority of history, the ancient lineage of the House of Windsor."[41]

As with Scotland, the royal visit to Wales received considerable coverage on the Welsh regional station and in the *Radio Times*. Like Dinwiddie, Rhys Hopkin Morris, the Welsh Regional Director, wrote an article for the *Radio Times* in which he discussed the extensive coverage BBC Wales was planning for the visit of the King and Queen. These included a running commentary of their visit to Cardiff and the ceremonial opening of the National Library of Wales in Aberystwyth. BBC Wales also covered the visit by the King and Queen to Caernarfon Castle, where the investiture ceremony had taken place in 1911.[42]

BBC Northern Ireland likewise made the most of the King's brief visit to the province. In his piece on the visit of the royal family, George Marshall, the Northern Ireland Regional Director, dwelled on the special bond between Protestant Ulster and the King. After an introductory paragraph, Marshall unleashed a paean to Northern Ireland's British patriotism, noting that Coronation Day saw passionate displays of loyalty to the new King and Queen and predicting even more fervent expressions of allegiance during their visit to Belfast. For Marshall, it was not merely the infrequency of royal visits to Northern Ireland that accounted for this enthusiasm but rather an historic and deeply felt connection between the monarchy and the unionist community.

> It is not only the comparative infrequency of royal visits to Ulster that explains the fervid enthusiasm of her people; nor it is merely that additional stimulus of having the focal point of their loyalty in their midst … The loyalty of Ulster is deep-seated and traditional. It has its roots in a past more real in some respects to the Ulsterman than England's to the Englishman.[43]

Because the Windsors spent only one day in Northern Ireland, Marshall praised the work of the BBC in enabling all "Ulster men and women" to experience the royal visit. Reporting "disappointment" in the countryside and Derry "that the King and Queen will have only one day to spend in the province," Marshall expressed his hope that BBC Northern Ireland would "soften the blow" for those unable to visit Belfast. The "sound picture of the royal visit" produced by BBC Northern Ireland included commentaries on the arrival of the King and Queen at Belfast Lough by John Snagge, and their procession from the dockside to Belfast city hall by Henry McMullan. Recordings were made of the day's ceremonies, including the inspection of a parade of Northern Ireland ex-service men and women, a youth gathering at Stormont, and the presentation of addresses of loyalty from the Churches in Northern Ireland, the Belfast Corporation, and the Derry Corporation. The evening program, based on these recordings, concluded with the departure of the King and Queen, "leaving behind them hundreds of thousands of loyal citizens grateful to have had the opportunity, however short, of demonstrating their allegiance to their new King and Queen."[44]

Throughout the late 1930s the new King broadcast intermittently. Perhaps the most elaborate of these events was his 1939 Empire Day address from Winnipeg. He was touring Canada at the time, and the tour as a whole received enormous coverage from the BBC.[45] The Empire Day program, consisting of a "salute by radio which has now become a traditional form of allegiance to the crown from all the people of the Empire," concluded with a broadcast by the reigning monarch.[46] Perhaps the new King chose to broadcast on Empire Day, something his father never did, because he hoped to discontinue the traditional Christmas Day address. He did not give a Christmas address in 1936 or 1938, and only a brief one in 1937, "to send a further word of gratitude for the love and loyalty" expressed during the coronation year.[47] Self-conscious about his slight stutter, George VI doubted his ability to measure up to the standard of his father, whose final Christmas Day broadcasts had been warm and poignant.[48] He also held a deep antipathy for the microphone, confessing to his diary that "I don't begin to enjoy Christmas until after it [the Christmas Day broadcast] is over."[49] However, the course of events would prevent the King from retiring the Christmas Day broadcasts and limiting his appearances before the BBC microphone, for less than two and a half years after his coronation, Britain was at war.

The wartime monarchy and the BBC

Although the Second World War ultimately strengthened the bond between the monarchy and the British people, this was hardly a foregone conclusion. The war could easily have caused the monarchy to fall into disrepute. George VI and Queen Mary had been keen supporters of appeasement, appearing with Neville Chamberlain on the balcony of Buckingham Palace after the Munich settlement. Further, the Duke of Windsor's Nazi sympathies might have caused considerable embarrassment to the royal family. The large-scale civilian involvement in the war, the "people's war," could easily have created skepticism towards an institution that represented hierarchy and social inequality. Yet, by 1945, *The Royal Family in Wartime*, an official account of the monarchy at war, could claim that the King was "the most English Englishman, the most British member of the British Empire."[50]

The King and Queen retained their place of esteem among the British public by successfully embodying the pluck, sacrifice, and stoic determination of their subjects. Instead of fleeing London for the countryside or moving overseas, the royal family remained in London, even during the worst parts of the Blitz. The bombing of Buckingham Palace on September 13, 1940, epitomized the image of the King and Queen as sharing in the dangers of their working-class subjects, with the Queen remarking, famously but apocryphally, "we can now look the East End in the face."[51] Yet the monarchy was still somewhat marginalized during the conflict. Propaganda and news tended to celebrate the bravery, virtue, and sacrifice of the people, not the King, who represented the class-based and undemocratic nature of British society. The powerful personality of Churchill also undermined the symbolic importance of the King. "To a great extent," notes Richard Weight, "Winston Churchill *was* Britishness during the Second World War."[52] It is Churchill's words that are burned into Britain's collective popular memory—"we shall never surrender;" "their finest hour"—not the utterances of the shy, stuttering George VI.

Nevertheless, public affection and esteem for the monarchy increased during the war years, and the BBC was a key conduit in maintaining the connection between King and people. After Britain's declaration of war on September 3, George VI broadcast to Britain and the empire. Striking the right notes with a British public that accepted, but did not welcome, war, George VI spoke of the failed attempts "to find a peaceful way out of the differences between ourselves and those who are now our enemies," and urged his people to "stand calm, firm, and united." Although the King was no orator, "no one doubted his sincerity as he concluded:"

> There may be dark days ahead, and war can no longer be confined to the battlefield. But we can only do the right as we see the right, and reverently commit our cause to God. If one and all we keep resolutely faithful to it, ready for whatever service or sacrifice it may demand, then, with God's help, we shall prevail.[53]

With war upon his people, George VI resumed the Christmas Day broadcasts he had wished to bring to an end. In the first of his wartime Christmas addresses to the nation and empire, the King sought to dispel any complacency or apathy brought on by the "Bore War." He praised the efforts of the Royal Navy "which … [had] burst the storm of ruthless and unceasing war," and the Air Force, "our sure shield of defence"[54] And he heaped acclaim on the armies of the Dominions and the colonies, assuring listeners of the unity of the King's people:

> The men and women of our far-flung Empire working in their several vocations, with one same purpose, all are members of the great Family of Nations which is prepared to sacrifice everything that freedom of spirit may be saved to the world. Such is the spirit of the Empire; of the great Dominions, of India, of every Colony, large or small. From all alike have come offers of help, for which the mother country can never be sufficiently grateful. Such unity in aim and in effort has never been seen by the world before.[55]

George VI's decision to resume the Christmas Day broadcasts did not mean that he was to become a frequent or enthusiastic contributor to the BBC. The Corporation had a difficult time convincing him to speak after the 1940 Empire Day program, which chronicled the empire's war effort.[56] But in the end the King consented, giving a broadcast that starkly contrasted his—i.e. the British—vision of empire with that of the Nazis. The speech is noteworthy not only because of its content, which like George VI's earlier speeches highlighted the empire's contribution to the war, but also because it was a direct rebuttal to German propaganda. "There is a word," spoke the King, "which our enemies use against us—Imperialism." He continued:

> By it *they* mean the spirit of domination and the lust of conquest. We free peoples of the Empire cast the word back in their teeth. It is *they* who have these evil aspirations. *Our* one object has always been peace: peace in which our institutions may be developed, the condition of our peoples improved, and the problems of government solved in a spirit of good will [emphasis text].[57]

More often the King spoke in more general terms—praising the efforts of the armed forces, lauding the sacrifices of the people, hoping for peace and an end to the conflict, and asking Britons to put their faith in God. Churchill's words inspired; the radio speeches of George VI during the war provided comfort and reassurance.

The King rightly adjusted his addresses for the changing circumstances of the war. If, in 1939, he made sure to praise the Navy and Air Force so as to assure his subjects that there indeed was a war being fought, later broadcasts focused more on the home front. The 1940 Christmas speech, broadcast during the Blitz, focused on the resilience and common sacrifice of all of the King's people: "we are all in the front line and the danger together." George VI lauded his listeners: "I have seen for myself the battered towns and cities of England and I have seen the British people facing their ordeal. I can say to them all that they may be justly proud of their race and nation."[58] He struck similar notes in 1941, praising the "women and girls as well as men, who at the call of duty have left their homes to join the Services or to work in factory, hospital, or field," singling out the Civil Defence for acclaim. In 1942 the King again mentioned the home front, as well as the armies overseas, speaking frankly of his "admiration" for workers in war industries and his gratitude to farm laborers.[59]

Although George VI was not an orator of Churchill's caliber, it is important to remember that his broadcasts were extremely popular. The King spoke to numbers that only Churchill himself could surpass. Approximately 46 per cent of the listening population of Great Britain heard *The Empire's Greeting*, and *Christmas Under Fire*, the feature programs that preceded the King's Christmas Day broadcasts in 1939 and 1940 respectively. In 1941, 32.4 per cent of Britons listened to the Christmas Day feature *Absent Friends*, but an additional 27.9 per cent (over 60 per cent of listeners total) tuned into hear the King speak after the feature ended.[60] In 1944, the Listener Research Department reported that 55.9 per cent of British listeners heard the feature *The Journey Home*, the largest audience for a Christmas Day broadcast, excepting the King's speech which followed it.[61]

By the end of the war, the King had achieved a closer bond with the British people than any previous monarch, and he remained a symbol of British and imperial unity. The BBC played a vital role in this; in his Christmas addresses and other speeches he defended British war aims, re-assured listeners of the strength and unity of the empire, and expressed his gratitude, on behalf of the nation, to the nation, notably the armed forces, war workers, the Civil Defence, and the Home Guard. Yet, from 1939 to 1945, the BBC could not possibly promote the monarchy as extravagantly as before the war. Except for Christmas and Empire Day, there were few royal ceremonies for the BBC to celebrate: no coronations, jubilees, royal weddings, or grand tours.

The coming of peace to Britain meant more opportunities for the BBC to cover the royal family. On the tenth anniversary of the King's coronation, the Home Service broadcast a special program highlighting the events of May 12, 1937.[62] Princess Elizabeth, who gave her first radio address during the war, began to give radio speeches with increasing frequency. In 1946, the BBC broadcast her talk to the youth of the empire from Royal Albert Hall on Empire Day.[63] For Elizabeth's twenty-first birthday, which took place while she was on tour with her family in Africa, BBC correspondent Frank Gillard described the celebrations in South Africa that preceded the speech by the heir to the throne. In the speech itself, which one biographer called "the climax of the tour," Elizabeth promised to devote herself to a life in "the service of our great imperial family to which we all belong."[64] The most important single broadcasting event of 1947 was the wedding of Princess Elizabeth in November. It was still very much a "radio" event. The ceremony was carried live on the Home Service and repeated, in the evening, on the Light Programme.[65] Cameras were barred from the inside of Westminster Abbey, so television could only carry the procession and events outside.[66]

Radio covers the royal tour of Africa

Although the wedding of Princess Elizabeth was an important media event during the post-war period, two other episodes exemplify the role of the BBC in promoting the monarchy as a symbol of a pluralistic Britishness: the royal tour of South Africa in 1947 and the coronation of Queen Elizabeth in 1953. Not only did the BBC provide extensive coverage for both the royal tour and the coronation, but each time it emphasized the nature of the monarchy as head of a multi-national state and a multi-racial Commonwealth.

The idea that the King should visit South Africa on his last imperial tour came out of discussions between George VI and Jan Smuts during the latter's trips to London during the Second World War. George VI was personally interested in visiting the Dominion, having immensely enjoyed his visits to Australia, New Zealand, and Canada. Clement Attlee approved of the trip, feeling that a personal visit by the King would help strengthen the relationship between Britain and South Africa, while Smuts hoped that the King's visit would help him stave off an election challenge from the Afrikaan nationalists.[67]

The BBC began to make plans soon after the King officially accepted the invitation of the South African government, resolving in the summer of 1946 to "cover the visit fully."[68] In August, J. Grenfell Williams, the BBC's African Service Director, was dispatched to South Africa to begin to make arrangements with the South African Broadcasting Corporation.[69] The BBC made extensive plans for the royals' four-month tour of Africa. Three news reporters covered the tour, all of them veteran war correspondents: Frank Gillard, who joined the Royal Family aboard the H.M.S. *Vanguard*, then the world's newest battleship, for the trip to South Africa, Bob Dunnett, and Wynford Vaughan Thomas. The team was responsible for daily news dispatches and extensive coverage of the major tour events, such as the Royal Procession through Cape Town. Additionally, the reporters' material, recorded on disc and flown back to London, was edited into a weekly feature program, *Royal Progress*.[70] Geoffrey Bridson, perhaps the BBC's most talented producer, joined Gillard, Dunnett, and Thomas in South Africa, where he collected material and prepared feature programs to supplement the news coverage of the royal tour.[71]

The BBC wanted to provide listeners with extensive news coverage of the Royal Family, but also a "vivid picture of … a great sister nation."[72] This picture consisted of radio images of Victoria Falls, the grave of Cecil Rhodes, diamond mines at Kimberley, and the modern skyscrapers of Johannesburg. It also included a good deal of material—interviews, performances, and songs—from the indigenous African peoples. Reflecting on his coverage of the royal tour, Vaughan Thomas noted that, "from the point of view of new experience the highlights have been our trips to native territories—Basutoland, Transvaal and Zululand."[73]

The most spectacular broadcasts of the tour were those that included elements of the indigenous cultures of Africa. On March 12, as part of his tour of Basutoland, George VI was welcomed by fifty thousand Basuto riders, "probably," suggested Bridson to readers of the *Radio Times*, "the largest gathering of horsemen that Africa or the King himself has ever seen."[74] Bridson also produced a feature program on the Basutos, which included interviews and dancing. "One of the most striking [performances]" according to Bridson, "was made for us by little Jobo, son of the chief Goliath … he recited in Basuto the praises of King George VI with all the forceful assurance of a born orator."[75] Still, for Bridson, the climax of the royal visit to South Africa was the Royal Dance at Eshowe, where a crowd of thirty thousand had gathered to see the King and Queen and witness the Zulu dance *Ngoma Umkosi*. Bridson describes the spectacle in some detail:

> Hemmed in by the vast crowd, they [Zulu warriors] advanced upon the royal dais from the far end of the arena, their piebald oxhide shields a moving wall of white and black and brown against the dark sepia of their bodies … After the men, it was the turn of the women, and to them the day really belonged. They flooded onto the field in so many dark waves, their bodies bare to the waist, their necks festooned with white and coloured intricacies of beadwork, their loins gay with beaded aprons. As they came on, the field rang with their shrill cries, their glistening breasts bounding and slapping against their bodies in a

staccato accompaniment to the prancing of their feet … Finally, as the women retired, the impis gathered for their charge—the *ukuqubula*. Their ranks drawn up behind their shields, their weapons raised in a shout of battle, they charged headlong towards the royal dais … stopping dead in their tracks a few yards before the Royal Family … they shouted out their royal salute—*Bayete! Bayete! Bayete!*[76]

The Royal Dance is an example of spectacular political theatre, and Bridson's description of it conveys its fantastic nature and the extent to which even he, left-wing in his politics and an opponent of South Africa's color bar (see below), could romanticize imperial subjects and British imperialism. The Royal Dance and other events along the tour emphasized the authority of the King over his colonial subjects but also the consensual nature of British rule. Through its coverage of these events and its own creative programming, the BBC produced an image of a multi-national empire, under the clear command of the monarchy and, by extension, Britain. In covering these displays, the BBC enabled British listeners to affirm the virtue and the stability of the empire and understand the central role of the monarchy in keeping it together.

It should be noted that while the BBC's primary concern in Africa was to relay various events and produce programs that verified the unity of the empire and the prestige of the monarchy, it did not conceal the injustices of South African society. Vaughan Thomas, summarizing the BBC's coverage of the tour, claimed that he and his fellow correspondents gave listeners "an idea of the some of the problems that lie below the surface … [of South Africa,] problems of colour bar, race, soil erosion and drought," while in another article, Gillard noted "the complex problems of this sub-continent—the problems of race, outlook, colour, language, and of civilization itself."[77] Bridson, upon his return from Africa, used some of the material he had compiled to produce an episode about South Africa for *Focus*, the Light Programme's weekly current events show. Bridson's program covered South African racial policy and the social conditions of the African population in the Dominion. When officials at South Africa House saw the script, they sent an official deputation to Broadcasting House to prevent the airing of the program. Basil Nicolls, now Senior Controller and Controller of Programmes, refused to pull the episode of *Focus*. South Africa House then threatened to lobby the Deputy Prime Minister, Herbert Morrison, to shut down the BBC transmitter, "in the interests of Commonwealth solidarity."[78] Up until the time of the broadcast, Bridson did not know if the program would be transmitted in a heavily censored version, if at all; in the end it went out without official intervention.

National and imperial diversity: broadcasting and the coronation of Elizabeth II

The broadcast of the coronation ceremony of Elizabeth II in June 1953 represents one of the most important moments in broadcasting history. It was by far the most elaborate broadcast the BBC had attempted to that point, and it attracted an enormous audience; only 12 per cent of the adult population of Great Britain neither watched nor listened to the broadcast of the coronation ceremony.[79] It marked the first time that television cameras were allowed, at the insistence of the British Cabinet, inside Westminster Abbey. The coronation also saw a shift in the relationship between radio and television, with the latter becoming the dominant medium. Not only did more Britons watch the coronation (56 per cent) than listen to it, but also the coronation ably demonstrated the power of television, which gave viewers, in a way that radio could not, a sense of being included in the ceremonies themselves. The coronation also marks the first chapter in the development of global television. The BBC made recordings of the proceedings, which were flown to North America on the fastest jets in the British Air Force, and broadcast on Canadian and American networks.[80]

Rather than focus on the technical accomplishments of the coronation broadcasts, or its role in the rise of television, or its significance as an international media event, the remainder of this chapter will focus on the BBC's presentation of the monarchy as a symbol of Britain's multi-national identity and the "unity in diversity" of Britain and the empire. The coronation of Elizabeth II, and the BBC's coverage of it, brought together the imagery that dominated the BBC's coverage of the 1937 coronation and the royal tour of Africa; monarchy as the symbolic head of a cohesive British state and monarchy as a projection of British authority overseas in the form of a united Commonwealth and loyal empire. And as important as the BBC's coverage of the coronation ceremony was, it is through the complementary programming that preceded the coronation that one best gets a sense of the BBC's projection of the meaning of the monarchy.

Although the coronation did not take place until June 2, programming to honor the new Queen began in early April. The Light Programme's Wednesday short play, *Curtain Up*, was renamed *Coronation Curtain Up*.[81] In the subsequent months the BBC bombarded listeners with a variety of patriotic radio and television programs on every facet of the ceremony: the history of Westminster Abbey, preparations for the coronation in London and the rest of the country, and the origin of *God Save the Queen*, "the best-known tune in the world."[82] A series of six plays entitled *Sovereign Ladies*, about the past queens regnant of Britain, was broadcast during *Children's Hour*.[83] In April, the Home Service broadcast a series, *Throne and People*, which examined the evolution of the monarchy since Victoria. John Connell, one of the program's authors, wrote an article in the *Radio Times* in which he described the monarchy as "the symbol and the focus of loyalty and love, of personal and public virtue, of a Commonwealth's faith and conscience, self-knowledge, and self-interest."[84] More suitable, perhaps, to social democracy and the first coronation follow-ing the "people's war," was *The Queen's People*. The aim of the series was to show how "the Queen's people fought and worked to preserve the heritage of Britain."[85] The first episode of the series, "Ourselves and Our Land," paid homage to the infantry soldier as well as the factory workers, miners, and farmers of Britain, while the last, "Ourselves and the Air" dealt with the Battle of Britain.[86] During "Coronation Week" the BBC broadcast *Time Has Brought Me Hither* (the title came from a remark by Elizabeth I during her coronation procession) by veteran features producer Louis MacNeice. The *Radio Times* promoted the program thusly:

> This is a programme of facts but of facts which are also symbols. It has been compiled in the belief that symbols and ritual are important. It is a programme unified by the concept of monarchy but diversified both by the evolution of that concept and by the diverse characters of our monarchs. From another angle, it is unified by the constant elements in the British tradition and diversified by the diversity which is part of our tradition.[87]

Although a bit convoluted, the *Radio Times* write-up neatly encapsulates the contradictions of monarchy, the very things that made it so successful and such a widely acknowledged representation of British national identity: tradition and change, unity and diversity, empiricism, yet love of myth and ritual.

During the run-up to the coronation, the BBC broadcast several programs on the imperial nature of the monarchy, emphasizing the crown as the link between Britain and the Commonwealth. In the week before the corona-tion, the Home Service broadcast a series of talks, *Commonwealth Stocktaking*, while Light Programme listeners enjoyed concerts by Pakistani, Canadian, and Indian military bands.[88] The BBC prepared a series of special variety programs for the coronation, including *The Commonwealth Gala*, which featured enter-tainers from Canada, Jamaica, and Malta. In an article describing the Variety Department's preparations for the coronation, the *Radio Times* noted:

> Many months ago … it was decided that one highlight must be a show given as their own tribute by artists of the Commonwealth. It should not be a studio

broadcast, but a full-dress affair, played before a 'full house' with all of the atmosphere that a London theatre can command. The *Commonwealth Gala* will be the most important show ever to be broadcast 'live' from the stage of the London Palladium.[89]

A children's program, *The Queen's Commonwealth*, employed recordings of children from Australia, New Zealand, Canada, South Africa, India, Pakistan, and Ceylon describing their plans for the coronation. A promotional article for *Queen's Commonwealth*, noting that Empire Day fell on Whit Sunday, only nine days before the coronation, concluded, "it is a very special day for remembering all those children in Commonwealth countries right around the world who owe allegiance to Queen."[90]

The Commonwealth was also to play a central role on the day of the coronation itself. In terms of the treatment of the event, the Commonwealth representatives were given special privileges. "In our planning," wrote Charles Max-Muller, the BBC's Director of Outside Broadcasts, "one factor has always been foremost in our minds—the coronation of Elizabeth II is a Commonwealth affair."[91] The commentary team included a representative of the Australian Broadcasting Commission and the Canadian Broadcasting Corporation, and a BBC employee to act as a "Colonial commentator." Unlike the 1937 coronation, two commentators were allowed inside Westminster Abbey itself; one to broadcast in English and the other in French, to accommodate Francophone Canada.[92] In addition to making these special provisions for Commonwealth broadcasting, the BBC made the Commonwealth and empire a major component of the programs broadcast on the night of the coronation. Elizabeth's speech to the nation at 9:00 p.m. was sandwiched between two major broadcasts, *Long Live the Queen*, and *Coronation Day Across the World*. The former, broadcast at 8:00, was a "radio pageant" in which messages from the Commonwealth were linked by commentary and song, a format by now familiar to any Briton who had listened to the BBC's Christmas Day programs. The latter, broadcast immediately after the Queen's address, was billed as "a living, instantaneous sound picture of rejoicings and celebrations … and loyal messages, on a scale as great as anything ever attempted in the history of broadcasting." Although the microphone made stops in parts of western Europe and the United States, *Coronation Day Across the World* was largely a Commonwealth program, and included the sounds of Zulu chieftains saluting the new Queen, Accran children singing songs of loyalty, and "drums of joy" from Ceylon.[93] As with the royal tour of South Africa, the BBC's coronation coverage encouraged British listeners to think of themselves as part of a wider British world which, even in the era of decolonization, still expressed allegiance to the British monarchy and amity towards the British people.

If the coronation of Elizabeth II was a "Commonwealth affair," it was also very much a British affair. As with her predecessor, George VI, the BBC made sure that Elizabeth's coronation, and the fanfare leading up to it, emphasized the multi-national nature of the Queen's kingdom. Throughout May, the Home Service carried a series of programs entitled *Scottish Journey*, designed to "emphasise the diversity that underlies the unity of the different parts of the United Kingdom, and to make them better known to one another."[94] Similarly, the Home Service carried *Ulster Journey*, a radio picture of Northern Ireland written by Graeme Roberts and Sam Hanna Bell, while Richard Hughes, author of *Danger*, the first play to be broadcast by the BBC, contributed *A Welsh Journey*.[95] Like the Commonwealth, Britishness played a prominent role in the programs on the day of the coronation. *Coronation Day Across the World*, mentioned above, included scenes from the Margam steelworks in Wales, Bangor, Northern Ireland, and Ben Nevis, as well as York and Merseyside, before moving to Europe and the Commonwealth. And the *Radio Times* promoted the BBC's broadcast of Elizabeth's speech from Downing Street in a way that made explicit the multi-national character of Britain:

> Through the dusk of the June evening, her clear young voice will go out across England, past the familiar landmarks of church steeple, hedgerow, and white winding lane; over Welsh mountain, Scottish moor, and Irish lough; and out across the seas and continents with the speed of light, round the circle of the earth … and in those minutes, and through the act of listening, the family of the Commonwealth will be joined and reunited.[96]

As it had in so many other programs, the BBC made manifest the intimate links between monarchy, empire, and Britishness.

Conclusion

From its origin, the BBC sought to ingratiate itself to the monarchy. This was, in part, an attempt to legitimize the new medium of radio by attaching to it the authority and prestige of monarchy. But it was also personal. Reith strongly believed in the monarchy and its symbolic role, and it was largely through his efforts that George V finally consented to broadcast his speeches. When Reith succeeded in this endeavor, by getting the King to broadcast at the Wembley Empire Exhibition and years later on Christmas Day, he forged a powerful and mutually beneficial relationship between two fundamental British institutions.

The BBC used monarchy to pique interest in radio and enjoyed enormous audiences every time the monarchs came to the microphone; the monarchy was given an opportunity to project itself to the British people on a grander scale and with greater intimacy than ever before.

The BBC was pivotal in creating an image of the British monarchy as truly "British," an image that the Windsors themselves had been constructing since at least 1911. The BBC was careful to make the coronations of George VI and Elizabeth II truly "British" affairs, by encouraging contributions from the regions and providing extensive local coverage of the royals' visits to Scotland, Wales, and Northern Ireland. In addition, the BBC depicted the monarchy as a powerful symbol of empire and Commonwealth. The monarchy as a source of loyalty to Britain may have been especially comforting in 1953. Britain had already lost India, its most important colony, in 1947, and suffered through an embarrassing withdrawal from Palestine. Monarchy, then, as presented by the BBC in 1947 during the royal tour and the 1953 coronation of Elizabeth, could assuage listeners concerned with Britain's decline.

Although the monarchy was a powerful symbol of British unity, the Windsors pressed for this to be unity as diversity. The BBC was eager to comply and reproduce this image, not the least because it was also in keeping with the self-image of the BBC. Like the monarchy, the BBC also promoted a unitary from of Britishness, but one that recognized and celebrated the multi-national character of the United Kingdom.

Notes

1 Jeffrey Richards, "The Monarchy and Film, 1900–2006," in *The Monarchy and the British Nation: 1780 to the Present*, Andrzej Olechnowicz, ed. (Cambridge: Cambridge University Press, 2007), 258.

2 Colley, *Britons*, chapter 5. Of course the monarchy became the center of patriotic celebrations only after the threat of a Stuart restoration was finally disposed of at Culloden.

3 John Plunkett, *Queen Victoria: First Media Monarch* (Oxford: Oxford University Press, 2003); William M. Kuhn, *Democratic Royalism: The Transformation of the British Monarchy* (New York: St Martin's Press, 1996); Tom Nairn, *The Enchanted Glass: Britain and Its Monarchy* (London: Vintage, 1994). David Cannadine, "The Context, Performance and Meaning of Ritual: The British Monarchy and 'The Invention of Tradition,' c. 1820–1977," in *The Invention of Tradition*, Hobsbawm and Ranger, eds. Cannadine interprets the monarchy's move to public display as a maneuver by elites to create popular affection for a decidedly un-democratic institution, to manage social change, and to retard the modernization of Britain.

He also sees it as part of a rise in popular, but conservative, patriotism, centered on the Queen and the empire. Tom Nairn makes similar arguments in "Britain's Royal Romance," in *Patriotism: The Making and Unmaking of British National Identity*, vol. 1, *History and Politics*, Raphael Samuel, ed. (London: Routledge, 1989), 78–83. Kuhn argues that the new popularity enjoyed by the royals in the nineteenth century reflected genuine affection as opposed to elite manipulation. In a similar vein Frank Prochaska argues that the monarchy's patronage of charitable organizations helped cement its popularity among the mass of British citizens. See *Royal Bounty: The Making of a Welfare Monarchy* (New Haven: Yale University Press, 1995).

4 Quoted in Cannadine, "British Monarchy," 125. Gladstone was perturbed by the inclusion imperial elements in these celebrations and found the diamond jubilee "artificial and unreal." See Kuhn, 52.

5 Cannadine, "British Monarchy," 120–3.

6 Ibid., 122.

7 Philip Williamson, "The Monarchy and Public Values 1900–1953," in *Monarchy and the British Nation*, Olechnowicz, ed., 223–57.

8 Ward, *Britishness*, 23.

9 Nairn, *Enchanted Glass*, xvii.

10 On George IV's famous visit to Edinburgh in 1822, see John Prebble, *The King's Jaunt: George IV in Scotland, August 1822 "One and Twenty Daft Days"* (London: Collins, 1988); Hugh Trevor-Roper, "The Invention of Tradition: The Highland Tradition of Scotland," in *The Invention of Tradition*, Hobsbawm and Ranger, eds.

11 John Davis, "Victoria and Victorian Wales," in *Politics and Society in Wales, 1840–1922*, Geraint H. Jenkins and J. Beverley Smith, eds (Cardiff: University of Wales Press, 1988), 7.

12 John S. Ellis, "Reconciling the Celt: British National Identity, Empire, and the 1911 Investiture of the Prince of Wales," *Journal of British Studies*, 37 (1998): 391–418.

13 Ibid., 396–8, 403–4.

14 Chandrika Kaul, "Monarchical Display and the Politics of Empire: Princes of Wales and India 1870–1920s," *Twentieth Century British History*, 17 (2006): 464–88.

15 This, of course, became an untenable position after the Anglo-Irish War and the partition of Ireland. Thereafter, the monarchy would become a powerful symbol of Protestant loyalty to the British state.

16 Anne Spry Rush, "Imperial Identity in Colonial Minds: Harold Moody and the League of Colored Peoples, 1931–40," *Twentieth Century British History*, 13 (2002): 372–3. A recent issue of the *Journal of Imperial and Commonwealth History* was devoted to the imperial dimensions of the British monarchy. See *Journal of Imperial and Commonwealth History*, 34 (2006): 1–154.

17 Reith, *Into the Wind*, 28–9.

18 Reith quoted in Scannell and Cardiff, 280–1.

19 Scannell and Cardiff, 281; Briggs, *Birth of Broadcasting*, 265. For statistics on licenses, see Mark Pegg, *Broadcasting and Society* (London: Croom Helm, 1983), 7.

20 *Oxford Times*, 25 April 1924, quoted in Pegg, 192.
21 J. C. W. Reith, *The Reith Diaries*, Charles Stuart, ed. (London: Collins, 1975), 133.
22 Ibid., 181–2, 183.
23 Ibid., 183.
24 *BBC Annual, 1936*, 10.
25 Robert Wood, a BBC engineer, quoted in Scannell and Cardiff, 284.
26 McIntyre, 229.
27 Boyle, 281–4.
28 Reith diary, quoted in McIntyre, 230.
29 Reith, *Diaries*, 194.
30 *Radio Times*, May 7, 1937, 10–12; *BBC Handbook, 1938*, 31–6.
31 *Radio Times*, April 23, 1937, 4.
32 *Radio Times*, April 30, 1937, 34, 79.
33 *Radio Times*, April 23, 1937, 80.
34 *Radio Times*, April 30, 1937, 78–9.
35 Ibid., 4.
36 Ibid., 79.
37 This and following taken from an article by Laurence Gilliam in the *Radio Times*, May 7, 1937, 13.
38 French-Canadians often featured in Empire Day and Christmas Day broadcasts similar to *The Empire's Homage*. The fact that they were trotted out as "loyal outsiders" says much about British views towards Catholicism in the first half of the twentieth century. Ibid.
39 Ibid.
40 Melville Dinwiddie, "Scotland's Royal Salute," *Radio Times*, July 2, 1937, 6.
41 *Radio Times*, June 11, 1937, 78.
42 *Radio Times*, July 9, 1937, 15. The Caernarfon Castle ceremonies were carried on the National Programme.
43 George Marshall, "Royal Visit to Ulster," *Radio Times*, July 23, 1937, 14.
44 Ibid.
45 Simon Potter, "The BBC, the CBC, and the 1939 Royal Tour of Canada," *Cultural and Social History,* 3 (2006): 424–44.
46 *Radio Times*, May 19, 1939, 7.
47 King George VI, *George VI to His Peoples, 1936–1951: Selected Broadcasts and Speeches* (London: John Murray, 1952), 4.
48 In his 1937 Christmas Day address, George spoke of his father's broadcasts: "Many of you will remember the Christmas broadcasts of former years, when my father spoke to his peoples at home and overseas as the revered head of a great family … I cannot aspire to take his place—nor do I think that you would wish me to carry on, unvaried, a tradition so personal to him." Ibid.
49 John W. Wheeler-Bennett, *King George VI: His Life and Reign* (New York: St Martin's Press, 1958), 429.
50 Weight, 34–5.

51 Weight, 34; Williamson, "Public Values," 241.
52 Weight, 35.
53 George VI, 17–18; Calder, *People's War*, 57.
54 George VI, 19–20; Wheeler-Bennett, 429.
55 George VI, 20.
56 Home Board, February 9, 1940; February 23, 1940; May 3, 1940; May 10, 1940; BBC WAC, R3/16/1. The BBC received such a late response from Buckingham Palace that the broadcast could not be publicized in the *Radio Times*.
57 George VI, 23.
58 Ibid., 26.
59 Ibid., 28, 31–4.
60 Listener Research Report LR/551, January 9, 1942, BBC WAC, R9/54/1.
61 Listener Research Report LR/3130, January 11, 1945, BBC WAC, R9/54/3.
62 *Radio Times*, May 9, 1947, 1.
63 *Radio Times*, May 17, 1946, 1.
64 Robert Lacey, *Monarch: The Life and Reign of Elizabeth II* (New York: The Free Press, 2002), 156.
65 Programme Policy Meeting, 23 September 1947, BBC WAC, R34/615/6.
66 Briggs, *Sound and Vision*, 713.
67 Wheeler-Bennett, 685; Sarah Bradford, *The Reluctant King: The Life and Reign of George VI 1895–1952* (New York: St Martin's Press, 1989), 389.
68 Programme Policy Meeting, July 18, 1946, BBC WAC R34/615/5.
69 Programme Policy Meeting, August 1, 1946, Ibid.
70 *Radio Times*, January 24, 1947, 3; *Radio Times*, March 14, 1947, 4.
71 Geoffrey Bridson, *Prospero and Ariel* (London: Gollancz, 1972), 133–41.
72 *Radio Times*, January 24, 1947, 3.
73 *Radio Times*, April 18, 1947, 7.
74 *Radio Times*, March 7, 1947, 3.
75 Ibid.
76 Bridson, 137–8.
77 *Radio Times*, April 18, 1947, 7; Frank Gillard, "Covering the Royal Tour of South Africa," *BBC Year Book 1948*, 29.
78 Bridson, 139–41.
79 Asa Briggs, *The BBC: The First Fifty Years* (Oxford: Oxford University Press, 1985), 275.
80 James Schwoch, "Crypto-Convergence, Media, and the Cold War: The Early Globalization of Television Networks in the 1950s," unpublished paper delivered at the MIT Media-In-Transitions Conference, 2002.
81 *Radio Times*, April 10, 1953, 31.
82 *Radio Times*, April 24, 1953, 42; *Radio Times*, May 8, 1953, 15, 42; *Radio Times*, May 15, 1953, 1.
83 *Radio Times*, May 1, 1953, 12.
84 *Radio Times*, May 1, 1953, 1.
85 *Radio Times*, May 22, 1953, 1.

86 Ibid.
87 *Radio Times*, May 29, 1953, 11.
88 *Radio Times*, May 22, 1953, 1; *Radio Times*, May 29, 1953, 11.
89 *Radio Times*, May 22, 1953, 5. "The purpose of the program," went another promotional item in the *Radio Times*, "is to bring together leading artists of the Commonwealth and the United Kingdom in one great family party." *Radio Times*, 29 May, 1953.
90 *Radio Times*, May 22, 1953, 39.
91 Charles Max-Muller, "The BBC Prepares for the Coronation Broadcast," *Radio Times*, May 5, 1953, 5.
92 Ibid.
93 *Radio Times*, May 29, 1953, 9–10.
94 *Radio Times*, May 1, 1953, 1.
95 *Radio Times*, May 8, 1953, 7; *Radio Times*, May 15, 1953, 9.
96 *Radio Times*, May 29, 1953, 9.

4

Rethinking regional broadcasting in Britain, 1922–53

The first four chapters of this book examined the BBC as a nationalizing institution and its role in the construction of a British national identity inclusive of English, Scottish, Welsh, and Northern Irish identities. They highlighted the fluidity of British national identity, the tensions inherent in the BBC's construction of Britishness, and the contests over this version of Britishness inside the Corporation. The focus of this book now shifts to broadcasting within the nations that, along with England, make up Great Britain—Scotland, Wales, and Northern Ireland. The development of broadcasting, and the debates about how broadcasting could best represent the identity of these nations, will be considered in Chapters 5, 6, and 7.

The purpose of this chapter is threefold. First, it will furnish some necessary background information for the discussion of broadcasting in Scotland, Wales, and Northern Ireland to follow by providing an overview of local and regional broadcasting in Britain from 1923 to 1953. As discussed in the Introduction, the BBC, by the early 1930s, consisted of six separate services for domestic listeners: the National Programme, broadcast from the BBC's high-power transmitter at Daventry, and five regional services broadcast from medium-wave transmitters throughout Britain. The BBC originally based its regional networks in Scotland, Northern Ireland, the North of England, the Midlands, and the West. The BBC included, but hardly subsumed, Wales in the West region until 1937, when it was split into two distinct broadcasting regions.

Second, the chapter includes significant material on the regional programs produced during the Second World War, an almost completely ignored part of broadcasting history. The war saw the suspension of the individual regional networks, but by no means the end of regional programs. Ironically, 1939 proved to be an important moment in the "regionalization" of the BBC and its representation of Britain as a unified, but highly diverse nation. The suspension of the regional networks for the duration of the war forced the BBC, to a greater extent than ever before, to represent the multi-national character of Britain; regional programs had to be carried by either the Home Service or the Forces Programme, which were both national services. English listeners who may never have heard a Scottish, Welsh, or Irish program before the war found themselves exposed to broadcasts from around the regions. To further compensate for the loss of the regional networks the BBC also produced a number of programs that combined contributions from around the regions, giving them a British, as opposed to English, flavor.

Third, this chapter argues that current scholarship on the history of regional broadcasting in Britain provides an incomplete and narrow assessment of BBC broadcasting in the regions. The orthodoxy, "centralization," underestimates the willingness and ability of regional broadcasters to resist the authority of the BBC's London establishment and the extent to which regional broadcasters fostered national identity in the regions while also forcing the BBC to recognize the multi-national character of Britain. The most influential studies of regional broadcasting in Britain, Briggs's *Golden Age of Wireless*, Cardiff and Scannell's *Social History of British Broadcasting*, and Pegg's *Broadcasting and Society* all end in 1939, which can give the impression that the suspension of regional broadcasting was the logical outcome nearly two decades of centralization. By expanding our chronological scope to 1953 we get a different picture of regional broadcasting, one in which the Second World War appears as an aberration, not the culmination of BBC policy. Orthodox interpretations of regional broadcasting also tend to emphasize the brief period of 1927–32, during which the BBC consolidated its local stations into the five regional stations. But the second half of the 1930s saw the BBC loosen its control over its regional stations, and regional autonomy continued after the war. Finally, Briggs and Scannell and Cardiff share a certain nostalgia for local broadcasting in the 1920s, which they regard as more organic, and therefore genuine, than the regional broadcasting that replaced it. Local broadcasting represented a more democratic alternative to the system of broadcasting that did evolve in Britain. While there is much truth in these interpretations, they tend to overstate the independence and "localness" of the early BBC stations. At the same time, histories of early broadcasting which offer a "what could have been" lament for the demise of the local stations can fail to fully appreciate the possibilities and accomplishments of regional broadcasting.

Our understanding of the role and influence of regional broadcasting in Britain has been conditioned by the periodization of Briggs's *History of Broad-*

casting in the United Kingdom, and Scannell's and Cardiff's *Social History of British Broadcasting*, both of which conclude with the start of the Second World War and the suspension of the regional networks.[1] Of course, setting a chronological limit on one's work is a necessary, if somewhat artificial, task for the historian. Scholars have every right to decide the legitimate scope of their work, and there are few better "watershed" dates in the twentieth century than 1939. Yet studies of regional broadcasting that conclude in 1939 must, by definition, exclude the era of vibrant regional broadcasting that followed the war. They cannot help but leave the reader with the impression that after a heroic battle for a measure of independence in the 1930s, the BBC scuppered regional broadcasting at the outbreak of the war, never to return. Scannell and Cardiff, in an analysis of the work of the North region, write of the late 1930s as the "brief golden years before the war."[2] The following, from an article on BBC Scotland before the war, merits some attention because it is characteristic of how periodization shapes orthodox interpretations of regional broadcasting. In the piece, Adrienne Scullion claims that in September 1939:

> station independence was reset as fragmentation and unity was encouraged for patriotic reasons … after this disruption regional broadcasting only edged back into the schedules and never with the organic naturalness of the original broad-cast structure. After this a Scottish element was never assumed, always something to be aspired to and worked towards.[3]

The phrase "never with the organic naturalness of the original broadcast structure" is both ambiguous and an oversimplification of the nature of regional broadcasting. The BBC restored the Scottish regional network after the war. "Original broadcast structure" might refer to the first Scottish local stations, but 1939 was not an important year in terms of the consolidation of the Scottish local stations into one regional station; that process had been completed in the early 1930s. "Never" could mean never during the war, but this is both awkward and vague. Finally, the passage's reference to "organic naturalness" begs us to consider the extent to which even the early local stations could be characterized as authentic or "organic."

As noted above, the use of 1939 as the *terminus ad quem* has, in some cases, led to one-dimensional interpretations of regional broadcasting. Equally problematic is the fact that historians have placed too much emphasis on the demise of the local stations and the BBC's policy of centralization, and not enough on the slow but sure reversal of this policy, culminating in several years of noteworthy regional broadcasting before the war. The London-based hierarchy of the BBC began to exert more control over the local stations beginning in

1928, but this policy came to be tempered as early as 1932 with the appointment of Lindsay Wellington as Presentation Director and the creation of the position of Programme Director for each region. Briggs's section on regional broadcasting in *The Golden Age of Wireless*, itself only 45 pages out of over 650, spends a little less than three pages discussing regional broadcasting from 1936 to 1939. Briggs does little more than highlight some of the more outstanding regional programs produced during this period, and all but concludes his chapter on regional broadcasting by remarking on a stinging 1936 report by Charles Siepmann, which itself led directly to subsequent improvements for the regional networks. In his book, Pegg also gives the lion's share of his section on regional broadcasting to the process of centralization.[4] Scannell and Cardiff also end their chapter on local and regional broadcasting in *A Social History of British Broadcasting* with Siepmann's report, although in a subsequent chapter on the activities of the North region they do examine productions from the late 1930s.[5] The activities of BBC Scotland in the late 1930s seem to be an afterthought for Scullion as well. She writes that "devolution in the structure of the BBC … was formalised and curtailed with the regional scheme of the late 1920s and early 1930s and gradually reduced and eroded until 1939." Not only does this claim contradict the assertions of Scannell and Cardiff, two scholars hardly sympathetic to the BBC's regional scheme, that the period from 1936 to 1939 saw "innovative and exciting programmes from the regions,"[6] it does not fairly reflect the work of the staff of BBC Scotland and their relationship to BBC Head Office. Not only do we need histories of regional broadcasting that take a longer view, past the outbreak of the Second World War, but histories that more closely focus on the period from 1932 to 1939. Instead of lamenting the fall of local radio, histories of regional broadcasting need to focus more on what the regional broadcasters were actually doing, and the programs they were making, which were in turn consumed by hundreds of thousands, perhaps millions of listeners.

Why have historians of British broadcasting focused so much on the local stations and regarded the implementation of the regional scheme as a largely negative development? The answer to this question lies, in part, in the romanticization of early local broadcasting and an intense dislike for the more metropolitan values and undemocratic impulses of the early BBC. This nostalgic view of the activities of the local stations is based on a belief that the local stations represented the "reality" of genuine communities. In contrast, the BBC's regions, which replaced the local stations, lacked authenticity because of the geographical size and the social and cultural diversity of communities they represented. As Pegg states in *Broadcasting and Society*, "the BBC Regions were so large that it is difficult to see any rationale for them beyond that of administrative, economic or technical convenience. The North and West regions were particularly large, covering many hundreds of communities."[7] Briggs, author of *Victorian Cities*, perhaps could not help but see in the regional scheme a further blow to "the proud 'provincialism' of the Victorian era, already in tatters in many parts of the country."[8] Similarly, Scannell's and Cardiff's writings on local and regional broadcasting are, in part, an attempt to recover the engaging and friendly broadcasting that characterized the first BBC stations. They focus especially on the interactions between the local broadcasters and the audience, so uncharacteristic of the BBC in the 1930s. "The outstanding quality of radio at this time was its coziness and warmth," write Scannell and Cardiff of the early 1920s. "The local stations," they conclude, "adapted themselves to the areas they served and offered not only entertainment but a public service to their community of a rather different kind to that which was taking shape in London."[9] For Scannell and Cardiff, early broadcasting developed from the community it served, a point taken up by Scullion when she claims that BBC programming before the regional scheme "had a close and even organic relationship with the local culture it served."[10] Finally, there is a tendency in this scholarship to link regionalization with the imposition of "Reithian" standards on broadcasting—the fetishization of received pronunciation, the anonymity of the announcers, and the decision to make announcers wear proper evening attire—all of which professionalized the BBC and created distance between broadcaster and audience. As Scannell and Cardiff write, "the friendly informality of local broadcasting … was foreclosed in this country [Britain] … by the implementation of the regional scheme."[11]

The problem is not that these are all wholly invalid arguments. Local stations were less formal than the regional stations and more "in touch" with their listeners, but on balance this is all to take a rather romantic view of local radio in the 1920s. For example, over half the BBC's early local stations, the "relay stations," produced only a small amount of local programming; the rest of their output came from London via telephone lines. Listeners in these areas had the opportunity to listen to more "regional" broadcasting after the implementation of the regional scheme than "local" broadcasting from their relay stations. Even the main stations received a heavy dose of London programs. While the presence of a BBC studio might boost civic pride, local broadcasting in Britain was never entirely local. Further, while the character of radio did become more formal in the late 1920s, there is no necessary relationship between the implementation of the regional scheme and the formalization of radio broadcasting. Regionalization did facilitate Head Office's move to impose certain program standards on the provincial stations. Undoubtedly the BBC found it easier to monitor five regional stations than nineteen local stations. But it does not follow that the regional scheme caused broadcasting to become stiff and detached or that Reith would not or could not have impressed his vision of professionalism, cultural elitism, and public service broadcasting on the local stations. Even more apparent is the fact that the consolidation of the local stations and the implementation of the regional scheme did not require broadcasting to become distant and patronizing. Indeed, after the Second World War the regions led the way in developing informal audience-participation programs such as *Have A Go* and *Any Questions*. The demise of the local stations did not preclude the production of informal, populist programs. Finally, it is difficult to see how local broadcasting was more genuine or organic than the regional broadcasting that replaced it. The difference is one of degree, perhaps, but not kind. As Anderson notes in *Imagined Communities*, any social organization beyond the pre-industrial village is in some sense "imaginary." While it is true that the regions covered large tracts of territory and included several major cities, they were no more "imaginary" than the conurbations, some the size of small nations, served by the original main and relay stations. Is "Scotland" any more of an imagined community than "Glasgow?" Is "Manchester" any less of an imagined community than "the North?" Would Brummagems not recognize social and geographic differences within Birmingham and its suburbs? Diversity and differentiation is something that is national, regional, *and* local.

The common terminal date of 1939, the emphasis in the prevailing scholarship on the policy of centralization, and the romanticization of the work of the first local stations have resulted in a somewhat skewed interpretation of regional broadcasting in Britain. The key words and phrases in most of these texts are "centralization," "control," "standards," and "metropolitan bias." But these emphases obscure, as much as they illuminate, the relationship between London and the regions. The regions had more independence within the Corporation than the preponderance of scholarship suggests. This position also can distort the intentions of Head Office with regards to regional broadcasting. The original purpose of the regional scheme was to offer listeners a measure of choice in their programs. The department heads in London wanted authority over the regions in order to maintain artistic standards, not program content. BBC Head Office encouraged the regions to explore, examine, and reflect the way of life of the regions they represented. There was a certain danger of parochialism in this policy. BBC Scotland could not put on the plays of Brecht and the North region was discouraged from doing opera. Some members of the BBC's Head Office staff considered the regions poor relations that ought to bow to the demands of London, but historical narratives based solely on London's control undervalue the nature of regional broadcasting and the important role it played in constructing national identities in Scotland, Wales, and Northern Ireland.

The local stations and the coming of the regional scheme

Broadcasting in Britain was organized, initially, on a local basis. When the British Broadcasting Company formed in 1922, it acquired the three radio stations then operating in Britain: Marconi-owned 2LO in London, Western Electric's 5IT in Birmingham, and 2ZY, the Metropolitan-Vickers station in Manchester. The most pressing priority for the new company was to extend its service to as many listeners as possible. The radio manufacturers who created the BBC stood to benefit enormously from an expansion of the service; a wider service meant more consumers. Reith agreed, as he regarded the "extension of broadcasting facilities as justification of the national claims of broadcasting as a public service."[12] Given the technical limitations—both the low power of radio transmitters and the inability of most receivers to pick up distant signals—the BBC decided to construct a series of stations in Britain's main population centers. In addition to London, Manchester, and Birmingham, the BBC, by the end of 1924, had built stations in Newcastle, Bournemouth, Cardiff, Belfast, Aberdeen, and Glasgow. By 1925, these nine "main stations" were joined by ten low-power "relay stations." With the completion of relay stations in Sheffield, Plymouth, Liverpool, Leeds-Bradford, Hull, Nottingham, Stoke-on-Trent, Swansea, Edinburgh, and Dundee, 80 per cent of the population could listen to BBC programs.[13]

These first stations were, in some ways, extremely local. Each of the main stations included a studio for the production of programs, for and by the local population. The presence of a BBC main station often produced considerable civic pride. The Company encouraged station managers to make contacts with local dignitaries, and the BBC did broadcasts for the benefit of local charities. Yet in other ways, the BBC was already taking on characteristics of a unitary, national service. For one thing, the relay stations did not, by and large, produce many of their own programs, or even take programs from the nearest main station. Rather, they simply transmitted the output of 2LO, the London station. Sheffield, where the BBC built its first relay station, rejected the idea of taking programs from Manchester, the nearest main station. The Swansea relay station likewise refused to subordinate itself to Cardiff. Edinburgh and Dundee were not linked to the main station at Glasgow; rather, they carried London programs. In *Broadcast over Britain*, a perplexed Reith noted that "no city counted sufficiently important to have a relay station could listen to the programs of any station other than London without loss of dignity."[14] The result was that over half the stations in the BBC system broadcast London programs almost exclusively, and provided no alternative for the audience.

The BBC further took on the characteristics of a national broadcasting system with the institution of "simultaneous broadcasting." Simultaneous broadcasting, which began in 1923, allowed the program of any station to be carried instantaneously, via post office trunk lines, to all the other BBC stations. In theory, any station could provide a program for simultaneous broadcast, but in practice, London dominated the scheme. Shortly after the implementation of simultaneous broadcasting, the BBC decided that two evenings of programming a week would be supplied to the network by London. Programs of cultural or national significance also were broadcast from all stations. Almost from the inception of broadcasting in Britain, then, listeners were given a regular diet of London-produced programs.

Although the BBC found the main and relay stations expedient in extending its service, the system had several drawbacks. For one, the range of the low-power transmitters used in the scheme was limited. Listeners had to be within twenty miles of a transmitter to listen to the BBC, so large tracts of countryside remained outside of the reach of radio. The situation also undermined Reith's plans to make the BBC a public service corporation. Radio had to reach the whole nation for Reith to make claims for the BBC as a national institution. A more pressing problem for the Company was the decision of the *Union Internationale de Radiophonie* in July 1926 to limit the number of radio wavelengths available to each country in Europe in order to prevent multiple stations from trying to use the same frequency for broadcasting. The BBC's allocation of ten medium waves and one long wave precluded the building of additional low-power transmitters; rather, it required the BBC to make economies in this regard. The wavelength restriction also made it impossible for the BBC to offer alternate channels if they kept their system of main and relay stations intact. If the BBC failed to deliver alternate programming, the government might have considered revoking its monopoly status in order to give radio listeners a measure of choice.

The "regional scheme," devised by Peter Eckersley, the BBC's Chief Engineer, offered a solution to these pressing problems. Instead of a series of lower-power transmitters located in urban centers, Eckersley envisaged five high-power transmitters that would provide coverage to vast stretches of territory, thereby reducing the number of necessary wavelengths and providing coverage to rural areas. Further, the high-power "regional" wavelengths would give listeners an alternative to the programming carried by the BBC's long-wave station at Daventry, which could be heard the length and breadth of the United Kingdom. Finally, the regional scheme allowed the BBC to make economies of scale. The subsequent reduction in production centers, that is the closing of the relay and some of the main stations,[15] reduced the number of necessary staff and avoided the costly duplication of similar programs. When the regional scheme was completed listeners had a choice between two networks, the National Programme and the Regional Programme. The latter consisted of the North region, the West region (which until 1937 included Wales), the Midland region, the Scottish region, the Northern Ireland region, and the London region. London region provided most of the daytime programming to the regional stations, but regionally produced material filled the schedules of the regional stations during evening listening hours.

Concomitant with the regional scheme was the implementation of the BBC's policy of centralization. As early as December 1923 Reith was commenting on the need to forge a uniform policy for broadcasting across Britain and to increase the authority of Head Office with regard to the local stations. By 1924, regular meetings between Reith and the station directors allowed for closer oversight of provincial programs. Also in 1924, the BBC established its Programme Board, a body of Head Office staff "in close touch with the Directors of the provincial stations," to schedule programs and simultaneous broadcasts, and generally uphold program standards.[16] Part, indeed perhaps the key part, of centralization was the maintenance of London artistic standards at the local stations and the end of the friendly informality between local broadcasters and their audience. In November 1924 the BBC decided that all announcers should be anonymous, and in the autumn of 1925 the BBC implemented its infamous policy of having announcers wear dinner jackets. Head Office in London made clear its low regard for provincial staff in 1926, when each BBC station received a "book of instructions of the do's and don'ts of broadcasting," prompting protests from some of the local stations that Head Office was overbearing and condescending towards the their work.[17]

The concern with control from London, the insistence on high artistic standards, and the haughtiness with which Head Office sometimes treated the staff of the local stations reveal the cultural suppositions that underlay centralization. In short, much of the Head Office staff considered local and provincial culture to be inferior to that of London. Chief among them was Roger Eckersley, who held various posts at the BBC, including Director of Programmes; Val Gielgud, Director of Drama; and Charles Siepmann, Director of Talks. Despite his Scottish roots, Reith was also quite metropolitan in his outlook, but he often sympathized with Regional Directors. Indeed, his original conception of broadcasting was one of stations serving populations grouped according to their regional characteristics.[18] Nevertheless, Head Office prejudices became policy with the implementation of the regional scheme. Through 1929–30, centralization and the cultural baggage of the Head Office staff responsible for implementing the policy undermined the newly created regional networks. The BBC cut back on staff at the regional stations and the chief problem regional broadcasters had to surmount was overwork. Because Head Office decided that plays were to come only from London, except on special occasions, regional stations did not keep a member on staff for dramatic work. Most of the regional orchestras were reduced to octets and many of the staff members at the new regional stations became demoralized.[19]

The retreat from centralization

However, for all the emphasis it has received in the scholarly literature, centralization, within a few years, began to be retracted, or at least modified, as Corporation policy. This policy shift was in part a response to the overreaching ambitions of Gielgud and Siepmann. The latter was, at the time, one of the most powerful men at the BBC. The two pressed Reith to give them authority over regional program-making in their respective spheres of Drama and Talks. Ted Liveling, Cleghorn Thompson, and Gerald Beadle, Regional Directors for the North, Scotland, and Northern Ireland respectively, resisted. Liveling argued that Gielgud and Siepmann had little knowledge of provincial resources and program making. Beadle suggested the creation of a "Regional Assistant Director of Programmes" to mediate between the regions and Head Office. In 1932 Reith tabbed Lindsay Wellington, who had been responsible for simultaneous broadcasts, for the post.[20] Wellington's exact position in the BBC hierarchy was unclear. Although technically subordinate to Gielgud and Siepmann "his position to them would be advanced somewhat" and they would "in general be guided by his advice."[21] He was not, however, a Head

Office supremo in charge of regional programs. Although given "executive control" over shared programs from London regional, he could only advise on programs produced by the regions for their own regional audience.[22] Wellington provided the regions with a voice and could, when he saw fit, support their interests at Head Office. Although he was a Head Office man, and could be harshly critical of some regional productions, Wellington was, by and large, a supporter of regional broadcasting.

Another important step in the development of regional broadcasting was the appointment of Programme Directors for each of the regions in 1932. Again, the impetus for the creation of this post seems to have come from the feeling that centralization had gone too far. In making their decision, Control Board noted "a certain metropolitan bias ... present at Head Office" and complained that "officials at Head Office were ... not fully conversant with regional characteristics and conditions."[23] The new Regional Programme Directors had a dual mandate. On the one hand, Control Board expected them to "absorb Head Office outlook and standards," suggesting that the Regional Programme Directors could become a kind of "Trojan horse" that would allow Head Office to further erode regional autonomy. On the other hand, part of their remit was to "safeguard justifiable regional interests."[24] The Regional Programme Directors, especially in Scotland, Wales, and Northern Ireland, embraced this latter role. For example, Andrew Stewart, appointed to the post of Scottish Programme Director in 1935, often clashed with Head Office personnel over scheduling and other issues. Further, he claimed that his special knowledge of his region made him more qualified to make program decisions for Scotland than Head Office staff. E. A. Harding, the North Programme Director, also successfully resisted Head Office encroachment on the North region's schedules.

The conditions under which the regional broadcasters toiled continued to improve in the mid-1930s. Regional program staffs doubled in 1935, alleviating some of the problems of overwork.[25] More importantly, the Ullswater Committee, commissioned with investigating the state of broadcasting in Britain and making recommendations for changes, took a keen interest in regional programming and the relations between London and the regional offices. The Ullswater Committee interviewed three of the Regional Directors, Percy Edgar (Midland), Ted Liveling (North) and Melville Dinwiddie (Scotland); all three "vigourously defended the regional system as it operated at that time."[26] Still, a wide range of interest groups—academics, provincial newspapers, Welsh and Scottish MPs, Welsh and Scottish nationalists, cultural societies—criticized the BBC's regional policy. Worried about the possible recommendations of the Ullswater Committee, Reith strongly defended the practices of the BBC while at the same time promising reforms. In presenting his oral evidence to Ullswater, Reith defended central control because of the BBC's "nation-wide responsibility," and claimed that centralization had been necessary to "establish a settled policy and the beginnings of a tradition of public service broadcasting." But, Reith was quick to add, the BBC's newest policy was "regional devolution … as quickly and as comprehensively as is compatible with efficiency in the broadcast sense of the term." He assured the Ullswater Committee that regional staffs had been enlarged and told them of the creation of a new position, the Director of Regional Relations, who would be responsible for ensuring some measure of autonomy for the regions. Reith concluded by stating that the "*de facto* independence of the Regions" was progressing at a suitable pace.[27]

The Ullswater Committee initiated two major reforms of regional broadcasting. First, the BBC divorced Wales from the West region and established a distinct broadcasting region for the Principality. Second, Reith appointed Charles Siepmann as Director of Regional Relations. Siepmann's first task was to tour all of the regions and write a detailed report on the state of broadcasting in each of them. He spent between six days and three weeks in each region, and met with staff, inspected premises, and listened to programs. After visiting the provinces, Siepmann, who had been one of the most adamant centralizers in 1932, completely reversed his position on regional broadcasting. In his report, he argued that centralization had been a short-sighted policy. The regions, he argued, represented the "seed ground of talent and the ultimate source of supply for the London programmes." Although Siepmann certainly disparaged some programs from the regions, he criticized the application of London artistic standards to the products of the regional stations. Regional programs, he continued, had to be judged not only by their artistic merit but also by their patronage of local artists and by their ability to reflect local life. The activities of the regions, he concluded, were too standardized and needed to be more in touch with the communities they served.[28] Although some of Siepmann's recommendations were rejected (notably his proposal to create a "Southern" region), most of the senior staff and the BBC Board of Governors accepted his call for more independence and diversity in regional programs, and for the provincial stations to meet more effectively the needs of the regions they served. The BBC Governors regarded these changes as a "Charter of Rights" for the regions.[29]

Regional broadcasting during the Second World War

It was unfortunate that not long after receiving their "Charter of Rights" and engaging in diverse, exciting, and, at times, innovative broadcasting, the regions suffered a severe blow with the outbreak of the Second World War. The BBC synchronized all of its transmitters to the same wavelength and suspended the regional networks for the duration. Although some scholars see this as the final degradation of regional broadcasting and evidence of Head Office's contempt for the regions, the decision was made at the behest of the Air Ministry, which gave serious consideration to asking for the suspension of all broadcasting during the war. The Air Ministry was concerned that the Luftwaffe could use the BBC's transmissions to guide them to targets in Britain. Synchronization was the compromise solution, and it enabled the BBC to broadcast throughout the war. Indeed, the great benefit of synchronization was that it allowed the BBC to be heard, without interruption, throughout the whole of Britain. If an air raid forced the closing of one of the BBC transmitters, listeners in that area could still receive their programs from another nearby transmitter.[30] Of course, the synchronization of the BBC's transmitters benefited the government and the BBC in another way; it was much easier to monitor and censor the output of a single national program than that of six regional networks.

The suspension of the regional networks in 1939 did not mean, however, the suspension of regional programs. This is a crucial distinction, and one that often gets lost due to the failure of scholars to give due consideration to the importance of regional programs during the war. For the duration of the war the BBC kept up its production of regionally flavored programs for both its Overseas services and the Home Service and Forces Programme. This is essential to understand, for while propaganda during the war emphasized national unity, it did so in a way that necessarily recognized the national diversity of Britain. The presence of regional programs on the Home Service and Forces Programme allowed the BBC to acknowledge Britain's multi-national character and create a less homogenous representation of Britain and Britishness.

On one level, the BBC was well prepared for the outbreak of the war. Synchronization prevented interruptions in the service and program departments were evacuated to production sites away from London. However, the BBC misjudged its audience when it came to actual programming. A steady diet of tedious programming created a backlash from listeners who craved entertainment as well as information. This dissatisfaction extended to regional programming as well, but by early November 1939, the BBC realized that it needed to include more regional programs in its schedules.[31] After a complaint from the Midland Region Director, the BBC's Home Service Board resolved "as a general tendency," to "greater employment of regional artists and representation of regional resources in the Home Service programs, particularly in variety and features."[32] Laurence Gilliam later assured the Home Board that regional representation in features "would increase very largely" by January 1940.[33] Regional contributions included outside broadcasts, special programs (such as those for St Patrick's, St Andrew's, and St David's Day), and talks. Welsh region prepared talks in Welsh and Scottish region prepared talks in Gaelic for broadcast in the Home Service, much to the chagrin of English (and most Scottish and Welsh) listeners.[34] In addition to producing their own programs, the regions also contributed to myriad "all-regional" programs, many with a propagandist purpose. The series *Land We Defend* included contributions from Scotland and Wales. *Go To It* and similar programs designed to inspire workers on the home front included contributions from all the regions, including Northern Ireland.[35] The BBC broadcast the popular program *Ack-Ack, Beer Beer* from anti-aircraft installations across the United Kingdom, including Scotland, Wales, and Northern Ireland. By 1941, each region had its own war correspondents contributing to the Home Service news broadcasts.[36]

The most notable achievement of wartime regional broadcasting was the series *In Britain Now*, which, like other popular wartime programs, continued after 1945. A magazine program under the direction of the Talks Department and edited by the West Region Programme Director, C. J. Pennethorne-Hughes, *In Britain Now* provided short, "everyday life" vignettes from each of the BBC's regions. Its purpose, noted Maconachie, was "to give a picture of the national effort seen in a diversity of aspects but with the unity of a common aim."[37] The program, meant in part to deflect criticism of the BBC, provided a forum for regional contributions and it admirably represented the multi-national character of Britain. Pennethorne-Hughes bluntly described the objective of *In Britain Now*: "The idea is consciously to counteract any suggestion of metropolitan bias in our programmes."[38] Indeed, the original *In Britain Now* included contributions from the Scottish, Welsh, North, Midland, West, and London regions. BBC Northern Ireland, always anxious to be included in all-regional programs, did not appear in the initial installments of *In Britain Now* due to technical reasons.[39] When Northern Ireland entered the mix in early 1940, Pennethorne-Hughes agreed that London contributions to the program would be infrequent "as London is already very fully represented in the Programmes."[40] The Britain represented by *In Britain Now* was truly the Britain of the provinces, with all the nations of the United Kingdom providing material for the program.

Because its primary purpose was to simply get regional voices and regional subject matter on the air, much of the content of *In Britain Now* reflected "everyday life" in a kind of banal, uncontroversial manner. Something like "Donkeys in Ireland," a piece produced by BBC Northern Ireland, was not untypical. But, at times, *In Britain Now* strayed into more propagandistic territory. For example, listeners reacted negatively to a talk on West Indian workers in Britain, criticized for being "patronising," and "official propaganda by an official."[41] In another installment, broadcast on February 7, 1941, *In Britain Now* took on the issue of evacuees, emphasizing the theme of "unity within diversity." Doing its best to support what Angus Calder has called the "myth of the Blitz," the program focused on the "social and regional distinctions, which provoke interest, and barriers which are being broken down by this transplanting of populations." Pennethorne-Hughes was more than willing to ignore the class tensions which manifested themselves when urban evacuees arrived in the countryside. "Where such barriers are not being broken down or even being accentuated," he wrote of the above episode, "it would be better to say nothing about it!"[42]

Above all, *In Britain Now* tried to be "regional" in the strictest sense. The BBC encouraged the regions to use dialect speakers and make local references in the program.[43] Pennethorne-Hughes reiterated this to the Regional Programme Directors just before the series was to be transferred to the Forces Programme:

> The regional and even local atmosphere should be stressed as much as possible. The nostalgic appeal of place names would perhaps be particularly valuable, and I think we should not be afraid of mentioning even quite small places … Dialect remains extremely valuable.[44]

In contrast to the pre-war period, the BBC was making an attempt to be overtly provincial in encouraging the use of broad dialect on the national network. Pennethorne-Hughes even suggested that its use of dialect might make *In Britain Now* an ideal program for the dissemination of propaganda. Listeners found propaganda dull, he reasoned, "because it is in the official terms of London representatives." But, "conveyed obliquely in provincial example, the rough coating may deceive for a time when the chocolate metropolitan coating is becoming too smooth or well known."[45]

The regional nature of *In Britain Now* clearly resonated with domestic listeners, especially at the beginning of the war. Pennethorne-Hughes commented several times on the positive responses he received from listeners' letters and from the statistics provided by the Listener Research Department. On a given evening, 20–23 per cent of British radio listeners tuned in to *In Britain Now*.[46] Pennethorne-Hughes was also pleased to note that, so far as Listener Research could tell, *In Britain Now* attracted a regular audience of devotees, as opposed to casual or occasional listeners.[47] A number of things account for the success of *In Britain Now*. The pace of the program was quick: each of the regional contributions in a thirty-minute episode of *In Britain Now* lasted no more than five minutes. The topics of the regional talks were eclectic, and only occasionally and incidentally related to the war. Most important perhaps was the use of regional voices and dialect. "The few complaints" about the use of dialect, wrote Pennethorne-Hughes, "usually come from the Surrey Foothills, where there appears to be a considerable population which still cherishes the belief that anything but the use of sub-standard southern English is an affectation."[48] Although a temporary move to the Forces Programme caused a significant drop in the audience for *In Britain Now*, its reappearance on the Home Service revived its ratings. In 1942 the BBC tabbed the series to replace the venerable and popular *In Town Tonight* during its hiatus.[49] The BBC cancelled *In Britain Now* in December 1943, although it returned to the BBC's schedules after the war.[50] Its space in the Home Service was made available to the regions on a competitive basis. "There is no reason," noted Barnes to BBC Scotland's Programme Director, "why regions should lose any space by the change."[51]

Despite the success of *In Britain Now* and the opportunities the BBC provided for regional programs, the relationship between the regions and Head Office were not unproblematic. At the beginning of the war, regional representatives showered Head Office with memoranda protesting the lack of regional representation in the programs,[52] and intermittently continued to complain about a lack of adequate representation in the Home Service.[53] As late as 1943 Percy Edgar, the Midland Regional Director, who had been with the BBC since the beginning, called for more "regional-mindedness" in the program departments in London, complaining "that programme suggestions from his region were sometimes accepted and then not heard of again, and in some cases not even acknowledged."[54] As happened before the war, regional producers could find Head Office criticism of their programs too severe.[55] In turn, Head Office personnel thought, at times, that the regions were making unfair and unjustified grabs for broadcast time.[56] "Anglo-centric blunders" such as the extensive radio celebration of St George's Day in 1944 or the use of "England" for "Britain" angered regional listeners and brought frequent protests from BBC Scotland.[57] The Programme Directors in Wales and Northern

Ireland had to fend off an attempt to curtail their representation in *In Britain Now.*[58]

Another issue of contention between the regions and Head Office was the placement of regional talks, which counted for a high proportion of regional contributions to the Home Service. Many of these were scheduled for either 9:20 or 11:00 in the morning, and attracted only small audiences. Early in 1941 Moultrie Kelsall, the Acting Scottish Programme Director, claimed that these morning slots were unsuitable for regional talks, as the audience at these times was "likely to consist of the aged and infirm."[59] Christine Orr, a Talks Producer in Edinburgh, broached the subject of morning talks again in 1942.

> Is there an audience worth considering at 9:20 a.m., and even if one [or] two percent do listen, does that justify the trouble and expense? Might not a purely "background" programme at that hour be better planning? I know your answer before was definite. You felt early talks were justified, and you in London appeared to find no problem in getting either listeners or talkers. I am afraid our experience shows the very opposite. If any comment on morning talks is forthcoming at all, its either "Oh yes, looked good—but of course I missed it. How can you expect people to listen at that hour?" or with extreme annoyance "I heard it—a good talk, but what a waste to put it on then. What is the BBC thinking of?" … Even households—in the minority!—anxious to listen, interested personally in the subject and speaker, and willing to sit down and concentrate, find morning domestic interruptions intolerable.[60]

Getting well-known and competent speakers, "offended by the poor time slot," proved to be an even more pressing problem for regional producers and the policy, Orr contended, could be damaging to the BBC's standing in the regions.[61] Orr's complaints did not change BBC policy, but it made an impact; she secured an afternoon and an evening slot for two Scottish talks "too good for early-morning periods."[62] And, despite his own policy, Barnes disclosed to the Director of Programme Planning that all the Regional Directors shared Orr's concerns. Listener Research confirmed Orr's claim that the 9:20 a.m. talks attracted small audiences.[63]

Despite the not infrequent disputes over the use of precious broadcast time, an acceptable *modus vivendi* was established between Head Office and the regions during the war. By 1941, the *BBC Handbook* could report, "in some regions programme output reached its peacetime level."[64] The following year the same publication claimed that the output from the BBC's Northern studios was greater in 1942 than in the pre-war days, although "a considerable proportion" of its material was for listeners overseas.[65] Complaints from regional broadcasters never disappeared, but they became fainter and less frequent by the middle of the war. By then, regional broadcasters and Head Office staff increasingly began to contemplate the nature and scope of regional broadcasting after the war.

In March 1943, Robert Foot, the Director-General, circulated a paper on the post-war organization of the BBC. His memo, concerned with various issues from accommodation to sponsored programs, provided an opportunity for regional broadcasters to weigh in on the post-war regional organization of the BBC. Their responses to Foot's memorandum were as diverse and eclectic as the regions themselves. Scottish broadcasters advocated for something along the lines of the pre-war regional scheme: the restoration of Scotland's own wavelength, with the regional staff producing a large proportion of Scottish material, while also taking the best British programs available. BBC Scotland was against a return to the local broadcasting characteristic of the early 1920s, while a proposal for a Celtic wavelength, combining the Scottish and Welsh regions, was rejected outright.[66] Scottish broadcasters gave primacy to the national differences between the Scots, the Welsh, and the English; they championed regional networks for Scotland and Wales, but were equivocal towards English regional broadcasting. In the case of Scotland, being a regional broadcaster did not necessarily mean strongly supporting regional broadcasting. Andrew Stewart, the Scottish Programme Director, advocated "distinct services" for Wales and Scotland only, on "the basis of national character." "In my view," he continued, "regional development in England went too far before the war."[67]

John Coatman, North Regional Director, took quite a different view. In the summer of 1943, the Regional Directors jointly drafted a proposal for post-war development, which asserted that "Scotland, Wales, and Northern Ireland should have their territorial broadcasting rights restored and extended," but suggested that English broadcasting be developed "on the basis of county and/or city constituencies … as soon as technical developments make it possible."[68] Coatman wrote his own "dissenting opinion" to this draft, in which he laid out his vision of regional broadcasting. He advocated decentralization along regional lines, arguing that it would put the BBC in step with government policy (he thought the appointment of a Secretary of State for Wales was imminent) as well as the public mood. But Coatman strongly rejected any idea of altering the nature of the English regions. "It is not possible," he wrote, "to have any scheme of British Broadcasting which does not include English territorial regions."[69] His argument for maintaining the English regions stemmed from his belief that the North constituted a distinct, historic, cultural community. But Coatman, a staunch imperialist, had a more pressing reason for timely return of the English regions:

> It would be extremely dangerous to propose to have only three territorial broadcasting regions, namely Wales, Scotland and Northern Ireland, on the grounds of their separate nationalities … if we make them, and them alone, into territorial broadcasting regions because of their separate nationality, then it is quite certain that they will be drawn into politics and twisted and warped away from their primary business of broadcasting as parts of the inclusive nation to which they belong, namely the British nation. Scottish nationalists, Welsh nationalists, Roman Catholics in Northern Ireland would all demand their share of broadcasting, and it would not be possible to deny them … But, on the other hand, if these three regions are merely three out of six territorial regions, then we present to the country a scheme based in purely broadcasting principles, and the danger to which I have drawn attention can be averted.[70]

There is more than a little irony in the fact that Coatman "perhaps the most passionate supporter of Regional claims within the Corporation"[71] would deny the BBC in Scotland, Wales, and Northern Ireland the right to engage in legitimate regional activities (this is especially true in the case of Northern Ireland). "Leaving out this elusive concept of nationhood," Coatman concluded, "the three English regions which I propose have exactly the same claim to be allowed to broadcast to their own people as Wales, Scotland or Ireland."[72] The English regions would undermine any claim by nationalists and Catholics to the airwaves. Indeed, they would undermine the status of the Scottish, Welsh, and Northern Irish regions within the BBC itself, for they would simply be British regions, as opposed to "national regions." In a separate paper Coatman all but equated the English regions to the "national" regions. Just as "the 'historic north' and the West country … are individual entities inside England … Wales, Scotland and Northern Ireland are individual entities inside Great Britain."[73]

The Directors of the other English regions did not share Coatman's opinions on the dangers of broadcasting in Scotland, Wales, and Northern Ireland. Nor did they accept Coatman's arguments concerning the cultural unity of the English regions, which, in Coatman's view, made them like the national regions. For Gerald Beadle, Director of the West region, it was the cities and counties that were the "historical" communities of England: "when that adjective [i.e. historical] is applied to English regions it does not seem to me to be very valid … [it] does not exist in the minds and consciousness of ordinary English men and women."[74]

While the Regional Directors contemplated the scope and nature of the regional networks, staff at Head Office also began to consider the restoration of regional broadcasting after the war. Basil Nicolls, the Controller of Programmes, and Maurice Farquharson, the BBC Secretary, implied that the regional networks might not return after the war. William Haley, soon to become Director-General of BBC, similarly expressed the opinion that development of broadcasting on a national basis should come before any talk of "regionalization." Later, when Haley commented publicly that the post-war Home Service would be "capable of regionalisation in the same way as programmes were regionalised before the war," his ambiguity aroused considerable suspicion in the provincial press.[75] Yet, the idea that the BBC would not re-establish the regional networks after the war was simply untenable. The objections from provincial elites, Scottish and Welsh MPs, cultural groups, and the press would have been too much for the BBC to bear. Haley and his colleagues in London eventually accepted the idea that the regional networks would have to be quickly restored after the end of the war. In the *BBC Yearbook* for 1945, commentator L. A. G. Strong could write a paean to regional broadcasting in which he advocated a "comprehensive service of regional broadcasting," giving the regions "the greatest possible freedom to organize and plan."[76] Haley himself came out as a public supporter of dynamic regional broadcasting. "It will be the BBC's aim," Haley wrote in the *Radio Times*, "to make its six regionalised Home Services alert, living things … their existence should lead to rivalry both of creativeness and of craft, and to the fostering of those national and local cultures which are an enduring part of our heritage."[77]

The end of the war and the return of the regional services

The BBC duly restored regional broadcasting in July 1945 on lines almost identical to 1939, except that the regions enjoyed even more autonomy than they did before the war. The six pre-war regions remained intact, although the staff of the West region had to fight off an attempt to merge it with the Midland region in 1946. And, due to a shortage of available wavelengths, Northern Ireland had to share its wavelength with a transmitter serving the Newcastle area. As before the war, listeners had a choice between their regional program and a nationally broadcast service. But instead of the pre-war National Programme, the regions had to compete against the Light Programme (joined by the Third Programme in 1946). The basic Home Service, like the pre-war London Regional Programme, supported the regional networks when necessary. The regions took material from the London-produced Home Service, but they were able, when they liked, to drop the Home Service to broadcast their own regional programs. Moreover, under the new system, BBC Head Office in London encouraged the regions to make more contributions to the Home Service and the Light Programme, on the basis of merit. This marked a continuation of the war-time practice of including a significant portion of regional material in the Home Service. It also created a certain amount of competition within the BBC, which would hold on to its monopoly until 1954. The position of the regions was further strengthened by the creation of Regional Advisory Councils.[78]

With their networks secured and their autonomy guaranteed, the regions enjoyed something of a golden age from 1945 to 1953. Indeed, after the war, it was the regions that produced some of the most popular and enduring of all BBC radio programs. *Have A Go*, which originated from the North region, quickly became a hit, and within six months the BBC began to broadcast it nationally on the Light Programme. An audience-participation quiz program with the affable Wilfred Pickles as quizmaster, *Have A Go* allowed the BBC to interact with the communities that hosted each episode of the series. The program opened with community singing and Pickles was an expert at bringing out the personality of each participant, giving the program a human touch.[79] A similar regional success was *Any Questions*, the brainchild of Frank Gillard, the Head of Programmes for the West region. Like *Have A Go*, the success of *Any Questions* depended on a genial host (Freddy Grisewood) and a strong measure of local pride. The program traveled to "the far corners of the West Region," and enjoyed the avid support of its live audiences.[80] Finally, there is *The Archers*, launched on the Midland region in late 1950, moved to the Light Programme at the beginning of 1951, and broadcast to this day on BBC Radio 4. Conceived of as a "farming *Dick Barton*" designed to provide an "accurate" and reassuring picture of country life, as well as educational material, *The Archers* soon had an audience of 9.5 million.[81]

The Beveridge Report on broadcasting, published in 1951, recommended further regional devolution. As a result of the report, the BBC established Broadcasting Councils for Scotland and Wales in 1952. Like the Board of Governors, the Councils initiated and oversaw policy for their respective regions. Beveridge also recommended that the national regions have special representatives on the Board of Governors. Lord Clydesmuir, already a governor, was tabbed to represent Scotland, and in 1952 Churchill appointed Lord Macdonald of Gwaenysgor and Sir Harry Mulholland to represent Wales and Northern Ireland, respectively.[82]

After the implementation of the recommendations of the Beveridge Committee, the organization and powers of regional sound broadcasting remained stable for almost two decades, until the introduction of BBC local broadcasting in 1970. Indeed, regional policy for radio, which Beveridge himself fretted over, began to recede as a public issue. Competition, and the breaking of the BBC monopoly, quickly overtook regionalization as the main concern of policy makers. In so far as regionalization was in the public and official mind, it was the regional distribution of the newer, and soon to be dominant medium, television.

Concluding remarks

Rather than victims of hegemonic cultural domination from London, the BBC regional networks, specifically in Scotland, Wales, and Northern Ireland, were engaged in a kind of nation-building exercise. The extent to which broadcasters in Scotland, Wales, and Northern Ireland could undertake nation-building activities was, of course, limited. They were part of a larger British network, and financial control remained in the hands of London. The BBC had little sympathy for Scottish and Welsh nationalism, although this hostility was more characteristic of Head Office than the regional staffs. In turn, nationalist parties and cultural organizations were among the harshest critics of the BBC in Scotland and Wales. But, like the National Programme, which constructed a unitary British nation through its programs on the empire and the monarchy, the regional networks in Scotland, Wales, and Northern Ireland enabled listeners to imagine themselves as part of a historically and culturally coherent nation. Programs like Northern Ireland's *Provincial Journey* took listeners to all corners of Northern Ireland and structured these disparate communities into one common "Ulster." Weekly news and current events programs presented individual events as happening in "Scotland" or "Wales," as opposed to Cardiff or Britain. Regional programs celebrated the history and heroes of their respective communities. Scotland, Wales, and Northern Ireland made special broadcasts for their own "national" days, and important festivals, such as the Welsh Eisteddfod, received considerable coverage in regional BBC programs. As much as regional broadcasting elided local differences, it emphasized the cultural and historic differences between Scotland, Wales, and England, with Northern Ireland being a different case altogether. The chapters that follow examine the ways in which broadcasters in Scotland, Wales, and Northern Ireland conceived of and constructed "national identity" for their audiences.

Notes

1 For example, Scannell and Cardiff, *Social History of British Broadcasting*; Pegg, *Broadcasting and Society*; Briggs, *Golden Age of Wireless*. Briggs's multi-volume history of the BBC takes up, of course, the story of regional broadcasting in volume 4, *Sound and Vision*. Briggs does not at all discuss regional broadcasting during the war in volume 3, *War of Words*.

2 Scannell and Cardiff, 355.

3 Adrienne Scullion, "BBC Radio in Scotland, 1923–1939: Devolution, Regionalism and Centralisation," *Northern Scotland*, 15 (1994): 63–4.

4 Pegg discusses regional broadcasting on pages 22–35 of his *Broadcasting and Society*. He covers regional broadcasting after 1936 on pages 33–5.

5 Scannell and Cardiff, 330–2.

6 Ibid., 332.

7 Pegg, 23.

8 Briggs, *Golden Age of Wireless*, 285.

9 Scannell and Cardiff, 313, 314.

10 Scullion, 79.

11 Scannell and Cardiff, 320.

12 Briggs, *Birth of Broadcasting*, 195.

13 For the history of regional broadcasting in Britain before the Second World War, see Sylvia Harvey and Kevin Robins, eds, *The Regions, the Nations and the BBC* (London: British Film Institute, 1993), 1–8, 27–37; Scannell and Cardiff, 304–32; Pegg, 22–35; Briggs, *Golden Age of Wireless*, 271–314.

14 Reith, *Broadcast over Britain*, 62.

15 Six of the nine main stations became regional stations after the BBC implemented the regional scheme: London, Cardiff, Birmingham, Manchester, Belfast, and Glasgow. The relay station at Aberdeen also continued to produce local programs and broadcast on its own wavelength for the benefit of listeners in the north of Scotland who could not get Scottish regional.

16 Scannell and Cardiff, 315; Briggs, *Birth of Broadcasting*, 189.

17 Scannell and Cardiff, 316. D. H. Clarke, Director of the Belfast station, made the initial complaint to Reith. Reith then solicited opinions from the other stations. Of the responses that survive, Dundee agreed with Clarke, while Nottingham and Birmingham took the opposite position. Manchester felt that Clarke's claims were "far too overstated." Ibid., 317.

18 Paddy Scannell, "The Origins of BBC Regional Policy," in *Regions, Nations, BBC*, Harvey and Robins, eds, 29.

19 Briggs, *Golden Age of Wireless*, 292.

20 Scannell and Cardiff, 325–6; Briggs, *Golden Age of Wireless*, 301–2.

21 Control Board, July 19, 1932, BBC WAC, R3/3/8. See also Briggs, *Golden Age of Wireless*, 302.

22 Control Board, Ibid.

23 Control Board, May 24, 1932, Ibid.

24 Ibid.

25 Briggs, *Golden Age of Wireless*, 305.

26 Ibid., 451.

27 Ibid., 453–4.

28 Ibid., 306–7. See also Scannell and Cardiff, 330.

29 Scannell and Cardiff, 330; Briggs, *Golden Age of Wireless*, 309–11.

30 Briggs, *The First Fifty Years*, 175–6; Briggs, *Golden Age of Wireless*, 583–4.

31 Home Service Board, November 10, 1939, BBC WAC, R3/16/1.

32 Home Service Board, November 17, 1939, Ibid.

33 Home Service Board, December 1, 1939, Ibid.

34 The BBC began broadcasting in Scots Gaelic during the week of November 19, 1939. See Home Service Board, November 3, 1939. It had been decided earlier to include one school broadcast each in week in Welsh. Home Service Board, October 30, 1939, Ibid.

35 *Go To It*, BBC WAC, Scripts, Northern Ireland Region Scripts, Reel 144/145.

36 *BBC Handbook 1942*, 29.

37 Richard Maconachie, "Broadcast Talks in Wartime," *BBC Handbook 1941*, 61–2.

38 C. J. Pennethorne-Hughes to Peter Creswell, February 25, 1942, BBC WAC, R51/249/2.

39 Pennethorne-Hughes to Ursula Eason, February 2, 1940, BBC WAC, R51/249/1.

40 Pennethorne-Hughes to Regional Programme Directors, February 9, 1940, Ibid.

41 Pennethorne-Hughes to George Barnes, July 7, 1942, BBC WAC, R51/249/2.

42 Pennethorne-Hughes to Regional Talks Assistants, January 20, 1941, BBC WAC, R51/249/1. See also Angus Calder, *The Myth of the Blitz* (London: Pimlico, 1992), 60–4.

43 After its initial success, the regions were encouraged to "make contributions [to *In Britain Now*], so far as it is possible, even more regional in character than they have been." Pennethorne-Hughes to Regional Programme Directors, January 31, 1940, BBC WAC, R51/249/1.

44 Pennethorne-Hughes to Regional Programme Directors, February 9, 1940, Ibid.

45 Pennethorne-Hughes to Barnes, December 16, 1941, Ibid.

46 Percy Edgar to Pennethorne-Hughes, April 19, 1940, Ibid.

47 Pennethorne-Hughes to Maconachie, March 7, 1940. See also Pennethorne-Hughes to Regional Programme Directors, January 31, 1940, Ibid.

48 Ibid. Upon reading Pennethorne-Hughes's memo, one staff member from BBC Scotland replied: "I am very much interested by your news about the aborigines of the Surrey foothills. I always felt there was a solid nucleus of provincialism somewhere ... but I had imagined it as being located in London itself." Programme Assistant, Edinburgh, to Pennethorne-Hughes, March 12, 1940, Ibid.

49 Barnes to Assistant Controller (Home), Maconachie, January 23, 1942, BBC WAC, R51/249/2.

50 See BBC WAC R51/249/3.

51 Barnes to Andrew Stewart, December 15, 1943, BBC WAC, R51/249/2.

52 A. Watkin-Jones to Maconachie, December 11, 1939, BBC WAC, R51/631/2; Home Service Board, November 17, 1939, BBC WAC, R3/16/1; Programme

Board, January 11, 1940, BBC WAC, R34/600/12.

53 Barnes to Watkin-Jones, October 31, 1941, BBC WAC, R51/631/3.

54 Programme Board, September 29, 1943, BBC WAC, R34/600/13.

55 Eason to Barnes, December 23, 1943, BBC WAC, R51/356/3. "Thank you for sending on Hilton Brown's [Head Office Talks Producer] comments on Northern Ireland morning talks," jibed Eason, "do please continue to send them, even when Hilton Brown is allergic to them. I find his adverse criticism most stimulating."

56 Harman Grisewood to Barnes, June 7, 1940, BBC WAC, R51/631/2.

57 Nicholas, *Echo*, 231–2; George Burnett to Controller (Public Relations), October 23, 1939, BBC WAC, SC5/2; Alan Melville to Moultrie Kelsall, July 15, 1940, Ibid.; Home Board, July 19, 1940, BBC WAC, R3/16/1; John Stewart to Robert Foot, September 13, 1943, BBC WAC, SC5/2; Andrew Stewart to Barnes, October 23, 1944, Ibid.

58 Godfrey Adams to Pennethorne-Hughes, August 21, 1943; Watkin-Jones to Adams, n.d.; Eason to Adams, August 26, 1943; Barnes to Regional Programme Directors, August 31, 1943, BBC WAC, R51/249/2.

59 Kelsall to Barnes, February 22, 1941, BBC WAC, R34/869/5. Barnes replied that it "was not the experience of the Corporation" that daytime audiences consisted largely of the aged and infirm, and tried to assure Kelsall that "a good talk, at whatever time it is broadcast, is never wasted." See Barnes to Kelsall, March 5, 1941, Ibid.

60 Christine Orr to Barnes, October 31, 1942, BBC WAC, R51/535/3.

61 Ibid.

62 Orr to Barnes, October 29, 1942; Barnes to Orr, October 31, 1942, Ibid.

63 Barnes to Director of Programme Planning, November 2, 1942, "Note on Listener Research Figures for Early Talks," n.d., Ibid.

64 *BBC Handbook 1942*, 28. In the first year and a half of the war, the *BBC Handbook* could only claim that the regions had "contributed their special quota to the home and overseas programmes." *BBC Handbook 1941*, 16.

65 *BBC Yearbook 1943*, 30.

66 Notes on Meeting of Post-War Committee, April 14, 1943, BBC WAC, R34/731/3.

67 Stewart to Melville Dinwiddie, April 27, 1943, BBC WAC, SC34/1.

68 Regional Directors, "Proposals for Post-war Development," quoted in Briggs, *Sound and Vision*, 82.

69 John Coatman, "Problems of Post-War Re-Construction," June 23, 1943, BBC WAC, SC5/34/1.

70 Ibid.

71 Asa Briggs, "Local and Regional in Northern Sound Broadcasting," *Northern History* 10 (1975): 180.

72 Coatman memorandum, June 23, 1943, BBC WAC, SC5/34/1.

73 Coatman, "Reconstruction," June 23 1943, BBC WAC, SC5/34/1. Wales had its own language and Scotland is own civic institutions. Coatman's claim for the West was that it constituted the "old boundaries of Wessex!" It seems that Coatman

resented the amount of time given to Scottish, Welsh, and Northern Irish programs during the war. In a memo on "the North of England's Contributions to Programmes" Coatman made several references to the "special treatment" of Scotland, Wales, and Northern Ireland while protesting the dearth of North Region programs. Coatman to Foot, February 21, 1944, BBC WAC, R34/731/3.

74 Gerald Beadle to Regional Directors, August 4, 1943, BBC WAC, SC34/5/1.

75 Briggs, *Sound and Vision*, 84.

76 L. A. G. Strong, "Long Live Regional Broadcasting," *BBC Yearbook 1945*, 24, 25.

77 *Radio Times*, July 27, 1945, 1.

78 Briggs, *Sound and Vision*, 94.

79 Ibid., 100–2.

80 Freddy Grisewood, *My Story of the BBC* (London: Odhams Press Limited), 1959, 173–4.

81 Briggs, *Sound and Vision*, 99–100.

82 Ibid., 413. Briggs provides a detailed account of the activities of the Beveridge Committee and the fallout from the report in *Sound and Vision*, 265–385.

5

Broadcasting a nation: the BBC and national identity in Scotland

This chapter argues that the BBC and its station in Scotland played an important role in sustaining and reinforcing a complex sense of Scottish national identity during the period from 1923 to 1953. The BBC did not act as an agent in the anglicization of Scotland, nor did it seek to impose a wholly metropolitan, southern English culture or identity on Scotland. Rather, the BBC, perhaps the most powerful institution for the dissemination of information and entertainment in Scotland, constructed a powerful sense of "Scottishness" through its organizational structure, policy, and programs.

Technical and financial considerations may have, in part, driven the regional scheme, but BBC Scotland existed to reflect the politics, society, life—in short the culture—of Scotland. Special days such as St Andrew's Day or Burns Night allowed for the expression of Scottish nationality. Further, BBC Scotland did not represent Scottishness in a caricatured, one-dimensional way. It did indulge in its fair share of nostalgia and kailyard and just plain stereotype, but the BBC's representation of Scotland was diverse and complex. Not surprisingly, the BBC utilized images of Scotland's rural and romantic past in programs, but it also represented modern, industrial, urban Scotland. Both nationalist and unionist Scotland, and their respective histories, myths and politics, were represented on the Scottish airwaves.

It is perhaps worth reiterating here that "Scottishness" and "Scottish national identity" are not synonymous with Scottish nationalism. As noted in the Introduction, Scottishness and Britishness were not mutually exclusive identities, nor was it impossible to hold a Scottish identity and be politically unionist. It is undeniable that the BBC as an institution was hostile towards Scottish political nationalism. It did not, for example, allow representatives of the Scottish National Party (SNP) to make political party broadcasts before general elections.[1] But neither did it wholly ignore political nationalism, broadcasting several debates on the issue in the 1930s.

One of the challenges of discussing the history of BBC Scotland and its role in constructing and reinforcing Scottishness is the paucity of historical work on radio broadcasting in Scotland. W. H. McDowell's meticulously researched *The History of BBC Broadcasting in Scotland* provides an introduction to Scottish broadcasting, and it is a valuable resource. But it is unabashedly an "institutional history of the BBC."[2] McDowell discusses facilities, finances, personnel, and engineering in detail. As for programs, he does little more than compile lists of some of the more important Scottish productions. Furthermore, McDowell largely focuses on the more recent history of the BBC in Scotland, after the advent of television.[3] Briggs's multi-volume work and other general histories of the BBC similarly offer little on early Scottish radio. Only a few articles and essays supplement McDowell's *History*. These include Adrienne Scullion's "BBC Radio in Scotland, 1923–1939: Devolution, Regionalism and Centralisation," which focuses on the drama productions of the early Scottish radio stations, a contribution by Ian Bell to Paul H Scott's *Scotland: A Concise Cultural History*, an article on broadcasting in Scots Gaelic, and a brief essay on German propaganda to Scotland.[4]

McDowell, Scullion, and Bell, all, to a greater or lesser degree, apply the standard model of centralization to Scottish broadcasting. Drawing on Briggs, McDowell provides a balanced account of the regionalization of the BBC, being careful to note its many benefits: almost complete coverage of the United Kingdom, better reception for valve-set users, higher-quality programs for less money, and most important, choice for Scottish listeners who could listen to either the National Programme or the Scottish Regional Programme; but on balance, McDowell emphasizes centralization and rise of national (i.e. British) culture at the expense of local (i.e. Scottish) culture.[5] Scullion also embraces centralization as the organizing theme of early Scottish broadcasting, and invokes theories of hegemony to explain the relationship between the BBC in London and BBC Scotland. Employing a kind of cultural imperialism model to describe the relationship between London and BBC Scotland, she claims:

> The BBC as an institution seemed to connote a metropolitan outlook, a centralised structure that broadcast from London to the provinces, and at the same time drew towards it all that was best, or most appropriate from elsewhere, in a kind of classic core-periphery model of cultural theory.[6]

Bell takes a similar tack, savaging the BBC in his essay as representing "Unionism." BBC Scotland's status as a "National Region" represents, for Bell, "tortured logic."[7] There may be some truth in this, but only in the most narrow political sense.

Such claims may confirm the beliefs of Scottish nationalists and fit nicely with Gramscian theory, but they oversimplify a complex set of negotiations between periphery and center. When Scullion claims that the autonomy of BBC Scotland was "gradually reduced and eroded until 1939," she ignores the real gains made by regional broadcasters from the mid-1930s. Similarly, she argues that "the BBC ... increasingly eschewed the regional in favour of the centralised, the national, the British."[8] This may have been true for the BBC's National Programme, which underrepresented regional productions, but it was not true of BBC Scotland. Scullion's suggestion that Scottish regional broadcasting entered into a terminal decline culminating in the domination by London of Scottish broadcasting is flawed. Scottish broadcasters frequently fought London to defend Scottish program interests and attempted to establish themselves, with some success, as arbiters of Scottish culture and identity. While they could do little to stop the suspension of the Scottish Regional Programme when the war began, the BBC's Scottish staff fought effectively to gain maximum consideration of Scottish needs in the unified Home Service. And, of course, BBC Scotland's transmitter reopened after the war, with Scottish broadcasters more independent than ever to schedule and develop programs for Scottish listeners.

Historically, Scottish nationalism and national identity originate from multiple sources and have followed several different trajectories. The 1707 Act of Union (Treaty of Union in Scotland) guaranteed the survival of several key Scottish institutions. Scotland maintained its own distinct legal code and educational system. And Presbyterianism, not Anglicanism, remained the established religion. A far more romantic strain of Scottish nationalism found inspiration in "tartanry," an eighteenth-century invention that conflated authentic Scottish culture with the pre-industrial lifestyle of the Highlands.[9] And, of course, Scottish national identity draws strength from Scotland's long history as an independent nation, a nation often engaged in conflicts with its neighbor to the south. William Wallace, Robert the Bruce, and Mary Queen of Scots, all, at different times and in different ways, symbolized Scottish nationhood. Jacobitism also could be used as a focal point for Scottish nationalism.[10] In presenting "Scotland" to their listeners, Scottish broadcasters frequently pulled program material from this rich store of myth and history; it would have been surprising if they had not.

Early Scottish broadcasting

As with the rest of the United Kingdom, broadcasting in Scotland began on the local level. The BBC opened its first Scottish station in Glasgow, on March 6, 1923, and quickly built another main station in Aberdeen, which opened on October 10 of the same year. The BBC then added relay stations in Edinburgh and Dundee on May 1, 1924, and November 12, 1924, respectively. The programs broadcast by these first Scottish stations varied, but the main stations in Glasgow and Aberdeen enjoyed a substantial degree of independence. They produced a large portion of their own programs, exploiting local sources for material. The Edinburgh and Dundee stations took a great deal of material from London, but also broadcast some locally produced material, including their own *Children's Hour*. Music accounted for much of the early output of these local stations, along with agricultural bulletins, appeals, religious programs, and special broadcasts for Scottish days such as Burns Night and St Andrew's Day. It was taken for granted that the Glasgow and Aberdeen main stations would draw on local talent and broadcast a significant amount of specifically "Scottish" material.[11] In addition to special shows for Hogmanay and St Andrew's Day, Glasgow and Aberdeen put on regular "Scottish programmes," which consisted of music "of a Scottish character," performed by local musicians.[12] One Aberdeen "all Scottish programme" featured the Aberdeen city Police Pipe Band. Aberdeen also produced a series of Scottish community singing concerts.[13] Each week Edinburgh's *Children's Corner* included a special Scottish program.[14]

Significantly, the first play broadcast by Glasgow was an adaptation of *Rob Roy*, Walter Scott's romantic paean to the Highlands. In publicity that reflected both the newness of the medium and the immediacy of radio, the *Radio Times* exalted:

> One of the most interesting radio events of the week will be the broadcast version of *Rob Roy* which is to be transmitted from Glasgow to three other stations—Newcastle, Cardiff and London—when this romance of old Scotland, adapted for broadcasting by Mr. R. E. Jeffrey, will unfold in a way never dreamed of by its originator, Sir Walter Scott, even in his most imaginative moments … this will be an unprecedented pleasure for thousands south of the Border.[15]

After the first performance of *Rob Roy*, the BBC decided to put it out over the network, making it the first program from a provincial station to enjoy a simultaneous broadcast. However, many early Scottish programs were not so well regarded. The "poor quality" of Edinburgh's Burns Night program in 1926 led the BBC's Programme Board to resolve that "broadcasts from provincial stations to London or Daventry will, in future, be more closely scrutinized."[16]

Although the 1923 broadcast of *Rob Roy* represented a high point in early Scottish broadcasting, the program was not unique in drawing on Scotland's literary past, particularly romanticized representations of its struggles with England. Indeed, the Dundee station broadcast its own version of *Rob Roy* in 1925; in the same year Glasgow broadcast a program, *The Rob Roy Country*, which included music and scenes from Walter Scott's novel.[17] Both the Edinburgh and Glasgow stations broadcast radio adaptations of another famous Scott novel, *The Heart of Midlothian*, while Scott himself was the subject of a special program created by the Edinburgh station and relayed to the network, in 1927.[18] Scott was later the subject of several programs on the Scottish Regional Programme in 1932, in honor of the one-hundredth anniversary of his death.[19]

Early Scottish broadcasters also turned to Scottish history for program material, again favoring the romantic heroes and heroines of Scotland. In 1924 the Aberdeen station, whose director, R. E. Jeffrey, had produced the original *Rob Roy*, broadcast a play based on the life of Mary, Queen of Scots written by John Drinkwater.[20] Edinburgh broadcast a one-act play, *Chastelard*, based on "a little-known incident in the unhappy career of Mary, Queen on Scots, and … having great dramatic power."[21] Glasgow evoked the Scottish past with a series *Clan Nights*, in which listeners heard a brief history of one of Scotland's famous clans, followed by songs and pipe music arranged by clan members.[22]

As the BBC began to implement the regional scheme, broadcasting in Scotland started to resemble something like a national network. The four Scottish stations began sharing programs with greater frequency. Throughout 1928 the BBC in Scotland broadcast a series of "Scots Concerts," carried simultaneously by all of the Scottish stations.[23] On November 1 of the same year, Dundee and Edinburgh ceased to produce their own *Children's Hour*, instead taking Glasgow's *Children's Hour*.[24] In 1929 the Scottish stations "broadcast every week a special programme originating in one of the four Scottish studios and broadcast to all Scots listeners."[25] As Scotland prepared for the opening of its high-power regional transmitter, the *BBC Yearbook* noted:

> a system of co-ordination was instituted; the several [Scottish] stations ceased to broadcast talks, concerts, and services independently to the same extent, and were concentrated on the task of specialising in their individual and characteristic contributions to an all-Scotland programme pool.[26]

Of course, as the Scottish stations prepared more programs to be broadcast throughout Scotland, program production and administration became centralized in Glasgow. Changes in title and nomenclature reflected the new policy. By November 1928 Edinburgh and Dundee were no longer considered "stations," although their studios remained active. Less than a year later the BBC closed the Dundee studio. "Station director," became a redundant position. In 1928, Cleghorn Thomson exchanged his title as "Northern Area Director" (in addition to the four Scottish stations, the Belfast station had been under his purview) for "Scottish Regional Director."[27]

Scottish regional broadcasting, 1932–39

A new chapter in the history of broadcasting in Scotland opened when the medium wave, high-power, "Scottish national transmitter" at Westerglen came on line on June 12, 1932. Eighty per cent of the Scottish population could receive transmissions from Westerglen, which carried the new Scottish Regional Programme, while most of the remainder was served by the BBC's transmitter in Aberdeen.

Westerglen did more than allow a larger proportion of the population to hear Scottish broadcasting: listeners to the new Scottish Regional Programme became part of a community, bound together, and in part defined, by radio. Scottish Regional and its programs helped to identify "Scotland" and delineate it from England or Britain. Programs on Scottish Regional were specifically designed to cater to Scottish tastes, explore Scottish history and tradition, and reflect "Scotland" back to itself. BBC Scotland thus helped to create a common, recognizable culture within the region. In his history of the BBC in Scotland, McDowell recognizes the significance of this new regional broadcasting, even if he does not explore its potential implications. "The output of the Scottish station was designed to cater for the whole of Scotland, not local areas," he notes, "and this resulted in some degree of submerging of cultural diversity within Scotland."[28] Quite true; but the corollary to this homogenization was that the BBC in Scotland defined and reflected the *Scottish* community as opposed to the local urban community. This allowed, in turn, BBC Scotland to foster a sense of Scottish national identity for its listeners. Nationalism and national identity must, by definition, paper over class and especially local differences, but scholars have focused too much on what was lost through regionalization, and not enough on what regional BBC stations provided.

BBC Scotland celebrated Scottish history and the Scottish way of life (or at least some versions of it). Although the Scottish Regional Programme could not take into account all of the diversity of Scotland, broadcasters were cognizant of the divisions within Scotland itself. An article on Scottish broadcasting in the *BBC Handbook* noted that if broadcasting were to sufficiently represent "the colour and characteristics" of Scotland, it "must not rely overmuch on the supply of talent in the cities and industrial districts." It was from the countryside, the article noted, "that we must seek the most authentic supply" of Scottish programs. Although BBC Scotland distanced itself from the Scottish political nationalist movement, neither did it simply ignore the nationalists. The BBC, both in London and Scotland, broadcast debates and talks on the question of nationalism in 1929, 1931, 1936, and 1938. Undoubtedly this seemed insufficient to the Scottish nationalist, but it did represent an implicit recognition of the legitimacy of Scottish nationalism. Finally, BBC Scotland occasionally indulged in a kind of cultural nationalism, invoking heroes and movements of Scotland's independent past.

BBC Scotland enjoyed the services of a staff that was strongly committed to making the BBC's service there as "Scottish" as possible. In contrast to Wales and Northern Ireland, most of the staff of BBC Scotland was, from the beginning, native Scots. These included Melville Dinwiddie, the Scottish Regional Director, Moray McLaren, the first Scottish Programme Director, and his successor, Andrew Stewart. There were also a number of talented producers and writers of Scottish descent, including John Gough, Moultrie Kelsall, and James Fergusson. Further, while the designation of Scotland as a "region" by the BBC offended some, the Scottish staff almost always talked of serving the "nation" of Scotland. In an essay on Scottish broadcasting titled "Broadcasting a Nation," Dinwiddie observed that, "on the whole, to be a nation in broadcasting is an advantage [for] it gives scope for the expression of the national character and outlook."[29] In the same publication Andrew Stewart explained his understanding of the role of broadcasting in Scotland:

> First of all, what in general does broadcasting set out to do? From its very nature, its reaching into the homes of a country, and its perennial accessibility, it has become an integral part of our life. So it seems to me that its first job is to reflect the character of the people of the country it serves: so that listeners should feel that their broadcasting programme is theirs by reason of something of themselves in it which makes it unique as they are unique; which reflects their tastes in entertainment and in music; which sets out their character in drama; and which discusses their problems as they themselves approach them.[30]

The vital, underlying assumption of Stewart's words is that the "country" he refers to is Scotland, not Britain. And Stewart seems to recognize the power of broadcasting to create "community," and not just because of his interest in reflecting "the character of the people." Like Benedict Anderson's newspapers, BBC Scotland fostered an imagined community that shared tastes (*their* tastes), character (*their* character), and problems (*their* problems).

Internal correspondence also reflects the desire of the staff of BBC Scotland to develop it into a truly national service, with its own standards and priorities, whose first priority would be serving the Scottish (as opposed to the British) listener. When, in 1934, BBC Head Office complained about the small number of programs that the Scottish region contributed to the national networks, Moray McLaren responded by asserting that his first priority was not the national networks or English listeners, but Scotland. "Practically all of my energies" he wrote to Lindsay Wellington, "are devoted to providing Scottish listeners with the best possible programmes I can arrange for them." McLaren claimed that it was more difficult for Scotland to provide programs to the national network because of the essential differences between the English and the Scots. Genuinely Scottish programs were inherently unsuitable for a British audience.[31] Andrew Stewart expressed almost identical sentiments four years later when asked by the Director of Regional Relations to provide more dramas and features for the National Programme. The request, he claimed, went against BBC policy, which mandated that programs on regional culture and concerns should be the first priority of the regional stations. "There will be serious difficulties and dissatisfaction," he concluded, "internal difficulty in having one department (i.e. Drama and Features) out of step with the others, and external dissatisfaction with a less good regional service."[32]

Stewart was appointed Scottish Programme Director in 1935 when Moray McLaren left for a Head Office position, and he held that post until 1948.[33] In that position Stewart did not inhabit the highest echelons of the BBC hierarchy, but it was his job to interpret and implement BBC program policy in the region. He was the key figure in the scheduling, arrangement, and broadcasting of programs in Scotland. Not surprisingly, this led to several clashes with Head Office in which he emerged as a staunch defender Scottish interests. In one important showdown with Head Office over Scottish program policy Stewart was forced to give in; but on other occasions he successfully fought off the encroachment of London staff. His willingness to clash with Head Office over program policy, and often prevail, problematizes the notion that the BBC simply imposed London norms and English programs on Scotland at will. Although Dinwiddie's claim that there was "no such thing as control of Scottish broadcasting in London"[34] oversimplifies the relationship between Scotland and Head Office, Scottish broadcasters resisted the pretensions of London staff.

BBC Scotland and the fight for independence
in programming

During the second half of the 1930s, Stewart repeatedly frustrated Head Office decisions when these, in his judgment, were not in the best interest of Scottish listeners. In 1936 the Drama Department in London was preparing a series for the National Programme on famous trials, and wanted to include the trial of Mary, Queen of Scots. Naturally, Val Gielgud expected to broadcast the drama from Scotland. But when he sent the script to BBC Scotland, the staff there found it utterly unacceptable. John Gough, a features producer, lamented the inclusion of the trial of Mary in the series, "*unless it be to expose it for the travesty it was* [emphasis text]." He complained that the script "comes almost to the point of persuading one that Elizabeth might have been honourable and right," and concluded "we [i.e. BBC Scotland] can do better." In another memo, Gough referred to the script derisively as "Hollywood."[35] When Stewart sent Gielgud an alternative script by a Scottish academic, the latter, somewhat bemused, reminded Stewart that their first priority was to produce an entertaining program, not defend the honor of Scotland.[36] The matter was settled only after a third script was produced under Gough's supervision. This fight over *Mary, Queen of Scots* is significant, for it demonstrates the pressure that BBC Scotland could put on the London program departments when Scottish material was at issue. It also shows the high regard among the staff of BBC Scotland for Scottish history and culture. In short, Gielgud was right: Gough and Stewart really were trying to defend the honor of Mary, Queen of Scots, and by extension, Scotland.[37]

Another important clash between BBC Scotland and Head Office concerned a debate over the broadcast of the opera *Acis and Galatea*. In 1937, Head Office decided to broadcast Handel's opera on the regional network. Although it was no longer compulsory, Head Office strongly encouraged the regional stations to take culturally significant programs like *Acis and Galatea*. When Charles Siepmann, now the Director of Programme Planning, saw that instead of the opera the Scottish Regional Programme was planning to broadcast a local entertainment program titled *Pursuit of Pleasure*, he fired off a memo to the Assistant Controller of Programmes, complaining that Stewart was acting contrary to Corporation policy. The Assistant Controller replied that Siepmann could do nothing to overrule Stewart's decision given his claim that carrying the opera on Scottish Regional would cause serious difficulties for Scottish staff.[38] Siepmann persisted, and composed a memo asking Stewart to reconsider his position. Stewart's reply is worth quoting at length:

> We discussed very carefully the "Acis and Galatea" question at [Scottish] Pro-
> gramme Board last week, and I consulted privately with Music Director before
> coming to a decision. In brief, our feeling is that it is too long a block at a peak
> period to give what is in Scotland a small minority interest … I am always glad
> of your advice, but I do want you to understand that the omissions which I
> make are not in ignorance or stubbornness but out of a pretty fair knowledge
> and assessment of broadcasting values and an understanding of, and alignment
> with, the Scottish character.[39]

In contrast to an earlier memo outlining his reasons for rejecting the opera,
Stewart made no mention of technical or staff difficulties, but rather asserted
two important principles in his decision to reject *Acis and Galatea*. First, he
claimed that as Scottish Programme Director he was competent, by virtue
of his broadcasting expertise, to decide which London programs to broadcast in Scotland. More importantly, he defended his decision not to take the
opera based on his special appreciation of the distinct Scottish character of his
listeners. This was nothing less than a declaration that, because he was a Scot,
Stewart knew better than English staff how to best program for Scotland. The
logical conclusion of such a position would be to grant regional staff broad
powers in putting together their programs because of their national or cultural
background.

Siepmann recognized the implications of Stewart's claim and immediately
replied that while Stewart had an obligation to reflect the "character and resources
of Scotland" in his programs, he did not agree with the rest of the argument: "it
seems to me a very bold extension of that function for you to claim the right to
modify our considered programme policy in light of your better knowledge of
the listener's interests." Stung by Stewart's refusal to cooperate, Siepmann went
further, noting, "if the BBC (not I as DPP or London as the capital), decides
that *Acis and Galatea* is a work of musical significance that it desires listeners to
hear, that should be enough."[40] In reaction to this last memo, Dinwiddie wrote
to an increasingly angry Stewart that Siepmann "appear[ed] to be exercising
his known desire for centralisation" and agreed with his Programme Director
that "only those in touch with a Region can decide what is best for the listeners
in it." But he warned Stewart to proceed with great care in matters of regional
autonomy.[41] In this case, Scotland acceded to the demands of Head Office and
carried the opera.[42] But Stewart wrote one last memo to Dinwiddie conveying
his irritation with Siepmann, asserting his authority as Scottish Programme
Director, and making a claim for the importance of his own nationality in
programming for Scotland:

As I see it, if I am to be of any use, it is because I … have an understanding of and sympathy with the Scottish people who are our listeners … We, as the BBC in Scotland, must surely use our discretion in agreeing to the selection which DPP makes of the weeks most significant programmes.[43]

Stewart found Siepmann's phrase "if the BBC decides" particularly objectionable, because of its implication that only Head Office constituted the BBC, therefore only Head Office should make program decisions. "You and I are as much the BBC as he is," Stewart bristled, "where is our part in such decisions?"[44]

The fight over *Acis and Galatea* was only part of a broader battle with Head Office over his authority and, more generally, the purpose and nature of BBC Scotland. For Siepmann, the job of regional broadcasting was first and foremost to provide programs that contrasted with programs on the National Programme. If the National Programme carried music, Siepmann wanted the regions to have talks; if the National Programme was broadcasting undemanding fare, the regions should broadcast something more substantial. For Stewart, the *raison d'être* of Scottish broadcasting was to serve Scottish listeners. Given the divergence of these two points of view, conflict between Stewart and Head Office became inevitable.

Although Stewart conceded in the specific case of *Acis and Galatea*, he prevailed in many of his other clashes with Head Office. In 1936, Lindsay Wellington questioned Stewart's decision not to carry the drama *Siegfried*. Stewart explained that, in addition to wreaking havoc with his schedule:

the sunless pomposity of *Siegfried* has never had much of a following in Scotland. I can bear this out, for I went to the last performance of it in Glasgow a week ago and the audience was much smaller than usual and not enthusiastic. In fact, to the Scots mind there is something a little comic in it, to which an occasional titter (in which I am ashamed to say I joined) testified.

As with *Acis and Galatea*, Stewart defended his decision not include *Siegfried* based on the peculiar tastes of the Scottish listener. In this case, Wellington deferred to Stewart's judgment.[45] On another occasion Siepmann asked Stewart to take a concert by the Royal Philharmonic Society. Instead, Scottish listeners were treated to a program on Jaime Fleeman, "the Laird of Udny's Fool."[46]

Siepmann and Stewart were at loggerheads again in 1939. "I hope you won't resent my questioning your arrangements," wrote Siepmann, but you "eliminate for Scottish listeners the whole of the operatic element both light and serious for the week." Stewart prevailed again this time, scheduling instead a Gaelic Concert and "Old Glasgow Favourites" instead of the opera.[47] Shortly thereafter, Stewart refused to broadcast a series of talks on health in Britain because Scotland's health service differed from England's. In one of their last exchanges, a somewhat battered Siepmann began, "useless as I know it to be, to suggest modifications of your plans, I yet hazard a further comment."[48]

By the mid-1930s then, BBC Scotland enjoyed the services of a confident and strong-willed staff whose first priority was to provide quality Scottish programs for Scottish audiences. In this sense BBC Scotland resembled a national broadcasting network rather than an *entrepôt* for English culture. Although ultimately part of the larger, British, BBC, there are other reasons to regard BBC Scotland as akin to a national broadcasting network. It possessed a transmitter that broadcast a single program available to almost the entire Scottish population. Although only about 40 per cent of BBC Scotland's material was produced in Scotland, the majority of this programming appeared in the evening, when audiences were their largest; London material was taken in large part to fill in the long daytime hours. BBC Scotland was more than willing and capable of representing Scottishness. The question to consider now is exactly how BBC Scotland constructed Scottish national identity. What did the BBC's programs in Scotland sound like?

Scottish regional programs and Scottishness

One of the simplest but most powerful ways in which BBC Scotland fostered the growth of Scottishness was by reflecting the peoples, customs, and events of the region to its listeners. The first, and most numerous, of these types of programs was *Frae a' the Airts*, a program that BBC stations in Scotland carried as early as 1928, and which remained a staple of Scottish broadcasting until the mid-1930s.[49] The purpose of these programs was to bring to Scottish listeners something of the genuine folk culture that still existed in the Scottish countryside and "reflect the diverse spirit of Scotland."[50] Because producers worried that rustic villagers would not perform as well in the somewhat stultifying environment of the studio, BBC Scotland broadcast these programs on the spot, in the inns, pubs, and halls of rural Scotland. This added a certain amount of authority and authenticity to the programs.[51] *Frae a' the Airts* culminated in a broadcast, carried by National Programme, entitled *Scottish Characters*. "A symposium of those local programmes which the Scottish Regional Director has broadcast during the past year," *Scottish Characters* served "the commendable purpose of introducing English listeners to the real Scotland."[52] One might add that the program also served the purpose of introducing *Scottish* listeners to Scotland, although whether or not *Scottish Characters* accurately reflected peasant culture, and whether this, in turn, constituted the "real" Scotland, is debatable.

In 1934 BBC Scotland offered a similar series, *In Praise of Scotland*. The program was part tourist information and part paean to the Scottish country-side, and consisted of a talk, music, and information. Each broadcast con-tained practical information including material about when and how to travel in Scotland.[53] Moray McLaren noted that *In Praise* would "interest the Scot-tish people who are spending more of their holiday time ... travelling about Scotland."[54] But the Scottish Programme Director suggested that the series had a somewhat higher purpose than merely encouraging Scottish tourists to stay in Scotland. Calling it a "really ambitious" program that would encapsulate the BBC's continuing efforts to go out into the regions of Scotland, McLaren claimed that *In Praise of Scotland* "will also be a real help in interesting Scots people in their own country."[55]

These travel programs became quite common in Scottish broadcasting before the Second World War. At the same time as *In Praise of Scotland*, McLaren proposed to broadcast a fortnightly series of features on six differ-ent Scottish districts to be presented by some well-known personage. "He or she would give a talk under some such title as 'Why I love Galloway,'" wrote McLaren, and "this would be followed by music, and possibly a short drama illustrating the district, and finally facts about the best way to get to the dis-trict and ... news about its amenities."[56] The following summer BBC Scotland broadcast two more travel/tourist series, *The Weekend Out of Doors* and *Adven-tures in Scotland*, a series intended to "reflect ... the increasing discovery by our nation of the freedom of the countryside."[57] Andrew Stewart, who took over as Programme Director in Scotland in 1935, continued this trend. In the summer of 1936 BBC Scotland brought back *The Weekend Out of Doors* and *Adventures in Scotland*. These programs culminated in 1938, with the broadcast of a major series of talks on the National Programme, *Your Visit to Scotland*. All eight talks in this series were published in the *Listener*, and included contributions from Moray McLaren on "Travel and Hospitality in Scotland," Edwin Muir on "The Scottish Character," and Compton Mackenzie on "The Highlands and Islands."[58]

In addition to projecting the beauty and virtue of the Scottish landscape, BBC Scotland helped to foster Scottish national identity through the broadcast-ing of special anniversary programs—remembrances of famous Scots such as Burns, Walter Scott, and Mary Stuart, or historical events in Scotland, such as the Jacobite rebellion of 1745, the subject of many BBC Scotland programs.

From its earliest days, the BBC in Scotland produced special programs for three Scottish holidays in particular: Hogmanay, Burns Night, and St Andrew's Day. Perhaps the most ambitious of these were the programs produced to commemorate St Andrew's Day. St Andrew, the patron saint of Scotland, was a potent symbol of Scotland's distinct identity. By the mid 1930s, the programs were rarely about the saint himself; rather, BBC Scotland regarded St Andrew's day as an opportunity to project the best of Scottish culture and Scottish heritage to Scottish, British, and empire audiences, or to do a kind of reflective program on the state of the nation. Eventually, BBC Scotland came to regard the St Andrew's Day programs as expressions of Scottishness. The development of these programs, which evolved from nostalgic sentimentality meant primarily for emigrants to representations of Scotland's distinct national identity, also demonstrates the ability of Scottish broadcasters to resist the demands of London.

While the BBC always hoped that Scottish listeners would enjoy the St Andrew's Day programs, their original purpose was to give Scots living in England an opportunity to hear traditional Scots music and speech. They also provided a chance to represent Scotland and Scottishness to a broader English audience. In 1928, the St Andrew's Day program was entitled *The Scot in Exile*. Publicity for the program made clear the purpose of the broadcast and its assumed audience. Noting that St Andrew's Day "is an even greater occasion for the exiled Scot than for the Scot that still lives on the right side of the border," the *Radio Times* reported that the 1928 program "suggests the sort of quiet, homely evening which any exiled Scot might spend … in a mood of reminiscence."[59] The following year the St Andrew's Day program embraced similar themes, "a sort of haggis supper," according to Cleghorn Thompson, "with singing, speaking, and violin playing included in the evening's entertainment."[60] While appeal to emigrants remained an element in the St Andrew's Day programs, a conflict between BBC Scotland and the London office in 1930 resulted in significant changes to the program.

The 1930 program appears to have been little different from its predecessors. It was a combination of music and speech, including pipe bands, a Gaelic love song, and a recitation of Burns's *Scots Wha Hae*.[61] But in October 1930, staff in London informed the Scottish Regional Director that the St Andrew's Night special would not be broadcast from the Daventry transmitter on the National Programme. The news enraged Thompson, especially as the day was to mark the opening of the BBC's new Glasgow studio. In a memo to Reith and the London Director of Programmes, he accused the program planners in

London, including Lindsay Wellington, of lacking confidence in the Scottish staff, and worse, of implying that Scotland lacked a "national music, drama, and humor of a distinctive kind."[62] Head Office's decision produced a flurry of memos between Wellington, Thompson, and Reith. Wellington was adamant that the National Programme not broadcast the St Andrew's Day offering. Wellington did not, as a general rule, support these anniversary programs (see Chapters 6 and 7), and he accused the Scottish regional staff of not producing programs up to the standards of London. In the end, the BBC broadcast the 1930 St Andrew's Day program from Daventry and continued to broadcast the program nationally, in large part because of the intervention of Reith. Often characterized as a centralizer with little sympathy for regional broadcasting, Reith, in this case, came down against Wellington.[63] Wellington, undoubtedly stung by Reith's rejection of his decision, was unduly harsh in his criticisms of the St Andrew's Day program. "I did not enjoy it," he wrote to the Director of Programmes, complaining that he had scarcely understood the purpose of the program, or what it was trying to convey. "It was not beautiful, impressive, or tragic, nor did it give me any feeling of Scotland ... it seemed a tragedy to describe [the program] ... as 'a celebration of Scotland in poetry and song.'"[64] When Wellington received the proposal for the 1931 St Andrew's Day special, he passed it on to the Director of Programmes, meekly noting: "This isn't the St. Andrew's Day programme I should myself propose, but I don't think we can raise any objection provided that the ultimate programme is characteristically Scots."[65]

What seemed to bother Thompson most was Wellington's claim that programs from Scotland, particularly the anniversary broadcasts, were not up to London standards. For Thompson, this seemed to be a clear case of metropolitan bias, and his rebuttal reveals the extent to which Scottish broadcasters thought of themselves as having a different purpose than their English counterparts. "It is ... impossible," he lashed out at the Director of Programmes, "to please a body which is predominantly English by a programme that is genuinely expressive of Scotland." Thompson's final words on the matter reveal his frustration with the expectations of London and suggest that he was prepared to move in a new direction in regards to future St Andrew's Day programs. "If we have erred in the past ... it has been through attempting to give an English audience something near to its preconception of a Scots gathering and through not really trying hard enough to express something finer and deeper."[66]

Although it is difficult to tell how successful BBC Scotland was in expressing "something finer and deeper" after 1930, they did begin to alter significantly the St Andrew's Day programs. While BBC Scotland hoped the new type of program would appeal to "exiles," whether in England or the empire,[67] the use of overly sentimental pieces decreased. Rather, the St Andrew's Day programs came to be seen as opportunities to represent "Scotland," first and foremost, to listeners in Scotland. Further, the Scottish programmers made attempts to represent "Scotland" in all its diversity, yet a diversity that remained essentially Scottish. The 1931 program included broadcasts from both the Glasgow and Edinburgh studios: special effects to represent the shipyards of Glasgow, a Gaelic choir, and from Edinburgh, "half a dozen speaking voices from various parts of Scotland."[68] The 1932 program, *Hail Caledonia*, likewise expressed the diversity of Scotland, including "the Celt ... the Borderer ... the man from the north-east of his own ancient corner of Scotland, and the Ayrshire man."[69] Yet, the ultimate unity of Scotland, the commonality all these people shared as "Scots," was explicit. "The lesson for all us Scots people on St. Andrew's Night," went the *Radio Times*, is that "whether we live north of the Border or are in the south or across the seas ... we are all Scotsmen."[70]

With the exception of 1933, a concert, and 1935, a celebration of Scotland's contribution to the empire (see below), all of the St Andrew's Day programs up until the beginning of the Second World War were similar to *Hail Caledonia*. They were not sentimental appeals but rather attempts to represent "Scotland." Andrew Stewart, the new Scottish Programme Director, described what he had in mind for the 1934 program in a memo to Lindsay Wellington:

> You will remember that in the past we have had a number of programmes of different kinds [for St Andrew's Day], mostly of the sentimental (I use the word not wholly in the bad sense) kind. In other words, looking back on Scotland's music, poetry, etc., each one trying to present a recollection of the Scotland that was past for the benefit of Scots abroad or in the south ... This year I want ... a programme under some such title as "This is Scotland." The idea would be to tell people exactly what is going on in Scotland now in this year 1934.[71]

This transformation of the St Andrew's Day programs make them a useful window into the ways in which BBC Scotland debated and defined the meaning of Scotland and Scottishness.

A debate about the 1937 St Andrew's Day feature between Stewart and Moray McLaren, former Programme Director of BBC Scotland but by 1937 Assistant Director of Features in London, provides some insight into the changing meaning of these programs. Like previous versions, the 1937 program aimed to provide a snapshot of contemporary Scotland by presenting a radio glimpse of its various regions. McLaren found the program lacking in quality and emotional appeal. Writing that he found the St Andrew's Day program "uninspiring and even dull," McLaren suggested that the broadcast ought to be "emotional or provocative, rather than informative." It is not surprising that Stewart defended his program, but his response to McLaren is indicative of his understanding of its purpose. While he still maintained that part of the objective of the St Andrew's Day program was "to touch the exile," Stewart also saw it as an opportunity "for a kind of stock-taking" and to "interest others in Scotland." In taking stock of Scotland, Stewart was not afraid to point out Scotland's shortcomings. "If the programme was mediocre," he replied to McLaren, it was due to "some inescapable qualities of mediocrity in Scottish life." Further, Stewart defended the program by making an appeal to the "ordinary listener" who was interested in information and the actuality that the program presented. Calling the program a "solid admixture of the *Glasgow Herald* and the *People's Journal*" and claiming that it was popular with listeners, he asserted that St Andrew's Day was not the occasion for "what the man in the street regards as 'high-flown nonsense.'"[72]

These two ideas—attempts to inspire pride in Scotland while at the same time confronting the difficult economic state of the country in the 1930s— came together with Edwin Muir's 1938 program, the last before the start of the war. Muir was not shy about presenting Scotland's problems on the air. In his *Radio Times* article describing the broadcast, Muir was pessimistic in his evaluation of the current condition of Scotland, and promised that his program would deliver an accurate picture. "The bad sides of Scotland have been presented along with the good: the plight of the fisheries and the deplorable state of the Highlands, along with the attempts to plan and build better."[73] Indeed, Muir defended this type of broadcast by explicitly rejecting the nostalgia that characterized the earlier programs. A St Andrew's Day program that did not portray the failures of contemporary Scotland, Muir claimed, was "at best the rose-hued sentimentality of the Kailyard of which Scotland itself has been long tired."[74]

The BBC, Scottishness, and imperialism

Any evaluation of Scottish national identity must take into account the importance of empire. The windfalls of empire helped to forge the union between England and Scotland, as ambitious Scots found fame and fortune in distant lands. Scots, English, and Welsh people, when confronted by people of color, tended to bury their differences and forge "British" communities overseas.[75] The empire provided new homes and new opportunities to the millions who emigrated from Britain in the eighteenth and nineteenth centuries. Reminders of empire were ubiquitous in Britain in the nineteenth and first half of the twentieth century, in the form of exhibitions, news stories, street names, cinema, letters from relatives in the colonies, and, of course, radio. And "empire" was part of a larger Scottish-unionist discourse that saw the nations of the British Isles as inextricably bound in a common enterprise. I. G. C. Hutchinson has recently suggested that the success of the Conservative Party in interwar Scotland was partly due to the identification of the Tories with the empire, "which continued to exercise a powerful emotional and economic hold in Scotland."[76]

In the last decade, a number of scholars have begun to examine Scotland's unique contribution to British imperialism, and the relationship between imperialism and Scottish national identity. They are finding that the two did not represent starkly opposing ideologies, despite the strident anti-imperialism of Scottish nationalists such as Hugh McDiarmid. For example, Presbyterian Scottish missionaries did not simply abandon Scottishness and embrace Britishness but rather engaged in a contest with their Anglican counterparts in the conversion and education of colonized peoples. And Scottish nationalists in the Victorian and Edwardian period argued that Home Rule would strengthen the bonds of empire and guarantee Scotland's continuing role in the imperial endeavor.[77] In a series of articles, Richard Findlay and John MacKenzie have both assessed the impact of empire on Scottish national identity, and both broadly conclude that rather than undermining Scottish self-consciousness, empire served as a symbol of pride for Scots, the more so because of the disproportionate number of Scots that contributed to its making.[78]

Like the National Programme, the Scottish stations produced a flood of programs about the empire, with imperial settings, themes, and "heroes." From the beginning, empire was an important element in the programs of the BBC's Scottish stations. Early Glasgow programming included "interesting travel talks on 'A Cruise to the South Sea Islands,'" while one of the first series of talks produced by the Aberdeen station was on Egypt by a representative of the Egyptian Exploration Fund.[79] The Scottish stations also broadcast their own Empire Day celebrations. In 1926 Aberdeen aired a half-hour program while Glasgow put on two programs, *Empire Review*, from 8:30 to 9:30 p.m., and an *Empire Day Programme*, from 10:00 until 11:00 p.m., when the station closed down for the night. The opening of *Empire Review* quickly established for its listeners the intimate familial links between Scotland and the empire:

From the lone shielding of the misty island,
Mountains divide us and a waste of seas,
Yet still the blood is warm, the heart is Highland,
And we in dreams behold the Hebrides.[80]

The program closed with the playing of selections from *Under the British Flag*.[81]

Also in 1926, the Edinburgh relay station held a competition asking listeners to create their own program; the best submission would be broadcast from the Edinburgh studios. The winning entry, *To India with Private Fred Yeats*, was an ambitious broadcast that combined music, poetry, and the spoken word, and followed the "experiences of an English soldier sent out to India with his battalion."[82] Not to be outdone, the Glasgow station also ran a series of contest programs with an imperial theme, *Empire Slogans*. An early effort to bring together entertainment and education, the program was an acrostic quiz in which Glaswegians formed the "imperial solution" by using the initial letters of the names of the composers in the evening's program. The BBC promoted *Empire Slogans* as "an attractive entertainment as well as a thoroughly intriguing ... effort of the intellect," and offered three guineas to the first listener to submit the correct answer.[83]

Perhaps the most ambitious of the empire programs brought forth by the early Scottish stations was Glasgow's *Empire Phono-Flights*. Broadcast to coincide with the Wembley Empire Exhibition, *Empire Phono-Flights* appeared regularly throughout 1925 and 1926. Again, the purpose of the programs seems to have been part entertainment, part education. Lasting two hours, each episode of *Empire Phono-Flights* combined words and music in order give the listener a sense of the present state of the empire as well as its history, "a picture of ... [it] as it is today, with here and there a phrase from the past."[84] The programs were highly regarded by the BBC and enjoyed the blessing of the Dominion High Commissioners. The *Radio Times* referred to them as "the outstanding [dramatic] achievement of the [Glasgow] station" and noted the popularity of the programs on more than one occasion.[85]

Empire Phono-Flights tended to focus on the familial and cultural links between Britain and the empire. The first series was devoted largely to the white Dominions and included episodes on Australia, Canada, India, New Zealand, and South Africa. While publicizing the program, the *Radio Times* referred to New Zealand as "the Britain of the South." It noted: "special attention is being paid to 'The Landing of the Immigrant,' in which there will be the typical questions and answers of the average home-seeker as he reaches the shores of New Zealand."[86] In contrast, Burma, Malaya, Palestine, and West Africa were covered in a single episode titled "The Lesser-Known Possessions." Of course, actual inhabitants of the "lesser known possessions" did not actually speak at the microphone, and that particular episode ended with the playing of *Land of Hope and Glory*.[87] In 1926, the Glasgow station started up a new series of *Empire Phono-Flights* around the theme of "Men of Empire." Not surprisingly, the first broadcast recounted the life of David Livingstone, Scotland's greatest imperial explorer.[88]

When Scotland became incorporated in the regional scheme in 1932, BBC policy implied that "empire" would cease to be a significant element in Scottish programs. The mandate of the regional networks was to reflect the way of life of their area. Head Office frowned upon the regions broadcasting talks, features, or other programs of national or international significance. Yet the empire, it seemed, was as much a part of Scottish heritage and culture as haggis, Burns poetry, or Mary, Queen of Scots. Moray McLaren certainly recognized this when writing to Gerald Beadle and Charles Siepmann that Scottish connections to the empire were "more obvious and varied than those with any other part of Great Britain."[89] *Scotland on the Air*, the short history of BBC Scotland compiled by George Burnett, included a long chapter on Scotland's contributions to the Empire Service by J. G. S. Macgregor. And while the number of Scottish programs on empire pales in comparison to the output of the National Programme, it did produce more programs about its imperial ties than the other BBC national regions.

In 1933, McLaren proposed to broadcast a debate on the topic of "Scotland's Future—National or Imperial," between Lord Beaverbrook and Compton Mackenzie. Siepmann demurred, suggesting not only that Beaverbrook was not a genuine representative of Scotland but also that it was inappropriate for Scotland to broadcast talks of "such national significance."[90] Despite Siepmann's objections, BBC Scotland broadcast the debate in March 1934, with James Maxton and Alexander MacEwen in place of Mackenzie and Beaverbrook.[91] The year 1935 saw the production of a spectacular feature program, *The Man Livingstone*.[92] In 1937, BBC Scotland broadcast an important series of talks, *Scotland and the Empire*, without any apparent objections from the new Director of Talks, Richard Maconachie, himself a Scot and an imperialist.

The mutually reinforcing relationship between Scottish national identity and imperialism is best seen in BBC Scotland's St Andrew's Day program for 1935. The program, which included a twenty-minute contribution from Canada, consisted of "a survey of the part played by Scotland in the foundation, development, and consolidation of the Empire."[93] The program was surprisingly unabashed in its attitude towards the empire. In an article promoting the day's program, J. D. Mackie defended the record of the Scots as empire-builders. "We are a great imperial people," he stated, "and our record shows us not only as the consolidators and developers of the great Empire that had been gained by the all venturing English, but as expanders too."[94] The broadcast itself invoked an even more jingoistic tone, opening with the following boast:

> Since Scotland's entry into the imperial partnership they have been explorers, soldiers, administrators, missionaries, statesmen, financiers, scientists, doctors, preachers, educators, engineers and merchants; and there is not a Dominion of the British Empire without its formidable roll of Scottish names. So today, in Canada, Africa, India, Australia, New Zealand, and many another places on earth, men join to affirm a sentiment—and that thing which is stronger than sentiment, the blood tie itself, binding all to the same mother.[95]

The script also included historic speeches, including Lord Rosebery's famous address at the University of Glasgow in 1900, a roll call of famous Scots who helped subdue India, and a tribute to David Livingstone.[96]

Scottish broadcasting during the Second World War

The outbreak of the Second World War brought a radical change to the organization of broadcasting in Britain as the BBC suspended the regional networks for the duration of the war. Although some cultural bodies in Scotland protested, this decision was met with resignation among the staff of BBC Scotland.[97] This is not to suggest that the war years saw an end to the quarrels between BBC Scotland and the BBC in London. BBC Scotland vocally complained when the BBC used the term "England" on the unified Home Service instead of the more appropriate "Britain." Other conflicts arose out of the representation of Scotland and Scottish programming on the Home Service and the scheduling of Scottish contributions. As they had before the war, Scottish broadcasters succeeded in pressuring the BBC in London to change policies or offensive practices. Indeed, by the end of the war people both inside and outside the Corporation were complaining that the BBC was catering too much to Scottish demands.

In the decade before the Second World War BBC Scotland had made a habit of complaining about the BBC's tendency to use "England" when "Britain" would have been the correct term.[98] Although duly noted by Programme Board, such blunders continued. It is not unlikely that Head Office paid little attention to BBC Scotland's criticisms in this matter. However, as the war approached, the BBC began to take the issue more seriously. Following another complaint from BBC Scotland about the use of "England" for "Britain," a "well-known source of irritation to Scottish listeners," Basil Nicolls asked Gordon Gildard to submit a paper on the issue.[99] Gildard and Dinwiddie both submitted papers to Nicolls, repeating their concern that inappropriate usage of the words "offends Scots all over the Empire." Referring to the BBC as "the greatest instrument for the maintenance of national unity," Gildard warned Nicolls that misuse of "English" would "provide a serious stimulus for dissatisfaction and evidence for Scottish Nationalists' arguments of English domination."[100]

When the war began the BBC became more careful in its use of "England" and "Britain" so as not to offend Scottish listeners. The loyalty of certain segments of Scottish society caused concern in some quarters. The depression of the 1930s hit Scotland disproportionately, causing much disaffection, and the interwar period had seen the birth of small Scottish nationalist political parties.[101] In an Argyll by-election in April 1940, William Power, representing the Scottish National Party, received 37 per cent of the vote against the Unionist candidate.[102] The same month, Lindsay Wellington, now at the Ministry of Information (MOI), sent a memo to Basil Nicolls, suggesting the BBC broadcast a program to be called "The Week in Scotland," to help offset the inevitable "growth of Scottish nationalism and restiveness in the minds of more balanced and sensible people."[103] The BBC also grew concerned about Scottish listeners tuning into overseas stations. In addition to the "New British Broadcasting Service," which carried Lord Haw-Haw, the Germans established Radio Caledonia, which transmitted propaganda specifically for Scottish listeners and called for a separate peace between Germany and Scotland.[104] Gildard, who took over for Stewart as Scottish Programme Director, suggested that they get a Glasgow shop steward to broadcast against Haw-Haw.[105] In addition to Haw-Haw and Radio Caledonia, BBC Scotland became concerned about programs broadcast from Eire, which declared its neutrality in September and was determined to sit out the war. In December, Dinwiddie drafted a memo "emphasizing the adverse affects [in Scotland] of reception of Athlone," Eire's state-run radio station.[106]

These concerns did not, of course, prevent the BBC from making mistakes that seemed to exclude Scotland from the national community. The cover of the first edition of the *Radio Times* to appear after the declaration of war pictures a rustic old man outside a thatched-roof cottage with the caption,

"There'll always be an England." A program of the same title was broadcast the next week. A ham-fisted turn to the myth of "deep England"—the belief that the countryside represented the essence of Englishness and stood for all of England—Scots could scarcely identify with the image. And the natural corollary of the country representing England was that this "England" represented all of Britain as well. In a memo to Head Office, George Burnett again reminded the BBC to "exclude possible irritants" in its announcements, and quoted the following from the October 23 edition of the *Glasgow Bulletin*:

> It was heartening to hear from a news bulletin on Saturday that the BBC had at last learned ... that Turkey had actually concluded a pact with the whole of Britain, and not merely with England. Judging by the mail which has been arriving at this office since the original announcement was made, a lot of people up here have been wondering if it is worth Scotland's while doing anything more about a war which seemed so exclusively English ... We're fighting England's war, paying for England's war and standing up to England's air raids. Apart from that we have absolutely no reason to complain when the BBC indulges in its comic "This England" exhibitionism.[107]

While the *Bulletin* may have overstated the potential for Scottish disloyalty (or at least apathy), it is clear that the BBC's frequent use of "England" for "Britain," irritated Scottish listeners.

Relations between the BBC and its Scottish listeners deteriorated throughout the spring of 1940 and reached something of a crisis point in July 1940. Alan Melville, a producer for BBC Scotland, wrote to Moultrie Kelsall on July 15, 1940, warning of the anti-BBC feeling among Clydeside workers. "Two men who have broadcast for me before have refused to do again," wrote Melville, "they would prefer to have 'nothing to do with the English Broadcasting Corporation.'"[108] The same day, Kelsall sent a damning report on the BBC, based on his meeting with the MOI Committee for Western Scotland, to Dinwiddie and Stewart. "The Committee think that ... an anti-English feeling is already beginning and to quite a large extent blame the BBC for it." Kelsall made a number of suggestions for improving Scottish morale, including programs to directly "appeal to the patriotism of Scotland," the use of Scottish speakers for Postscripts, and, of course, the use of "British" instead of "English."[109] The situation also led to a visit to Scotland by Allan Powell, Chairman of the BBC's Board of Governors, and F. W. Ogilvie, the Director-General. They found "Scottish resentment at lack of representation in programmes ... [and they added] that "British" rather than "English" should wherever possible be used."[110] At about the same time, Kelsall sent a memo to Nicolls on the matter.

In response, Nicolls drafted "a strong directive about 'England'" and complained to Val Gielgud about its use in a recent features broadcast.[111]

It seems that with the Director-General himself sensing Scottish dissatisfaction with the BBC, the Corporation became more serious about the correct use of "Britain" and "England,"—not that it did not happen again.[112] But even if the BBC could demand the accurate use of these words from its own announcers, producers, and performers, it was difficult for them to account for the use of "England" and "Britain" by every one of its outside speakers. The BBC's enforcement of this policy created a backlash with some Head Office staff complaining that the BBC inadequately represented Englishness. Mail from listeners also complained that "England" was being disregarded. This prompted Maurice Farquharson to write to the Assistant Controllers for News, Programmes, and Home broadcasts in May 1944: "we nearly always describe English things as 'British' while making a point of calling Scottish things 'Scottish' and Welsh things 'Welsh.' The words 'England' and 'English' thus tend to be submerged."[113] A week later, Laurence Gilliam and Moultrie Kelsall exchanged a couple of terse memoranda. The former, with an air of triumph, sent Kelsall an extract of the minutes from the most recent Programme Committee, which read, "'English:' this term is to be used in preference to 'British' when appropriate." "No comment!" Gilliam concluded with a flourish.[114] Farquharson was convinced by the end of the war that the BBC had gone too far in labeling everything "British." In a memo to Dinwiddie he claimed, "the wrong use of the wording of 'England' and 'English' has been so drummed into the heads of the programme people here in London that they definitely err on the other side!"[115]

While BBC Scotland continued to monitor BBC broadcasts to insure the proper use of "Britain," their main concern was arranging programs for all of the BBC's radio services (e.g. Empire Service, European Service, North American Service). Getting programs on the Home Service for Scottish listeners was especially important to the Scottish staff. BBC Scotland may have accepted the closure of the Westerglen transmitter with resignation—a necessary decision in a time of national emergency—but it remained committed to representing Scotland as best it could under wartime conditions. As noted in Chapter 4, the BBC included little regional programming in the Home Service during the first months of the war, and Scotland was no exception. Other than a weekly broadcast in Gaelic, which began in November 1939, Scottish programs on the Home Service were incidental and topical, such as Glasgow's broadcast with survivors from the liner *Athenia*, sunk by the Germans in September.[116]

But Scotland could not even take credit for this moving program. Due to strict security measures, the BBC was not allowed to even mention that the broadcast came from the Glasgow studio.

Scottish broadcasters often argued that Scotland's distinctiveness made it necessary to provide more programming from Scotland on the Home Service. But this claim could just as easily be used to exclude Scottish programs, and in part it helps explain the dearth of Scottish representation in the Home Service in the first months of the war. BBC Head Office was reluctant to take dialect plays or features from Scotland for fear that they would be unintelligible to the majority of listeners.[117] A Listener Research report on accents seemed to confirm this belief, concluding that English and Welsh listeners found both Lowland and Highland speech the most difficult to understand.[118]

Early in 1940, Dinwiddie sent a memo directly to the Director-General outlining his dissatisfaction with Scottish representation in the Home Service. He proposed regular times for Scottish music, variety, plays, Scottish farming talks, and a half-hour program that would be designed specifically for Scottish listeners. It produced few tangible results, but only because by the time Dinwiddie's memorandum had reached the Director-General's desk, the BBC had already resolved to place more programs from the regions on the Home Service.[119]

By the middle of 1940 the BBC began to give serious consideration to the status of Scotland within the Home Service. Again, it was the visit by Powell and Ogilvie to Scotland that seems to have been the main impetus, with Farquharson noting in a memo after their return that "various suggestions for increasing Scottish material are under consideration," including a series of Scottish "post-scripts."[120] Three days later, Nicolls wrote to Dinwiddie offering Scotland a weekly half-hour program in the Home Service at a fixed time and day. "With two Gaelic news periods, and the Gaelic half-hour, and the fairly regular Scottish contributions to the Forces Programme," Nicolls concluded, "Scotland will, I think, not be doing so badly."[121] Dinwiddie seemed to agree, and wrote a favorable article about the activities of the BBC in Scotland for the *BBC Handbook*.[122]

As the war progressed, the BBC expanded the number of hours allocated to Scotland in the Home Service. In 1941, it added *North of the Tweed* and *Scottish Magazine*, each broadcast once a month, to supplement the *Scottish Half Hour*. By comparison, Wales and Northern Ireland broadcast only one such summary of regional news. Hogmanay, Burns Night, and St Andrew's day continued to be represented in the BBC's schedules despite the fact that these programs remained much more popular in Scotland than in England and Wales. Nearly 38 per cent of Scottish listeners tuned into the 1943 St Andrew's Day program, compared with only 16.6 per cent of the total British audience.[123] Scotland also contributed several features to the Home Service, and more space was given to typically Scottish variety artists such as Harry Lauder, Will Fyffe, and Harry Gordon.[124] In talks, Scotland received a weekly space, whereas the other regions were guaranteed only a fortnightly space. The favoritism shown towards Scotland in talks provoked an angry memo from the Director of Programme Planning to George Barnes, the Head of the Talks Department, after Scotland asked for an extra afternoon space for an important speaker:

> D[irector] T[alks] … would you consider the desirability of writing Miss Orr [Scottish Talks producer], saying that at the moment they are in the position of the "most favored region"—i.e. they get weekly space [and] are allowed farming talks; afternoon space is few and far between … (I could go on for hours; maybe you won't feel as angry about this as I do. But please bring your cool calm judgment to bear).[125]

The Director of Programme Planning was not the only member of the London staff that had begun to resent the BBC's preferential treatment of Scotland. As early as 1941, London program planners were growing weary of the hectoring from Scotland's Acting Programme Director, Moultrie Kelsall.[126] When Kelsall wrote to the Director of Talks asking for a monthly late afternoon and evening talk for Scotland, Barnes flatly refused the request.[127] In 1943 Lord Derby, citing *Scottish Half Hour*, wrote to the Director-General asking that the BBC broadcast a special weekly program for the North of England.[128] In his reply refusing this request, Foot acknowledged that, because of their distinct national cultures, Scotland and Wales merited their extra spaces in the Home Service. "There seems to be no good argument," Foot wrote to Brendan Bracken, the Minister of Information, for treating a particular region of England in the same way as we do Scotland or Wales." Less than a year later, John Coatman wrote to Foot along the same lines as Derby. In a memo complaining about the lack of Northern programs in the Home Service, Coatman twice accused the BBC of giving "special treatment" to Scotland, Wales, and Northern Ireland.[129] Even after the war and the restoration of regional broadcasting, the status of Scotland in the BBC continued to rankle Coatman, who felt the Scottish broadcasters received an unfair share of BBC resources.[130]

While the coming of the war was a blow to Scottish broadcasting, the consolidation of all the BBC networks into a single Home Service should not be seen as an attempt at anglicization or cultural imperialism. When evaluating Scottish broadcasting during the war one must consider that domestic broadcasting was limited to one service; that special provision had to be given to the other regions, notably Wales and Northern Ireland; that government ministries demanded access to the microphone to make announcements and disseminate information; that the BBC had to participate in propaganda "campaigns" at the expense of other programming; and that during the war the BBC offered a steady diet of lighter programs, which were not one of BBC Scotland's strengths.[131] Given these constrictions, the amount of Scottish material that made it on the air during the war is impressive. After an initial period of neglect, the BBC gave considerable attention to Scottish issues and respect to Scottish concerns, to the point that both English listeners and BBC staff clearly thought the Corporation was going too far in its attempts to assuage Scottish opinion. This provoked a backlash when BBC Scotland staff seemed to be badgering Head Office personnel and overreaching in its demands for representation in the Home Service and Forces Programme.

Although the outbreak of the war retarded the development of BBC Scotland as a national broadcasting network, it did force the BBC to represent Britain as more "British" than ever before. If the radio was on, English listeners had no choice but to listen to Scottish contributions to the Home Service. The "Britain" represented by the wartime Home Service was more diverse than it was before the war, thanks in no small part to the efforts of BBC Scotland; and "Scottishness" was showcased for national and global audiences. Dinwiddie summarized it best in his piece on Scottish broadcasting during the war:

> The time and work which Scottish broadcasting ... had been compelled to take away from its own listeners has been put to the gain of Great Britain and the empire; and if Scotland cannot boast a separate programme in wartime, it may be consoled with the reflection that Scottish song and speech, Scottish wit and humour, have been made available as never before to the English-speaking peoples of the world.[132]

Conclusion

With the cessation of hostilities in 1945, the BBC quickly re-established broadcasting along regional lines. In yet another nod to its special status as a nation, the BBC dropped the term "regional" from its title for the post-war Scottish service, now dubbed simply the "Scottish Home Service." The new Scottish Home Service would have "virtual autonomy" with respect to the planning of its schedule.[133] It could produce its own programs or take them from London as it pleased. Andrew Stewart, who stayed on as Programme Director until 1948, remained committed to regional broadcasting. He was against the establishment of an independent broadcasting system for Scotland, but was adamant that "broadcasting should reflect the people it serves, and should partake of their character and habits of thought and mind so that it should be distinctly their own service."[134] Under Stewart's guidance, BBC Scotland quickly picked up where it had left off in September 1939.

Throughout the late 1940s and early 1950s further steps were taken to insure the freedom and viability of broadcasting in Scotland. In 1947, the BBC established a Scottish Advisory Committee (SAC). Like the BBC's General Advisory Committee, the SAC consisted of the good and the great in Scottish society. Its purpose was to keep the BBC staff in Scotland well attuned to movements in Scottish public opinion. Later, as a result of the Beveridge Report, the BBC's new charter established a Broadcasting Council for Scotland, "designed to keep the BBC conscious of its Scottish dimension." Unlike the purely advisory SAC, the Scottish Broadcasting Council could set policy, appoint advisory committees, and oversee the activities of the BBC in Scotland.[135] The new charter also strengthened the Scottish element at Head Office with its call for the appointment of a special "National Governor" for Scotland. BBC Scotland experienced a number of other changes by 1952. Dinwiddie would soon leave the BBC, while his more than capable lieutenant, Andrew Stewart, was made Controller of the Northern Ireland Home Service in 1949. But perhaps the most significant change was the coming of television to Scotland in 1952. Although radio, particularly the Scottish Home Service, remained important to the lives of Scots, its influence was undermined by the arrival of the new medium, whose production, at the time, was largely centralized in London.

Notes

1 In 1933, the Director of Programmes reported "that responsible opinion in Scotland was apparently unanimous … that the dis-association of the Corporation with the Scottish Nationalist Movement was welcomed. Programme Board, 19 October 1933, BBC WAC, R34/600/5. See also BBC WAC, R51/418.

2 McDowell, *The History of BBC Broadcasting in Scotland*, viii.

3 McDowell devotes eighty pages to the history of BBC Scotland up to 1951. Over two hundred pages of *BBC Broadcasting in Scotland* cover the period from 1952 to 1983.

4 Scullion, 63–93; Ian Bell, "Publishing, Journalism and Broadcasting," in *Scotland: A Concise History*, Paul H. Scott, ed. (Edinburgh: Mainstream Publishing, 1993), 385–95. See also John A. MacPherson, "The Development of Gaelic broadcasting,"

Transactions of the Gaelic Society of Inverness, 61 (2003): 251–79.

5 McDowell, 31–8.

6 Scullion, 65.

7 Bell, 392.

8 Scullion, 85.

9 On tartanry, see Hugh Trevor-Roper, "The Invention of Tradition: The Highland Tradition of Scotland," in *The Invention of Tradition*, Hobsbawm and Ranger, eds. On Scottish nationalism and national identity, see Neal Ascherson, *Stone Voices: The Search for Scotland* (New York: Hill and Wang, 2004); Christopher Harvie, *Scotland and Nationalism: Scottish Society and Politics, 1707 to the Present* (London: Routledge, 1995); Andrew Marr, *The Battle for Scotland* (London: Penguin, 1990).

10 On Jacobitism and Scottish identity, see Murray G. H. Pittock, *The Myth of the Jabobite Clans* (Edinburgh: Edinburgh University Press, 1996); Murray G. H. Pittock, *The Invention of Scotland: The Stuart Myth and Scottish Identity, 1638 to the Present* (London: Routledge, 1991).

11 *Radio Times*, July 10, 1925, 100.

12 *Radio Times*, April 16, 1926, 152.

13 *Radio Times*, April 30, 1926, 245; *Radio Times*, November 7, 1924, 287.

14 *Radio Times*, August 6, 1926, 256.

15 *Radio Times*, September, 28, 1923.

16 Programme Board, January 26, 1926, BBC WAC, R34/600/3.

17 *Radio Times*, November 27, 1925, 387; *Radio Times*, June 5, 1925, 507.

18 *Radio Times*, February 27, 1925, 453; *Radio Times*, May 7, 1926, 286; *Radio Times*, July 29, 1927, 163.

19 See BBC WAC, R34/868.

20 *Radio Times*, March 21, 1924, 505.

21 *Radio Times*, July 2, 1926, 48.

22 *Radio Times*, November 14, 1924, 335.

23 *BBC Handbook 1929*, 87.

24 McDowell, 16. Aberdeen continued to produce its own *Children's Hour* until September 1938.

25 *BBC Yearbook 1930*, 97.

26 *BBC Yearbook 1933*, 245.

27 McDowell, 23.

28 Ibid., 33.

29 See George Burnett, ed., *Scotland on the Air* (Edinburgh: Moray Press, 1938).

30 Ibid., 38.

31 Moray McLaren to Lindsay Wellington, August 21, 1934, BBC WAC, R34/869/1. McLaren's memorandum included the following: "I do not wish to be provincial in this matter or to stress what may seem to you an exaggerated difference, but after all, the other regions are English, or at least (as is the case with the West Region) have a large part of England in them, and it is to be presumed that a good deal of the stuff they provide is the same sort of stuff that English listeners in the South demand ... Scottish listeners appreciate the London Regional programmes that are

put out upon our regional wavelength [but] I am more convinced than ever of the essential difference in the fare which they expect to be provided for them from their own home station."

32 Andrew Stewart to Charles Siepmann, December 12, 1938, BBC WAC, SC9/108/2.

33 Stewart also served in the Ministry of Information from 1940 to 1944.

34 Burnett, 12.

35 John Gough to Stewart, October 1, 1936, BBC WAC, SC9/82/1. Gough to McLaren, July 12, 1937, BBC WAC, SC9/82/2.

36 Val Gielgud to Stewart, October 7, 1936, BBC WAC, SC9/82/1.

37 In a memo to Stewart, Gough railed against the English view of Mary Queen of Scots and the Scottish, in strong language: "It may be, of course, that DFD [Gielgud] will take the smooth English attitude that what happened four hundred years ago does not matter much now provided the script plays well. For myself, I cannot be party to that view … An event of such enormous historical importance must not be forced into the position of being a mere show; in other words, Mary Stewart must not be butchered all over again to make an English holiday." Gough to Stewart, October 23, 1936, Ibid.

38 Siepmann to Assistant Controller (Programmes), January 18, 1937, BBC WAC, R34/869/2.

39 Stewart to Siepmann, February 15, 1937, Ibid.

40 Siepmann to Stewart, February 17, 1937, Ibid.

41 Melville Dinwiddie to Stewart, February 19, 1937, BBC WAC, SC/9/108/1.

42 *Radio Times*, March 25, 1937, 30.

43 Stewart to Dinwiddie, February 21, 1937, BBC WAC, SC/9/108/1.

44 Ibid.

45 Stewart to Wellington, March 27, 1936; Wellington to Stewart, March 31, 1936, BBC WAC, R34/869/2.

46 Siepmann to Stewart, February 12, 1937; Stewart to Siepmann, February 15, 1937, Ibid.

47 Siepmann to Stewart, March 21, 1939, BBC WAC, R34/869/3.

48 Siepmann to Stewart, March 28, 1939, Ibid.

49 *BBC Handbook 1929*, 89. *BBC Yearbook 1934*, 227–30.

50 *Radio Times*, August 25, 1933, 411.

51 *BBC Yearbook 1933*, 255–6.

52 *Radio Times*, January 29, 1932, 238. The Borders, Aberdeenshire, Ayrshire, and the Highlands were represented in the broadcast.

53 McLaren to Siepmann, February 12, 1934, BBC WAC, R51/535/1.

54 McLaren to Dinwiddie and Wellington, February 28, 1934, BBC WAC, R34/869/1.

55 McLaren to Siepmann, March 6, 1934, BBC WAC R51/535/1.

56 McLaren to Siepmann, February 12, 1934, Ibid.

57 *Listener*, April 1, 1936, "Talks Supplement," XIII; McLaren to Director of Talks, March 20, 1935, Ibid.

58 *Listener*, June 16, 1938, 1271–3; *Listener*, June 23, 1938, 1323–5; *Listener*, June

30, 1938, 1383–4.

59 *Radio Times*, November 23, 1928, 552.

60 Cleghorn Thompson to Assistant Director of Programmes, September 10, 1929, BBC WAC, R34/235/1.

61 Thompson to Assistant Director Programmes, October 17, 1930, Ibid.

62 Thompson to Director of Programmes, J. C. W. Reith, and Assistant Controller (Information), October 14, 1930, Ibid.

63 Reith to Director of Programmes, October 20, 1930, Ibid.

64 Wellington to Director of Programmes, December 2 , 1930, Ibid.

65 Wellington to Director of Programmes, October 15, 1931, Ibid.

66 Thompson to Director of Programmes, October 20, 1930, Ibid.

67 Wellington to Thompson, October, 19, 1931, Ibid.; *Radio Times*, November 24, 1933, 555; *Radio Times*, November 23, 1943, 631.

68 Thompson to Superintendent Engineer, October 22, 1931, BBC WAC, R34/235/1.

69 *Radio Times*, November 25, 1932, 625.

70 Ibid.

71 Stewart to Wellington, August 13, 1934, BBC WAC, R34/235/1.

72 McLaren to Stewart, December 8, 1937; Stewart to McLaren, December 9, 1937, BBC WAC, R34/235/2.

73 *Radio Times*, November 25, 1938, 10.

74 Ibid.

75 Hall, *Civilising*; Colley, "Britishness and Otherness."

76 I. G. C. Hutchinson, "Scottish Unionism Between the Two World Wars," in *Unionist Scotland 1800–1997*, Catriona M. M. McDonald, ed. (Edinburgh: John Donald Publishers, 1998).

77 David S. Forsyth, "Empire and Union: Imperial and National Identity in Nineteenth-Century Scotland," *Scottish Geographical Magazine*, 113 (1997): 5–12.

78 John M. MacKenzie, "Empire and National Identities: The Case of Scotland," *Transactions of the Royal Historical Society* sixth series, 8 (1998): 215–31; Richard J. Finlay, "The Rise and Fall of Popular Imperialism in Scotland, 1850–1950," *Scottish Geographical Magazine*, 113 (1997): 13–21; John M. MacKenzie, "Essay and Reflection: On Scotland and the Empire," *The International History Review*, 15 (November 1993): 661–80; Richard J. Finlay, "'For or Against?': Scottish Nationalists and the British Empire," *Scottish Historical Review*, 71 (April, October 1992): 184–206.

79 *Radio Times*, April 11, 1924, 89; *Radio Times*, September 26, 1924, 5.

80 *Radio Times*, May 21, 1926, 343.

81 Ibid.

82 *Radio Times*, June 4, 1926, 402.

83 *Radio Times*, July 23, 1926, 176; *Radio Times*, July 30, 1926, 214; *Radio Times*, September 3, 1926, 434.

84 *Radio Times*, May 8, 1925, 229.

85 *Radio Times*, August 14, 1925, 320; *Radio Times*, September 25, 1925, 4; *Radio*

Times, November 6, 1925, 315.

86 *Radio Times,* August 14, 1925, 320.

87 *Radio Times,* July 17, 1925, 155, 169.

88 The program was sure to establish Livingstone's roots in both Scotland and the working class. Its description in the *Radio Times* included references to Livingstone's "Highland grandfather" and the "humble Blantyre Interior" of his childhood home. *Radio Times,* January 15, 1926, 168.

89 McLaren to Gerald Beadle and Siepmann, June 28, 1933, BBC WAC, R34/869/1.

90 Memo, n.d. "Proposed Talks for the First Quarter 1934;" Siepmann to McLaren, December 5, 1933, BBC WAC, R51/535/1.

91 McLaren to Siepmann, March 26, 1934, Ibid.

92 *The Man Livingstone,* 1935, BBC WAC, Script Library.

93 Stewart to Empire Service Director, September 23, 1935, BBC WAC, R34/235/2.

94 *Radio Times,* November 22, 1935, 7.

95 *Programme for St. Andrew's Day Broadcast, 1935,* Script, BBC WAC, R34/235/2.

96 Ibid.

97 McDowell, 44.

98 Programme Board, May 8, 1936, BBC WAC, R34/600/7; Programme Board, October 20, 1938, BBC WAC, R34/600/10.

99 Programme Board, March 30, 1939, BBC WAC, R34/600/11.

100 Gordon Gildard to Basil Nicolls, April 6, 1939; Dinwiddie to Nicolls, May 3, 1939, BBC WAC, SC5/2.

101 On the political aspects of Scottish nationalism in this period, see Richard Finlay, *Independent and Free: Scottish Politics and the Origin of the Scottish National Party 1918–1945* (Edinburgh: John Donald Publishers, 1994); Richard J. Finlay, "Pressure Group or Political Party?: The Nationalist Impact on Scottish Politics," *Twentieth Century British History,* 3 (1992): 274–97; Marr, 1–91.

102 Calder, *Myth,* 72–3. Neither Labour nor the Liberals had contested the election. "To oppose a government nominee at all," notes Calder, "could be constructed as unpatriotic."

103 Wellington to Nicolls, April 4, 1940, TNA: PRO INF1/162.

104 Briggs, *War of Words,* 144.

105 Programme Board, April 11, 1940, BBC WAC, R34/600/12. It is not clear if Gildard was reacting to a specific talk by Haw-Haw on Scotland.

106 Control Board, December 27, 1939, BBC WAC, R3/3/14.

107 George Burnett to Controller (Public Relations), October 23, 1939, BBC WAC, SC5/2.

108 Alan Melville to Moultrie Kelsall, July 15, 1940, Ibid.

109 Kelsall to Dinwiddie, July 15, 1940, TNA: PRO INF1/162.

110 Home Board, July, 19, 1940, BBC WAC, R3/16/1.

111 Nicolls to Dinwiddie, July 23, 1940, BBC WAC, R34/869/4.

112 After 1940 the BBC received at least two letters from the St Andrew's Society complaining of the inappropriate use of "England." One letter claimed that "the BBC is determined to work against British unity." John A. Stewart to F. W. Ogilvie,

March 21, 1941; John A. Stewart to Robert Foot, September 13, 1943, BBC WAC, SC5/2.

113 Maurice Farquharson to Assistant Controllers, May 15, 1944, Ibid.

114 Laurence Gilliam to Kelsall, May 22, 1944, Ibid. Kelsall replied, "I could not agree more so long as everybody concerned remembers the last two words—'when appropriate.'" Kelsall to Gilliam, May 25, 1944, Ibid.

115 Farquharson to Dinwiddie, December 20, 1945, Ibid.

116 *BBC Yearbook 1945*, 79.

117 Ibid.

118 Listener Research Report LR2186, "Dialects and Accents," November 17, 1943, BBC WAC, R9/9/7.

119 Nicolls to Dinwiddie, January 22, 1940, BBC WAC, R34/869/4.

120 Farquharson to E. Davies, July 20, 1940, BBC WAC, R34/731/3.

121 Nicolls to Dinwiddie, July 23, 1940, BBC WAC, R34/869/4. The MOI had encouraged the BBC to make room for a weekly Scottish program back in April. Wellington to Nicolls, April 4, 1940, TNA: PRO INF1/162.

122 Dinwiddie, "Scotland's Contribution in Wartime," *BBC Handbook 1941*, 84.

123 Listener Research to Scottish Programme Director, December 8, 1943, BBC WAC, R34/253/3.

124 *BBC Yearbook 1943*, 34–6.

125 Director of Programme Planning to Barnes, n.d., BBC WAC, R51/535/3.

126 Assistant Director of Programme Planning to Director of Programme Planning, February 15, 1941, BBC WAC, R34/869/5.

127 Kelsall to Barnes, February 21, 1941, Ibid.

128 Foot to Brendan Bracken, May 18, 1943, BBC WAC, R34/731/3.

129 John Coatman to Foot, February 21, 1944, Ibid. Coatman, incidentally, was right. Although Scotland had a much smaller population that the North Region, the Scottish Home Service received the same program allowance as the Northern Home Service after the war.

130 Nicolls, "Report by Senior Controller on Regional Matters," March 20, 1947, BBC WAC, R34/731/4.

131 Commenting on Scottish entertainment in 1941, the director of the BBC's Variety Department blamed its "minority appeal" on "the unintelligibility of the Scottish dialect to millions of Sassenachs and ... the tendency towards greater sophistication in Scotland than elsewhere ... The very "localness" of Scottish contributions to Variety programmes is a good reason for including them, and also a good reason for including them sparingly." Director of Variety to Dinwiddie, February 21, 1941, BBC WAC, R34/869/5. The BBC did broadcast nationally known Scottish comedians such as Harry Lauder and Harry Gordon.

132 Dinwiddie, "Scotland's Wartime Contribution," 84.

133 McDowell, 58.

134 Stewart to Dinwiddie, April 23, 1943, BBC WAC, SC5/34/1.

135 McDowell, 98–9.

6

BBC broadcasting in Wales, 1922–53

In 1949, Alun Oldfield-Davies, Controller of the BBC's station in Wales, declared: "the basic job of the BBC in Wales is to nourish and encourage national unity and to add wealth, depth, and value to all aspects of national life."[1] At first, this seems to be a rather straightforward testament to the role of the BBC in Wales. For Oldfield-Davies, Wales was not a region but a nation, albeit one that lacked a cohesive culture or identity. The BBC, he suggested, could and ought to participate in the process of forming a national identity in Wales. Yet, Oldfield-Davies's comments also raise some questions. Why, in 1949, did Welsh national unity require nourishment? What kinds of divisions existed within the Welsh nation? What could broadcasting do to paper over those divisions? How did Welsh broadcasters try to nourish a sense of national identity? In answer to these questions this chapter will examine the development of BBC broadcasting in Wales from the opening of the first BBC station in Cardiff, in 1923, to the coming of television to the Principality in 1952.

From the moment the BBC opened its first radio station in Cardiff, there was an expectation that the BBC stations in the Principality would express the "Welshness" of the areas they served, despite the fact that Welsh broadcasting was but a small part of a larger network of British broadcasting. BBC policy, at times, hampered the effort of Welsh broadcasters to represent the nation of Wales. During the 1920s, BBC broadcasting was limited to two stations in Cardiff and Swansea. Listeners in northern Wales were served by the BBC station in Manchester. From 1932 to 1937, Wales did not exist as a broadcasting region at all. As part of the original regional scheme the BBC included Wales in what was called the "West" region. And BBC Wales, like the other regional networks, was closed down for the duration of the Second World War. Yet, by and large, Welsh broadcasters had the will and ultimately the freedom to project a sense of Welshness for their local and regional audience.

Broadcasters charged with making the BBC in Wales adequately "Welsh" had a difficult task. On the one hand, the Welsh region had to battle with the BBC's Head Office in London over programs, scheduling, hours of operation, and the use of the Welsh language. On the other hand, BBC radio in Wales was never Welsh enough to satisfy the Welsh nationalists, who demanded more Welsh-language programs and eventually an independent broadcasting system for Wales. Caught between London and the nationalists, Welsh producers nevertheless managed to steer a middle course that in the end, perhaps, satisfied no one. Like BBC Scotland, BBC Wales was politically unionist, but that did not make it any less "Welsh." The early local stations, the West regional station, BBC Wales, and the Welsh Home Service all broadcast a considerable number of programs on Welsh history, culture, speech, and customs.

Besides the structural disadvantage of its union with the West region and the push and pull of the nationalists and Head Office, Welsh broadcasters faced another challenge: the extraordinary diversity of the Wales they were trying to represent. Language divided the Welsh more than it did the Scots, where Gaelic was the tongue of only a small minority. In Wales in 1921, 37.1 per cent of the population spoke Welsh.[2] In addition, Wales was divided between the industrial cities and mining villages of the south and the more rural north. And even if the large majority of the Welsh, including many Welsh-speakers, lived in the south and east, it was the north and west that represented, in the minds of most nationalists, the "genuine" Wales, with its rugged landscape, more traditional culture, and wider use of the language. Most of Wales had been anglicized and modernized to some degree, but the least anglicized and modernized minority was considered to be the most "Welsh." How to recognize and reconcile these various forms of Welshness proved to be one of the key challenges for the BBC in Wales.

Like almost all European nationalism, Welshness was forged into a conscious, articulate identity in the eighteenth and nineteenth centuries.[3] The Honourable Society of the Cymmrodorion was founded in 1751 and was to play a pivotal role in the revival of the Eisteddfod, a festival devoted to Welsh poetry and song. Edward Williams (1747–1826), who took the colorful name Iolo Morganwg, worked to restore the old bardic order. He invented and fostered the cult of druidism, and claimed that the Welsh bards were the heirs of the ancient Druids. Welsh antiquarians rediscovered the connections between the Welsh and the ancient Celts. Wales came to be constructed as a "land of song" (an image constantly exploited by the BBC). Welsh music proliferated, and wealthy patrons organized harp societies. In the nineteenth century, choral societies came to dominate the Welsh cultural scene, and in 1856 Evan and

James James composed *Hen Wlad Fy Nhadau* (Land of My Fathers), which became the Welsh national anthem. The eighteenth and early nineteenth centuries also saw the romanticization of the "wild" Welsh countryside, the establishment of Owain Glyndŵr, the fifteenth-century Welsh rebel, as a hero of national resistance, and the invention of "traditional" Welsh dress.[4] This was also the period during which the Methodist chapel would come to dominate Welsh social and cultural life.

Over the course of a century, the imagination of energetic dreamers, poets, and songwriters, the Methodist ministers, and organizational ability of Welsh nationalists in London and Wales forged together a romantic and largely backward-looking Welsh identity. However, a significantly different sense of Welshness sprang forth from the forces of industrialization in south Wales. From the middle of the eighteenth century, industrialization utterly transformed south Wales, called upon to supply the world with anthracite coal. Hundreds of thousands of people poured into the industrial valleys from England and the Welsh countryside to work in the mines and related trades. Unlike the romantic representations of Wales described above, this Wales was urban, modern, working-class, and largely Anglophone. The culture of this Wales had less to do with poetry and more to do with rugby, American popular culture, and the mine.[5] This "American Wales," to use Dai Smith's phrase, did retain or adopt certain aspects of "Welsh Wales," such as the centrality of the chapel and the musical tradition, but in other ways it differed sharply. In addition, as Gwyn Williams has argued, this modern, industrial Welshness had a "peculiarly *imperial* character [emphasis text]."[6] The Welsh, like the Scots, had reconciled themselves with "Britain" while at the same time maintaining a distinct sense of themselves as Welsh.

In attempting to "nourish and encourage national unity," BBC Wales faced a considerable challenge during the era of radio. No nation is homogeneous; but Wales after the First World War was particularly fractured. Divided by language, custom, history, and way of life, it was difficult for the BBC to construct a cohesive national identity for Wales. Further, Welsh broadcasters had to consider the British dimension of Welsh identity. If only because of the amount of material it broadcast, BBC Wales could, to a certain extent, reflect all of these versions of "Wales," although certain types, like the collier, appear repeatedly in BBC programs. Some programs tried to reconcile the many Wales with each other and encourage national unity. But the extent to which the BBC Wales was able to unify the Principality beyond its ability to reach the ears of the Welsh at any given time is difficult to determine.

The BBC in Wales before the regional scheme

Like Scotland, broadcasting in Wales began on the local level, in Cardiff, home to the first BBC transmitter in Wales. The station there broadcast its first programs, an hour of children's stories, on Tuesday, February 13, 1923. The formal opening of the station took place later that evening, with Reith, Lord Gainford, and the Lord Mayor of Cardiff, J. J. E. Biggs, in attendance. At 9:30, the Cardiff station carried Mostyn Lewis singing *Dafydd y Garreg Wen*, the first words in Welsh to be broadcast by a BBC station.[7]

Unlike Scotland, where Glasgow and Aberdeen were the obvious cities in which to locate main stations, the BBC's decision to erect a transmitter in Cardiff aroused some controversy.[8] With a population of 220,000 in 1922, Cardiff was the largest city in Wales, but only the twenty-first largest city in the United Kingdom. It was more than 50 per cent smaller than nearby Bristol. The BBC chose Cardiff largely to ensure that Wales had its own station, but even this concession met with controversy. The Swansea press argued that its city, with its large population, rich cultural history, and citizenry "imbued with a greater sense of Welsh awareness," was a better choice for the BBC station in Wales.[9] The Company did open a relay station in Swansea in December 1924, but like the other relay stations, it became one of "London's babies," taking most of its programs from 2LO. In 1925, the Swansea station produced only ninety minutes per day of its own programs, plus one local night a week.[10]

Although Cardiff and Swansea were only local stations with a limited range, there was an expectation that they would express Welsh culture and values in their programs. The BBC gave the Cardiff station the call sign 5WA, "implying that it had been conceived as some kind of gesture to Wales." Upon the opening of the new station, Lord Gainford read a statement from Lloyd George, expressing his hope that Cardiff's programs "would be enjoyed throughout the Principality."[11] Ironically, one of the most serious problems for the BBC through much of its early history was its inability to provide coverage for all of Wales. Before the regional scheme, Cardiff and Swansea were the only Welsh cities equipped with their own transmitters. From the perspective of the BBC this made perfect sense; Cardiff and Swansea were the two largest cities in Wales, and the Cardiff transmitter could reach most of the industrial areas of the southeast. Reith himself wanted to insure that the BBC reached the mining areas, "to combat the doctrines of Communism and Bolshevism so sedulously preached there."[12] Still, the mountainous topography of Wales prevented early BBC broadcasts from being heard in the Rhondda Valley and points north—meaning all of central and northern Wales—by anyone other than the owners of expensive valve sets. The BBC tried to rectify this problem, in part, by placing Welsh material on the newly opened long-wave transmitter at Daventry. Approximately once a month the BBC would broadcast songs in Welsh or talks in English, but on Welsh topics. Furthermore, much of northern Wales could receive broadcasts form Manchester and Liverpool, and these stations occasionally broadcast programs of Welsh interest.[13]

Although Welsh material did not make up the entirety of its output, the Cardiff station was responsible for producing programs for Wales that made use of local talent. "The spirit of 'Welshness' was not lacking in the programmes of the early years," notes Rowland Lucas of the Cardiff station. In late 1923 it broadcast the first of its series of *Welsh Nights*, and in August of 1924 it launched a series on *The Growth of Wales*.[14] Later that year the Cardiff station director, E. R. Appleton, met with *Cylch Dewi*, a Cardiff cultural nationalist group, proposing that they prepare a series of programs for the BBC. The result, *A Welsh Hour*, consisted of a mixture of Welsh song and English-language poetry and drama. Unfortunately, *Cylch Dewi* quickly fell out of favor with the BBC, in part because of a confrontation between Appleton and Saunders Lewis. Lewis, a member of *Cylch Dewi* and future leader of the Welsh nationalist movement, insisted on doing a St David's Day broadcast in Welsh. Appleton argued that such a program would encourage the English-speaking audience to "simply switch off."[15] *A Welsh Hour* ended its run in May 1925.

Appleton's experience with *Cylch Dewi* may have soured him on Welsh nationalism, but the Cardiff station continued to produce programs of Welsh interest throughout its existence. In 1925, it broadcast a series entitled *Cymric Genius*, based on Welsh folk songs, "the true national music of Wales."[16] Like the Scottish stations, Cardiff found program material in the heroic past of Wales, producing, in 1925, a two-hour dramatization of the life of Owain Glyndŵr that was also relayed on the Daventry long-wave station.[17] The Cardiff station also employed drama to reflect the life and culture of Wales. "Cardiff Station," announced the *Radio Times*, "is always on the look-out for plays about Wales, written by those who alone are competent to write about their own country-men."[18] The BBC even offered a prize for radio plays at the Royal National Eisteddfod, but as late as 1933, the Corporation had not yet awarded it.[19] On July 31, 1924, the Cardiff station broadcast *Y Pwyllgor* by D. T. Davies, the first play ever broadcast in the Welsh language.[20] Wales was also linked to another "first" in radio broadcasting. A Welshman, Richard Hughes, wrote the first play specifically for radio, *Danger*, set in a Welsh coal mine. The BBC broadcast the play first from London in January 1924 and then from

Cardiff on March 15.[21] In addition to being the first play ever written for radio, *Danger* established, within the BBC, the close association of Wales and Welshness with the coal industry and the industrial valleys of the south. Indeed, as early as 1927 the *Radio Times* commented, "most of the English-Welsh plays broadcast from Cardiff Station have been given an urban setting. Even when the mind picture is of a village, the action often takes place in a miner's kitchen or a shop back-parlour."[22]

As with Scotland, the implementation of the regional scheme began with the coordination of the activities of the two Welsh local stations, and the eventual subjection of the relay station at Swansea to Cardiff. In June 1927, Swansea produced over ten hours per week of its own programming; two years later, Swansea's functions were largely limited to producing a fifteen-minute *Children's Hour* and two programs a week to be simultaneously broadcast from Cardiff. Appleton, the station director at Cardiff, acquired the more august title of West Regional Director in February 1929, while C. K. Parsons, the Swansea station director, was relegated to the position of "Swansea representative."[23] Finally, in 1933, the BBC's medium-wave transmitter at Washford, south of the Bristol Channel in Somerset, became operational, providing uniform and widely available programs for Welsh listeners.

The BBC's West regional programme: the country, coal and Welshness

With the establishment of the Scottish regional transmitter at Westerglen, listeners to the Scottish station became part of a bounded, imagined community, defined, in part, by radio itself. The Scottish regional station helped to define Scotland and Scottishness, as distinct from England or Britain. Such could not be said for Wales with the opening of the Washford transmitter, for, as Appleton's new title suggested, the BBC did not initially provide a system of regional broadcasting specifically for Wales. Rather, the region was defined as the "West," and included the southwest of England as well as Wales. A shortage of available wavelengths and a desire to maximize the number of potential listeners compelled the BBC to create the unwieldy West region.

The linking of Wales and the west of England seems to support arguments that claim that the BBC implemented the regional scheme for no other reason than administrative convenience.[24] It was an arrangement that satisfied few on either side of the Bristol Channel. But perhaps nothing is more suggestive of the belief in Britain that broadcasting ought to be organized along ethnic and cultural lines than the debate and protest sparked by the BBC's decision to link Wales and the west of England. The BBC made some feeble attempts to argue that the clumsy region possessed some kind of organic unity. "The West Regional Station" proclaimed the *BBC Yearbook*, "reunites the Kingdom of Arthur after centuries of separation by the Bristol Channel."[25] In practice, however, the BBC conceived of its schedule as consisting of Welsh-interest programs (including, *de facto*, all Welsh-language programs) or English-interest programs. In June 1933, Appleton, in an article in the *Radio Times*, admitted, "the problem of giving to Wales and to the West Country their share on one wavelength is not an easy one."[26] The dissimilarity between Wales and England is nicely encapsulated in the series *Channel Currents*, which offered a regular review of events taking place in the West region. However, the program did not summarize the happenings in the West region as a whole. Instead, one edition was devoted entirely to Wales and the next to the west of England.[27] The West Regional Station did broadcast some programs that attempted to reconcile its Wales/west of England split personality. *Let's Do a Play*, broadcast in 1932, was a series of programs in which two amateur producers, "one from Wales and one from the West Country," discussed their problems with a professional assigned to help them.[28] But, on balance, the BBC did not attempt to build a sense of identity inclusive of Wales and the west of England, but rather tried to split airtime as evenly as possible between two distinct communities. It would have been foolish to try otherwise.

Although it had to provide an equal amount of programming for the west of England, the BBC's West region committed itself to producing "work in Wales which shall be an expression of the national consciousness."[29] In the first autumn following the opening of the Washford transmitter, the West region produced an ambitious series of talks, *Wales from Within*. The first three installments of the series concerned the economic problems afflicting Wales.[30] The second trio, named *The Wales of Tomorrow*, dealt with Welsh nationalism. In accordance with the BBC's strict policy of "balance" when handling controversial issues, BBC West dealt with the issue in a series of discussions between Welsh nationalists and opposition speakers. The proposal raised eyebrows at Head Office. "The discussions will need very careful vetting," wrote Charles Siepmann to J. T. Sutthery, then the West Region Programme Director, "and I shall be glad if it were possible for the manuscript to be sent to me in advance."[31] In addition to the suspicions of Head Office, the BBC West region had some difficulty getting suitable speakers. In September, Appleton complained that he was finding it hard "to get a really good statement of the anti-nationalism point of view from a man whose opinion carries sufficient weight."[32] Sutthery had proposed Caradoc Evans to take the "opposition" stance in a discussion of cultural nationalism, but discovered that Evans was "so personally disliked in Wales that his inclusion would tend to weight the scales seriously on the other side throughout the series."[33] Despite these difficulties, the BBC West region broadcast the first of these pioneering discussions on January 26, 1934, which opened with introductory remarks by Saunders Lewis, president of *Plaid Cymru* and a harsh critic of the BBC.[34]

Wales Today and Tomorrow marked the only series produced by the West region specifically on Welsh nationalism, but the region, from its consolidation in the late 1920s, regularly broadcast programs on the history, culture, and conditions of Wales. And, while the BBC West region covered a range of Welsh topics, two received an extraordinary amount of attention—rural, pre-industrial Wales, and coal.

In the winter of 1930, two series of West region talks focused on the former. Major Clough-Williams discussed threats to the Welsh countryside in *Wales and the Octopus*, while Iorwerth Peate gave a series of talks under the title *Life in Bygone Wales*. In the *Radio Times* a rather explicit link was made between Welshness and the countryside in publicizing one of Peate's talks, "Welsh Town Life." "The Welshman has always preferred the country," chimed the *Radio Times*, "the development of the modern Industrial centres produced a type of social unit previously unknown in Wales and bearing no relation to its culture."[35] A year later, Peate gave another series of talks, *Reminiscences of a Young Countryman*. Again, the *Radio Times*, in promoting the program, made explicit the links between language, countryside, and nation. After pointing out that Peate was raised in a rural village "where Welsh was the native language," it concluded, "Mr. Peate believes that the present generation in South Wales does not realize the rich and varied culture to be found in the Welsh countryside, and that an exposition of the wealth of country life may help people to guard their inheritance."[36] In February 1932, Sam Jones, soon to become the BBC's *de facto* director of Welsh-language programs and later head of the BBC's Bangor studio, gave a broadcast on thatched cottages, "many of them, curiously enough, in highly industrialised Glamorgan."[37] Later that year, he broadcast on a *Cyfarfodydd Pregethu*, or "preaching meeting," held in a "quiet backwater in Wales in which the *tempo* of an earlier generation is still preserved."[38]

Despite the regularity of these types of program, the BBC West region did not posit "rural Wales" as the dominant image for Wales in the same way that rural England often represented the authentic, genuine England. Just as often the BBC used the coal valleys to represent "Wales." Coal was the most important industry in Wales, but one that was under severe strain in the 1930s. Further, most of the BBC's listeners in Wales would have been more familiar with the industrial, urban life represented by the coal industry than the rural worlds described by Iorwerth Peate and Sam Jones. Rather than making either rural Wales or urban Wales the predominant representation of the nation, the BBC used the former to embody "Welsh Wales," while the latter came to symbolize the character and virtues of "Anglo-Wales."

In 1929, as the BBC began to consolidate the West region, the *BBC Handbook* could exclaim "the key to the situation in South Wales from a human standpoint is the mining village," adding that the Cardiff and Swansea stations "cannot forget the special needs of the depressed valleys."[39] Indeed, programs about, or set in, the coal mining areas provided regular fare for BBC West listeners. In talks, coal prominently featured in programs on economic development and, in 1934, the West region devoted an entire series of talks to the coal industry.[40] Drama productions included broadcasts of *Danger* and *Hard Graft*. The latter told the story of the winner of a local essay contest on mine safety caught in an explosion on the night he was to receive his award. The play, claimed the *Radio Times*, was "certain … to arouse great interest in the mining districts, because the scenes are absolutely typical of life in [these] districts."[41] Another play that also tried to capture the dangerous life of the Welsh collier was Evan Williams's *Flood*, broadcast by the BBC West region in 1936 and on the Home Service in October 1939. After listening to *Flood*, Charles Siepmann wrote to Appleton: "it made me feel that I was glad I had nothing to do with the mining industry, and I thought at times how much more it might frighten colliers' wives and so on whose relations were actually in the mines or going down into them." Siepmann asked if the Cardiff station had received any complaints regarding the broadcast. Owen Parry replied that the program had inspired one letter of protest but eleven of appreciation, and furthermore, "several members of the staff, who have been going about during the past week, tell that it raised a great deal of sympathetic interest among mining folk."[42]

The life of the miner continued to be an important theme in BBC broadcasts after 1937, when BBC Wales was separated from the West region and able to transmit programs exclusively for Welsh listeners. In some of these, BBC producers used life in the coal valleys as a backdrop to more general-discussion programs. In February 1938, BBC Wales introduced *Cross Section*, a current events program introduced to listeners in a way peculiar to collier life:

Few mining towns in South Wales are without their popular café. Many of the refreshment houses are the centre of a social life peculiarly their own, and tonight listeners will be taken to Aberdare to hear the habitués of a typical rendezvous discussing the world and its ways over their cups of coffee[43]

Later that year BBC Wales produced a similar program, *Mwcyn Gweld* taken from

the dialect term … [for] that short period of rest that the colliers used to enjoy after going down into the mine in the days before the Davy lamp. It took a little while for their eyes to become accustomed to the darkness and during this time they used to … chat … In a programme entitled *Mwcyn Gweld* … listeners will be taken on an imaginary descent into the pit to hear miners discussing one topic and another before they begin their day's work in earnest.[44]

Like *Cross Section*, *Mwcyn Gweld* was neither reportage nor dramatization of the miner's life. Rather, a way of life familiar to a large portion of the listeners of BBC Wales was used to introduce a series of generic talks.

BBC Wales did continue to produce several programs designed to reflect the life and values of the Welsh collier and by extension the life and values of the nation. To its credit, the BBC did not attempt to ignore the problem of massive unemployment in the coal industry. *The Changing Face of South Wales*, a series of talks broadcast in the winter of 1938 was subtitled "What are the causes of decline?" The *Radio Times* billed *Cold Coal*, written by E. Eynon Evans, as simply "a play of unemployment."[45] Perhaps the outstanding broadcast by the Welsh region in its two years of activity before the outbreak of the war was *Best Welsh*, produced by Jack Jones and T. Rowland Hughes. A radio picture of the Rhondda Valley, *Best Welsh* was meant to convey the "spirit and enduring courage of the people."[46]

In addition to these programs, the West region was responsible each year for the production of programs in honor of St David, the patron saint of Wales. These had been done since the beginning of broadcasting in Wales. Indeed, only two weeks after the opening of the Cardiff station in 1923, the Reverend Gwilym Davies became the first speaker to broadcast in the Welsh language during a St David's Day broadcast; later in the day Huw J. Huws, a Cardiff schools inspector, gave a ten-minute talk in Welsh.[47] The St David's Day programs quickly become more elaborate but consisted mostly of song. In 1924, the Cardiff station's St David's Day program was titled *Noson Lawen Mewn Hen Ffermdy* (A Happy Evening in a Welsh Farmhouse) and included Huw J. Huws as host, Lord Pontypridd as the "guest of honor," and a troupe of singers and performers. The program closed with the Welsh national anthem, *Hen Wlad Fy Nhadau.*[48] The following year the program, produced in London and carried by all BBC stations, consisted of two hours of the London Welsh Male Choir singing songs in English and Welsh.[49] In 1927 the Cardiff station broadcast, for the first time, from the St David's Day banquet of the Cardiff Cymmrodorion Society, which included a speech by Prime Minister Stanley Baldwin.[50]

As with BBC Scotland's treatment of St Andrew's Day, the early 1930s saw a shift in the way that broadcasters in Wales conceived of the St David's Day program. "I hope it may be possible," wrote Lindsay Wellington to Appleton in 1929, "to find something more specifically Welsh than a concert by Welsh artists."[51] Appleton eagerly agreed and informed Head Office that his staff had been working "on the lines of a Welsh Feature programme based either on a great national figure or a national event."[52] Although the feature did not pan out, the BBC West region broadcast, in addition to the relay from the Cymmrodorion Society, a talk, "St. David's Ideals and the Welsh People," and a program of Welsh music. Significantly, the latter, "to mark the national importance of the occasion," included music from "all parts of the Principality."[53] A memo on the program from Appleton to Reith on audience reaction reflects the desire, yet difficulty, of providing a comprehensive and fair representation of Wales in BBC programs. "Both North and South Wales," Appleton was quick to point out, "were … represented."[54] In 1932, the BBC West region prepared a St David's Day program not unlike what they had intended for 1930, *For the Honour of Wales* (Er Anrhydedd Cymru). A masque jointly produced by A. G. Prys-Jones and the BBC West region's Drama Director, *For the Honor of Wales* celebrated "the achievement of the Welsh people in history and in the realms of art, literature, and politics."[55] It represented the first attempt by the BBC West region to do more for St David's Day than a program of sentimental Welsh music and speeches, and it set the pattern that Welsh broadcasters would follow for the rest of the 1930s. Instead of devising a musical program for St David's Day, Welsh broadcasters used the holiday to explore and examine Wales and Welsh identity. The 1933 St David's Day program promised listeners "a journey through space and time" based on Filson Young's trip through Wales.[56] In 1934 the BBC West region produced another historical survey of Wales for March 1, *The Land of St. David*, while in 1935 Sam Jones and T. Rowland Hughes devised a "review of the chief happenings in the national life of Wales."[57]

The coming of BBC Wales

Despite its best attempts to serve its Welsh audience, it was impossible for the BBC's West regional station to fully satisfy the cultural and political leaders of Wales, especially those who regarded broadcasting as a necessary prop for the survival of the Welsh language. The West regional station broadcast approximately twenty hours per week. If those hours were to be divided between items of Welsh interest and west of England interest, that left only about ten hours a week for specifically Welsh broadcasting. A further division between English-language Welsh programs and Welsh-language Welsh programs meant a paltry four to five hours of broadcasting in Welsh every week. In 1935, Appleton claimed that the BBC West region produced six hours a week of "intrinsically Welsh material," although he defined such material to Head Office vaguely as "talks in Welsh, Welsh Feature programmes, concerts at which the majority of songs are sung in Welsh by Welsh artists, etc."[58] This dearth of Welsh programming, especially in light of the service provided for Scotland, created a strong reaction in Wales against the BBC.

Upon the opening of the Washford transmitter, the University of Wales Council agreed that there had been considerable improvement in the programs for Wales, and while it expressed its "sincere gratitude to Sir John [Reith]," it concluded that "we have to tell him that, like Oliver Twist, we are bound to ask for more."[59] Rather than assuage Welsh opinion, the opening of the Washford transmitter led to another round of deputations to the BBC and a press campaign against the Corporation's West region.[60] Welsh organizations contrasted the scope of broadcasting in Wales to that of Scotland. According to the *Daily Express*, the President of the Cardiff Cymmrodorion Society claimed, "Wales deserves recognition at the hands of the BBC and Wales should have its own broadcasting station just as Scotland has."[61] The University Council successfully convinced Reith to establish an advisory committee for Wales, the only BBC region to have such a committee at that time. Not surprisingly, it was the Welsh nationalists who expressed their dissatisfaction most loudly and in the most severe terms. In an article in the *Manchester Guardian*, Saunders Lewis complained that "the BBC administers Wales as a conquered province … this English Government Corporation flouts the Welsh nation and absolutely refuses to meet the most reasonable and moderate requirements."[62]

By this time, it was not only the Welsh who were expressing their frustration with the West region of the BBC. Listeners in the west of England, who were also served by the Washford transmitter, quickly grew weary of the Welsh content in the West region's programming. In May 1934, two western counties, Devon and Cornwall, sent their own deputation to the BBC to complain about the dearth of programs for English listeners. In July, the irascible radio critic Collie Knox used his column in the *Daily Mail* to disparage the Welsh content of the BBC's West region:

> As things are, it is ridiculous for this station to be called the West Region at all. It should be called the 'Welsh' Regional and left at that. Last week … there were no fewer than nineteen items, all of Welsh appeal. Does the BBC forget that this station serves listeners in Wiltshire, Dorset, Devon, Somerset, Gloucester, and Cornwall? … Naturally, as Wales is also catered for by that station, Wales should be served, but not to such an extent as to bring the entire West Country up in arms.[63]

The BBC met English demands in part by opening new studios in Bristol in September 1934. Shortly thereafter the BBC began to plan for the separation of the West region into a service for Wales and a service for the west of England. In April 1935, Reith met another deputation from the University of Wales Council and the Welsh Parliamentary Party. After the meeting, Reith issued a press release stating that the BBC had agreed to the creation of a separate Welsh region, pending the construction of a transmitter near Plymouth to meet the needs of listeners in the west of England. Further, the BBC decided to immediately separate Wales from the West region for administrative and program purposes. The fiction of the "West" region was coming undone. It was, for Rowland Lucas, an "acknowledgement of Wales's claim to be regarded as a nation separate from England."[64]

The two years from the summer of 1935 to the summer of 1937 were eventful ones for the BBC in Wales. In November 1935, the BBC opened a studio in Bangor, which allowed it to include more material from north Wales. The administrative division also meant that the BBC had to find a staff for the emerging Welsh region.[65] In 1935 the BBC appointed nine new staff members for Wales, and another in 1937. The new Welsh staff included T. Rowland Hughes, Alun Llywelyn, Geraint Dyfnallt, Arwel Hughes, and Mansel Thomas, "the cream of the Welsh-speaking intelligentsia of the 1930s."[66] Reith actively recruited Rhys Hopkin Morris, a former MP and critic of the BBC, for the position of Regional Director.[67] He was delighted when Hopkin Morris accepted the post.[68] Finally, the construction of a transmitter for the west of England was completed in 1937, clearing the way for the final divorce of Wales from the west of England. On July 3, 1937, the BBC West region broadcast *Coast to Coast*, a sound picture of daily life in the region. The opening announcement nicely captured the relations between Wales and the west of

England since the coming of the regional scheme in 1933:

> To-night is the last occasion on which the Welsh and West of England pro-
> gramme will operate on the same wavelength of 373.1 metres to put out their
> different programmes. To-night for the first and last time they unite to put out
> a joint programme.[69]

The program opened and closed, fittingly enough, with Welsh coal miners.

July 4, 1937 opened up a new era in Welsh broadcasting. With its own
wavelength, BBC Wales provided between twenty-two and twenty-seven hours
of Welsh programming per week. There were high hopes for the new station.
In addition to informing and entertaining its audience, BBC Wales was
expected to foster the Welsh language and traditional Welsh music, provide
careers for Welsh artists and performers, and give Welshmen overseas a sense
of connectedness to their homeland. Although they could not hope to satisfy
all Welsh interest groups, the staff of BBC Wales made an effort to fashion that
station into something akin to a national broadcasting network for Wales. The
Welshness of the new region was undeniable as it broadcast roughly half of
its programs in the Welsh language, including news. With studios in Cardiff,
Swansea, Aberystwyth, and Bangor, BBC Wales could draw on talent and represent all of the regions of Wales. Significantly, BBC Wales shared some of the
nationalizing pretensions of the BBC itself, but on a smaller scale. Alun Llywe-
lyn-Williams, who directed the Welsh announcers, hoped to use radio to create
a national, uniform version of the Welsh language for broadcasting. The BBC
in Wales patronized Welsh musicians and continued to broadcast the national
Eisteddfod. And BBC Wales sought to negotiate the traditional divisions
between south and north, industrial and rural, Anglo-Wales and Welsh-Wales.
For example, the new region broadcast quizzes and debates pitting coal miners
against northern slate quarrymen or farmers from different Welsh counties. In
1938, BBC Wales inaugurated two national lectures for the region, one to be
delivered in English, and the other in Welsh.[70] As one Welsh broadcaster noted
pithily, the new Welsh region should mean, "the unifying of North and South
which for centuries, to express the sentiment politely, have been indifferent to
each other."[71]

In terms of its organization, the outlook of its staff, and its activities, BBC
Wales represented something akin to a national broadcasting system in mini-
ature, and its programs reflected these ambitions. As with Scotland, BBC
Wales created talks, plays, and features that drew on the Welsh past, Welsh life,
and Welsh culture. In March 1937, BBC Wales broadcast a feature in Welsh,
Llewelyn Ap Gruffydd, the story of "the last Welsh Prince of Wales, and … the

final struggle for Welsh independence against the mighty forces of Edward I."[72] In April, the Owain Glyndŵr revolt was the subject of another BBC feature.[73] Glyndŵr, "the foremost national hero of Wales," became the subject of another BBC feature in 1938, *The Ballad of 1400*.[74] Inspired by Geoffrey Bridson's *The March of the '45*, which recounted the events of the Jacobite rebellion, *The Ballad of 1400* dramatized the Glyndŵr revolt in verse.[75]

The outstanding Welsh-language play produced by the region before the war was *Crugybar*, which told the story of the conversion of a Carmarthenshire district to Methodism and "the great influence of the eighteenth-century revival on the Welsh people."[76] The first talks schedule for the new region included a series of talks on Wales provisionally titled *As Others See Us*, another series, *Wales at Westminster*, which consisted of fortnightly talks by Welsh MPs, and *Around and About*. This last series was meant to be more than just a magazine of happenings in Wales; its aim was to "interpret events and tendencies in Welsh Wales to the English listener in the region."[77] The challenge for Welsh broadcasters was not merely to represent "Wales," but unify the distinct cultures of the region.[78]

Fighting for space on the wartime Home Service

After only two and a quarter years of broadcasting independence BBC Wales again found itself, in September 1939, linked to its English neighbor. But instead of having to split airtime with the BBC's West region, BBC Wales, like all the regional networks, was fully integrated into the BBC's unified Home Service.

In a move that demonstrates both the importance of the language to Welsh identity and Welsh broadcasters' sense of the importance of regional broadcasting to regional identity, Hopkin Morris made getting Welsh-language broadcasts onto the unified Home Service his top priority.[79] On September 18, Hopkin Morris wrote angrily to Head Office concerning the BBC's failure to make any provision for Welsh-language broadcasting during the war. Neither F. W. Ogilvie nor the deputy Director-General, Cecil Graves, reacted well to Hopkin Morris's request. They were prepared to concede a daily news bulletin and informational announcements, but nothing more. On October 4, Hopkin Morris sent Basil Nicolls a request and outline of what he saw as a suitable amount of Welsh-language broadcasting. He included one religious service each month, a studio service once a week, twenty minutes each week for school broadcasts, and a fifteen minute *Children's Hour* once a week, or at least once a fortnight. Nicolls proved to be sympathetic to these demands. In a memo dated October 12, he authorized two hours and fifteen minutes a week of Welsh-language broadcasting on the BBC's 261-meter wavelength, used primarily for broadcasts to Europe. The MOI approved of this measure, noting that Welsh-language broadcasts would undermine "subversive" tendencies in Wales.[80]

Hopkin Morris was satisfied with this arrangement, although Welsh broadcasts became a matter of controversy again in early 1940.[81] The establishment of the lighter Forces Programme and the subsequent rearrangement of trunk lines and transmitters re-opened the question of Welsh-language broadcasts. The Director of Programme Planning argued that Welsh ought to be dropped "for other more important services."[82] Hopkin Morris and Nicolls fought against this move, as did the government. Although, in contrast to Scotland, the Germans directed little radio propaganda directly to Wales, the fear of a Welsh Haw-Haw fostering discontent in Wales may have saved Welsh-language broadcasting for the duration of the war.[83] By February 1940 the BBC was broadcasting two hours and thirty minutes in the Welsh language every week, almost half of its pre-war level. When the BBC moved Welsh material to the Home Service it inevitably irritated English and Scottish listeners. In contrast, Welsh nationalists, not surprisingly, found the BBC niggardly in its use of Welsh and railed against the unified broadcasting system until the end of the war. But, given the demands made on the BBC during the war and the small number of monoglot Welsh-speakers in the United Kingdom, the amount of Welsh broadcast seems fair. Hopkin Morris himself thought Wales was getting "a very square deal" from Head Office.[84]

Although Hopkin Morris enjoyed some success in getting a modicum of Welsh on the air, he was waging a two-front war with Head Office. For, in addition to securing Welsh-language programs for Welsh listeners, Hopkin Morris and his staff also had to wrangle with London to get their English-language productions on the air as well. Throughout the war, Welsh staff, like all regional staff, wrote to Head Office to get more time for regional productions on the Home Service and better placement for their programs. As early as December 1939, the Acting Programme Director for Wales, A. Watkin Jones, wrote to Maconachie about increasing Wales's contribution to the Talks schedule.[85]

Watkin Jones attempted to increase the amount of Welsh broadcasting on the Home Service through a variety of methods. One was to simply ask for spaces in the Home Service beyond the agreed allotment by arguing that a particular program was unsuitable as merely a "Welsh regional" program, but rather important enough to merit an additional time slot in the Home Service.[86] In June 1940 Watkin Jones contended that two talks, "Workaday Thoughts in Wartime" and "Out of the Usual," should not be broadcast in the usual period given to Wales, "because we don't wish to use up our precious fortnightly period for a symposium or a discussion."[87] This immediately set off alarm bells in London. Had Watkin Jones's argument been accepted in principle, it would have given the Regional Directors a greater hand in scheduling, and more regional programs may have found their way onto the Home Service. Harman Grisewood, the Director of Programme Planning, warned George Barnes against acceding to Watkin Jones's request, calling it "a racket," and "a shocking encouragement to [the] other regions."[88]

Of course, if it was difficult for Wales to get material on the air beyond their regular periods, Watkin Jones could always ask for more regular spaces. In January 1941 he wrote to Grisewood asking for an additional thirty minutes a month for a "Welsh Half Hour" that would include regional news, commentary, and a few songs. London replied that Watkin Jones's suggestion would have to be considered by Home Board, which included the Director-General and was ultimately responsible for all of the output on the domestic service. A follow-up memo from Watkin Jones on the "Welsh Half Hour" exemplifies the problems that regional broadcasting in wartime created as well as the limits of Head Office's toleration for Welsh demands:

> We have to acknowledge your memo of January 28 in which you say that we may expect to hear further "towards the end of the week." As three weeks have now passed we begin to wonder whether you have found it impossible to consider our suggestions for this programme any further for the time being ... I must confess that it still surprises me that you should begin discussing so weightily a programme suggestion which strikes me at any rate as more or less routine.[89]

It seems clear from this memo that Head Office did not make the "Welsh Half Hour" a high priority; Watkin Jones's request was either forgotten or deliberately ignored. Yet, the fact the request was considered before Home Board demonstrates that London took regional broadcasting seriously for several reasons. On the one hand the BBC and the MOI worried that a lack of regional broadcasting, especially in the non-English regions, might undermine morale. For this reason alone Head Office often acceded to requests from the regions. On the other hand, had Head Office simply agreed to this appeal from Wales, the other regions would have flooded London with similar requests that would have to be honored. The Home Service schedule would have become even tighter, making it more difficult for programmers in London to accommodate all of the demands on the BBC.

The idea of a "Welsh Half Hour" gained little traction at Head Office in early 1941, but two years later the Talks Department began to reconsider the amount of contributions it would take from the regions. This created the opportunity for Wales to plead for special treatment in the new scheme, based on its distinct nationality. Aneirin Talfan Davies, then a Talks producer, made the case for Wales in late 1942:

> I wish to press the claim of Wales to special treatment in your new plans for the integration of the talks output of the various regions … Wales is a distinct National region, with very many problems peculiar to itself alone, and which can only be properly handled by the region concerned.[90]

Although the BBC had, since 1936, been more sympathetic to requests by the regions, what probably brought London around to the Welsh position was the fact that *Scottish Half Hour*, a summary of Scottish news and talks broadcast once a month, had already made its first appearance in the Home Service, a point Talfan Davies was careful to include in his proposal to the Director of Talks:

> In the granting of the Scottish Half Hour, the principle of separate treatment for a region which is itself a national unit has already been admitted, and we ask now that this privilege should be extended to Wales.[91]

Talfan Davies was making a perfectly reasonable request; indeed, he was only asking for something that the BBC had already agreed to in principle with regards to Scotland. Head Office now faced the situation they had hoped to avoid in 1940 when they rejected Watkin Jones's original proposal. This time London relented, and *Welsh Half Hour* debuted on the Home Service in early 1943.

By the middle of the war several factors had combined to maximize the number of Welsh programs, in both languages, on the Home Service. Welsh doggedness was perhaps the most important factor, as was the fact that important members of the London staff, notably Basil Nicolls, sympathized with the Welsh broadcasters. And, of course, Welsh members of Parliament, popular discontent in Wales, and sufficient noise from Welsh nationalists all played some role in the amount of programming from Wales that ultimately appeared on the Home Service.[92] Yet the question remains, what did Welsh broadcasting during the Second World War sound like? To what extent was Welshness expressed on the air?

From the beginning of the war, Welsh staff maintained that the output of

BBC Wales should remain fundamentally "Welsh;" catering to a large English audiences was less important for them than producing programs that accurately portrayed Welsh life. In a memo shortly after the outbreak of hostilities, the Welsh Programme Director wrote to Laurence Gilliam, criticizing his scheme for the BBC's *Home Front* program. The program, he complained, undervalued "the strength of Regional character at a time like this, when the Regions are everything."[93] And, in early 1940, Watkin Jones sent Barnes a thoughtful memo in which he argued that, because of the single service, it was more important than ever that regional broadcasting be truly regional. Before the war, Watkin Jones maintained, Welsh material that was too "regional" for the national audience could always be broadcast on the Welsh wavelength. However, since that option no longer existed, and since regional broadcasting needed to be more authentic than ever, Watkin Jones argued that London had to employ a different standard in terms of what they would broadcast in the Home Service. Welsh listeners needed Welsh programs (in Welsh and English) whether English listeners enjoyed them or not:

> What is of "National" interest, therefore, should no longer be assessed from the point of view of a National wavelength only, but from the point of view of a national unity, and the marshalling of national opinion in such a way as to secure as complete a co-ordination as possible and the maximum of goodwill between the different parts of the country … For instance, a talk by a man like Lord Derby about a subject which was of primary concern to Lancashire would, in the present circumstances, be of National interest, although its subject matter was local. Similarly, the reactions of Wales to the war effort, although of primary concern to Wales, are at the moment a matter of national concern.[94]

In this memo, Watkin Jones effectively turned on its head the notion of national unity. For, although Watkin Jones talked of "co-ordination" and "national unity," he was not suggesting that the BBC limit its broadcasts to the expression of a single, British, identity or national culture. Rather, he insisted that national unity could be achieved only if each region was fairly represented on the Home Service. Britain consisted of regions, each of which was contributing to the war effort. For Watkin Jones, the BBC had to reflect that truism.

The war and Welshness

BBC programs from and about Wales were typical of those produced by the regions during the war. For one, Welsh broadcasters focused on their region's contribution to the war effort and produced programs that connected the Welsh experience, or Welshness, to larger propaganda themes. For example, in

1941, Wales produced a program on an Indian contingent based in the Principality which meshed well with Head Office's commitment to highlighting the empire's contribution to the war effort.[95] In July of that year came "A Champion of Freedom," a talk on the nineteenth-century Welsh figure Bishop Thirwall of St David's, "a lifelong champion of Freedom in his generation."[96] The programs for St David's Day trumpeted Wales's contribution to the war. Welsh broadcasters, like their counterparts in London and the other regions, tried to use the countryside and its traditions to inspire and remind listeners "what they were fighting for" in programs such as *Land of Powys* by Geraint Goodwin or *This Shining Land*, a feature on Gwent.[97] BBC Wales was even able to broadcast programs on the importance of keeping Welsh culture vibrant during the war.[98] Perhaps most importantly, the BBC maintained, as no other institution could have during the war, the centerpiece of Welsh cultural nationalism, the national Eisteddfod.[99]

While the BBC in Wales drew on the range of Welsh life, especially as it contributed or had changed due to the war, the dominant image of Wales on the Home Front remained the coal miner and the industrial coal village. While, in one sense merely a continuation of the BBC's tendency to focus on life in the valleys, the image of the mining village carried special significance during the war. First, coal was vital to the war effort, and demand for fuel had revitalized the economy of the valleys. Second, the mining village powerfully represented the nation at war. The danger present in the life of a collier reflected the danger faced by the British people as a whole. More important, the values of the miners and the mining villages interlocked effectively with the ideals of a nation fighting a total war for its survival: community, camaraderie, resilience, and cheerfulness in the face of great tribulation.

Among the first Welsh plays heard on the wartime Home Service were a rebroadcast of Evan William's coal mine drama *Flood*, and a radio version of Jack Jones's *Rhondda Roundabout*. Another Jones novel, *Bidden to the Feast*, was broadcast in April 1941.[100] Jones, an author and native of industrial Wales, and T. Rowland Hughes, a talented BBC producer, together produced several programs based on life in the industrial valleys during the war.[101] In late 1939 and early 1940, the two collaborated on three Welsh programs for the BBC's *Home Front* series, each depicting some aspect of Welsh working-class life.[102] Later that same year, the two worked together to produce a radio version of the film *The Proud Valley*, which, more than any other BBC Wales production during the war, presented the collier's life as a representation of both Wales and the danger that all British civilians faced during the war.

The Proud Valley, first broadcast on the BBC on February 25, 1940, was an adaptation of the Ealing Studios film of the same name. Jones, who had a writing credit on the film, adapted the script for radio; Rowland Hughes produced. The radio version included several of the original actors from the film, although the cast did not include Paul Robeson, who starred in the motion picture.[103]

The Proud Valley tells the story of David Goliath, a black stoker seeking work in the Welsh coal fields. As Goliath tramps through the valleys singing, he is overheard by Dick Parry, the director of a local men's choir. Eager to add Goliath's deep booming voice to his choir Parry takes him in and finds him work in the Blaendy coal pit. However, on the day the choir is to compete in the Eisteddfod, an explosion causes the pit to collapse, killing Dick Parry, despite an heroic effort by Goliath to save him. Further, the collapse forces the closure of the mine.

After a period of unemployment, Emlyn Parry, Dick's son, vows to get the owners to reopen the Blaendy pit. He leads a march of colliers, including Goliath, to the owner's offices in London. As Emlyn's group approaches London, Britain declares war on Germany, increasing the nation's demand for coal. What was of local interest to the mining community of Blaendy has now become a matter of national interest. Despite the risks, the owner agrees to give Emlyn a chance to reopen the mine.

Upon returning to Blaendy, the colliers begin to prepare the mine for production, but another explosion traps Emlyn, Goliath, and two others in a small recess. Desperate and running out of air, the group decides to blast their way out of the alcove. However, the man who lights the blast will surely die because the group has only a short cord to use as a fuse. The men draw lots and it falls to Emlyn to light the fuse. Goliath offers to take his place on account of Emlyn's family. When Emlyn refuses, Goliath knocks Emlyn unconscious, drags him to a safe spot, and ignites the blast. Goliath sacrifices himself to save his comrades, the Blaendy pit, and by extension, Britain itself.

Although, notably, it is Goliath, a person of color, who emerges as the hero of *The Proud Valley*, the radio version constructs a powerful and vivid sense of Welshness centered on the mining village, the family, and the Eisteddfod, danger, camaraderie, and song.[104] At the beginning of the broadcast Goliath is told, by an English tramp, that the Welsh are a people of song: "When it comes to singing these 'ere Welsh people have forgotten more 'n you or me ever knew."[105] The listeners are first introduced to the colliers of Blaendy as they argue over the failure of their vocal choir at the last Eisteddfod, demonstrating the centrality of song, and the national festival, to the Welsh.[106] Indeed, the first half of *The Proud Valley* is driven by Dick Parry's desire to win the Eisteddfod. Song is central to *The Proud Valley*, from the Welsh choir to the songs themselves, which included the Welsh folk-song *All Through the Night* and "that most moving of all Welsh hymns, *Yn y Dyfroedd*." In a *Radio Times* article he prepared for the broadcast, Rowland Hughes wrote of the cinematic version of *The Proud Valley* that, "for the first time in the history of British films, the musical genius of the Welsh people has found strong and sincere expression."[107]

The Proud Valley also emphasized the warmth and solidarity of the Welsh working class. "David," notes the narrator, "becomes a member of the Parry household and of the warm-hearted mining community."[108] Although the feature opens with a fistfight between Emlyn and another collier, the two work closely to save miners after the first collapse, as "the perils of the mine wipe away all past differences."[109] Finally, Emlyn has the community behind him as he leads his march to London to get the owners to reopen the Blaendy mine.

The Proud Valley dramatically represented the life of the Welsh collier, but it also expressed the "dual identity" of many Welsh. The Eisteddfod, the song, and the coal village setting all make *The Proud Valley* unmistakably Welsh. The film, wrote Rowland Hughes, "expresses the undying spirit of the Welsh Proud Valley."[110] Yet, this Welshness is constructed firmly within a larger Britishness. The Blaendy mine must reopen to save not just the Wales represented in *The Proud Valley* but Britain itself. The violence and danger faced by the collier mirrored that of the British civilian population, a point made explicit by Emlyn as he argues for the reopening of damaged Blaendy mine:

> We heard you say that tomorrow we may be at war. In that case you know the risks that will have to be faced in the trenches, on the sea, and in the sky … ay, and by our women and children in their homes. Coal in wartime is as much a part of our national defense as guns or anything else. So why not let us take our chance down the pit?[111]

In *The Proud Valley*, Britishness and Welshness are complementary; Wales serves Britain and Britain depends on Wales. Emlyn and his fellow miners are no less Welsh because of their British citizenship and commitment to Britain's war effort.

The year following the first broadcast of *The Proud Valley*, Basil Nicolls gave the go-ahead for the BBC to adapt yet another film on the Welsh valleys for radio, Fox Studios' *How Green Was My Valley*.[112] Rowland Hughes adapted the film, itself based on the Richard Llewellyn novel, for radio.[113] In *How*

Green Was My Valley, Huw Morgan looks back on his childhood in a collier family in south Wales near the end of the nineteenth century. The village and the Morgan family are torn apart when the miners form a union and strike. Gwilym, the Morgan family patriarch, opposes the union; his sons (excluding Huw, who is still a boy), support it. The family is reconciled after the strike, but not before Huw is badly injured. Mr Gruffydd, the local minister, takes the bed-ridden Huw under his wing and arranges for the talented boy to attend the local National School. Although educated, Huw decides to return to the mine in order to support his widowed sister-in-law. The broadcast concludes with the death of Huw's father in a mine accident.

How Green Was My Valley is quite different from *The Proud Valley*. *How Green* lacks the backdrop of the war and the patriotic undertones of *The Proud Valley*. And, while *The Proud Valley* ended on an optimistic note, *How Green* tells the story of the dirtying of the Welsh valleys and the decline of the coal industry. Nevertheless, it is, like *The Proud Valley*, an elementary representation of Welshness. Dai Smith once referred to *How Green Was My Valley* as "the most important 'document' ever written about South Wales."[114]

Like the feature film and the novel, notions of community and solidarity drive the radio version of *How Green*. For Gwilym Morgan, the coming of the union threatened the community of the valley because it pitted the men against the owners. "The owners are not savages," Gwilym tells his sons, "they are men, too, like us."[115] Gruffydd, the minister, expresses a similar sentiment when he tells the young Huw, after the miners vote to strike, that "something has gone out of this valley that may never be replaced."[116] Class and national solidarity are also represented in the characters of Dai Bando, a former boxer, and his accomplice, Cyfartha. When Huw loses a fight with another boy at the National School, Bando trains him in the art of boxing. Further, when Huw is viciously beaten by his teacher Mr Jonas, a middle-class, anglicized Welsh-man, Bando and Cyfartha arrive at the school the next day and give him a thrashing.[117]

How Green also includes elements of Welshness not found in *The Proud Valley*. The chapel does not play a significant role in *The Proud Valley*, but it is central to *How Green Was My Valley*. It is true that the story reveals the negative aspects of Welsh Methodism in the person of the petty, jealous, and violently anti-union Deacon Parry. Yet, the hero of *How Green* is, arguably, Mr Gruffydd. Gruffydd represents the chapel at its best, for he is an exemplary minister. It is Gruffydd who mediates between the owners and men to end the strike and he helps reunite the Morgan family. Although Gruffydd opposes the union, he fights for the men, having spent ten years in a colliery himself before becoming a minister. Most importantly, Gruffydd mentors young Huw and encourages him to get an education. Huw represents two important aspects of Welsh identity—loyalty to the chapel and the pursuit of education. Indeed, the character of Huw in *How Green Was My Valley* is the embodiment of Welshness. He is educated, but not anglicized, he takes up the work of his brothers and forefathers, and he remains intensely loyal to his family and community: Huw stays in Wales after his remaining brothers have emigrated to America, Australia, and New Zealand. If *How Green* is about loss—the loss of Huw's father and brother in mine accidents, the loss of his other siblings to America and the Commonwealth, and ultimately the loss of the valley to unemployment and pollution—it is also about the undying spirit of the Welsh people. The feature finishes with the adult Huw contemplating his father's death. "Men like my father cannot die," he concludes, "they are with me still, real in memory as they were real in the flesh."[118]

As the war came to a close Hopkin Morris and his staff could justifiably look back on their accomplishments during the war with pride. Hopkin Morris was able to secure some representation for the Welsh language on the Home Service, no mean feat considering that Welsh was a foreign tongue to the vast majority of British listeners. Further, although the Welsh region produced fewer programs during the war, their quality increased. Features such as *How Green Was My Valley* and the BBC Wales-produced *San Demetrio*, the story of a tanker ship attacked by the Germans as it attempted to bring desperately needed fuel to Britain, enjoyed many repeat performances after the war, and *San Demetrio* became the first ever radio feature to be turned into a film.

Of course, not all Welsh listeners were satisfied with the service provided during the war. In 1943, Hopkin Morris had to meet with the Welsh members of Parliament to discuss complaints against the BBC. Criticism grew louder as the war drew to a close, no doubt because of concerns over the future of Welsh broadcasting. In the autumn of 1944, the journal *Wales* sharply criticized the BBC, claiming "a vague, undefined sort of narrow nationalism obtained at the BBC in Wales."[119] The *Caernarvon and Denbigh Herald* joined the chorus in November, but complained that BBC Wales "gave a very wrong impression … of our native characteristics and culture."[120]

The loudest critics were the nationalists, who had long accused the BBC of being hostile to the Welsh language. In a pamphlet written in May 1945, *Plaid Cymru* demanded that Wales be given a separate broadcasting system after the war. Although the nationalists had worthy goals, it is difficult to see how an independent Welsh broadcasting system could have thrived after the war. For example, in the year ending March 31, 1949, the BBC took £287,000 in license fees from Wales. The cost of operating the Welsh service for the same period of time was £372,000. In addition, Wales's share of the Basic Home Service, Light Programme, and Third Programme came to £164,000, meaning the BBC subsidized Welsh broadcasting £249,000 for the year.[121] In addition, any independent Welsh broadcasting network would have to purchase property and equipment and build transmitters and studios. Given these costs, a separate Welsh service would have broadcast fewer hours and provided programs of lower quality than BBC Wales before the war.

Representing Wales on the Welsh Home Service

There was little chance of an independent Welsh network emerging in 1945. The BBC was at the height of its prestige, and the new Labour government was disinclined to break the BBC monopoly. In 1946, a government white paper renewed the BBC's charter for five years and maintained its monopoly in broadcasting. Regional broadcasting returned to Wales along the lines established before the war. The new Welsh region, now referred to as the Welsh Home Service, enjoyed a greater degree of independence, if not enough to satisfy the BBC's critics. Engineering staff, for example, did not answer to the Regional Director, but to the Controller in London. Further, London kept its hands on the purse strings, in that Head Office parceled out an allowance to BBC Wales for their needs. But Regional Directors controlled their program budgets and, most importantly, BBC Wales could not be compelled to take a program from the Basic Home Service, the successor of the pre-war National Programme. Although limited by what London thought it could afford to spend on Welsh broadcasting, Alun Oldfield-Davies, the new Welsh Regional Director, had considerable control over the content of Welsh broadcasting.

In addition to asserting their independence after the war, Welsh broadcasters also asked that Head Office (or any other region) refer to them before making their own programs about Wales. "Consult us first," wrote Watkin Jones to London, "for our listeners in Wales hold us in Cardiff responsible for Welsh topics."[122] The significance of Wales's claim is twofold. First, it was an attempt by Welsh broadcasters to reverse their relationship with London and get a measure of authority over Head Office. Second, it reveals something about the self-image of Welsh broadcasters as important guardians of Welsh identity. Having been charged with representing "Wales" to the rest of the

United Kingdom and the world during the war, Welsh broadcasters tried to claim ownership of Welshness at the BBC, insuring that listeners through-out Britain heard depictions of Wales that met their standards.[123] While John Davies sees this tension developing after 1945, one can find evidence of these feelings during the war. For example, in 1941, when the Variety Department, then located in Bangor, proposed a program on the coal valleys, T. Rowland Hughes complained that Head Office was violating BBC Wales's turf and aping their own programming. "Several plays and features broadcast from here have dealt with kindred themes, most of them written by Jack Jones, who was responsible for the scenario for *The Proud Valley*." "The argument," he contin-ued, "that the Variety Department is in *North* Wales, hardly seems to warrant their tackling an ambitious plot about *South* Wales [emphasis text].[124]

Regional broadcasting returned slowly to Wales. Although the Welsh Home Service began operating on its pre-war frequency of 373 meters on July 29, 1945, shortages of staff (many had been reassigned during the war) and equip-ment (a German raid destroyed the Swansea studio) hampered Welsh broad-casting. After a month, BBC Wales was producing only eight hours a week of its own programming. Things improved dramatically in 1946. Much of the wartime staff had returned, and broadcasting hours had risen to their pre-war levels of approximately twenty hours a week. A reconstituted Welsh orchestra of thirty-one players gave its first performance on November 5, 1946. The same year BBC Wales established, for the first time in its history, its own reper-tory company of seventeen members. Plans were also laid down for a Welsh chorus, which began broadcasting in 1947.

The white paper of 1946 tried to encourage greater regional autonomy within the BBC by stipulating that each region should have its own Advisory Council. For Wales, a council of twenty-one was chosen by William Haley from a list of twenty-four names submitted by Oldfield-Davies. Hence, the Council was largely a creature of BBC Wales. It served as an important conduit between the Corporation and the public, and it was not uncritical of the BBC. Its chief cultural concerns included the quantity of Welsh-language broad-casts, a Welsh-language version of the *Listener*, and the playing of *Hen Wlad fy Nhadau* at the end of each broadcast day. BBC Wales met the Council at least halfway on these issues; in the first quarter of 1948, 60 per cent of BBC Wales's spoken-word broadcasts were in the Welsh language. In 1949 the BBC began to broadcast the Welsh national anthem to indicate the end of the broadcast day, but in recognition of the dual Welsh/British identity of the region, *God Save the King* followed it. The Council never did convince the BBC to publish a Welsh-language version of the *Listener*, for such a journal would have been unprofitable. But a Welsh edition of the *Radio Times* did debut in 1945.[125]

Issues of identity, of Welshness—the language and the use of the national anthem—received considerable attention from the Advisory Council. The writers and producers at the BBC in Wales shared this interest and tried to give expression to Welsh identity in their programs. Like the pre-war regional programs, the mandate of the new regional Home Services was to express the culture and character of their region. And, like its predecessor, the Welsh Regional Programme, the Welsh Home Service associated Welsh identity with a few easily recognizable characters, settings, and stories—the historical national hero, the mining village, the boy (never a girl) who, through education, leaves the valleys and their way of life behind him.

The representation of Wales through the values of the industrial valleys continued after the war, despite the early retirement of T. Rowland Hughes in 1945. Not only did coal remain a timely topic in the post-war years, but the supposed values of the collier—warmth, community, and hard work—accorded well with the mood of a nation that had to rebuild from the devastation of the Second World War. One of the first features offered by Wales to the Basic Home Service was *William Jones*. P. H. Burton, Rowland Hughes's protégé, described the program to Lindsay Wellington:

> It deals in a way both amusing and penetrating with a difference of temperament of the people of North and South Wales. The timid little man from the North, who was driven away from home by a nagging wife, finds himself very ill at ease among the noisy, boisterous community of South Wales miners. But he soon learns to estimate their true human warmth and becomes an essential part of the family with which he lives. He shares their joys and sorrows during the period of industrial depression, and changes his mind at the last moment about going back home—the South has become his home.[126]

Burton's reading of *William Jones* is interesting because it expresses two of the ideas that prevailed at BBC Wales. The first was the strong sense of community, but openness, of the Welsh people. Like the black laborer David Goliath in *The Proud Valley*, the "timid little man from the North" finds a home in the collier village. Second, *William Jones* metaphorically "unites" Wales; the man from the north finds a home in the south. It had always been a goal of BBC Wales to forge a common culture for the distinct communities of Wales, north and south. But in the case of *William Jones*, there is no common culture; rather, the culture of the south, of the miners, represents the culture of Wales.

The image of the miner as a national hero (both Welsh and British) presented in features such as *The Proud Valley*, survived the war. In 1946 Burton produced the *Battle for Coal*, a program that won the hearty endorsement of the Labour Minister of Fuel and Power.[127] Burton's collaborator on *Battle for Coal*, Islwyn Williams, wrote *Coal and Conciliation* the following year, a program that explained "the history of dispute in the industry and … aimed primarily at adjusting the attitude of the miner towards the new conciliation machinery."[128] BBC Wales also produced, in 1947, Williams's play *The Rescuers*, about an 1877 mine disaster. In 1948 Burton produced another series of programs designed to improve "the atmosphere in the [coal] industry." The Welsh Home Service was preparing yet more programs on coal in 1948 until it was informed by London: "the Governors [of the BBC] think we should damp down on the miners. We have praised them a little too much."[129] However, this admonition did not prevent BBC Wales from broadcasting *The Rescuers* again in 1949.[130]

In addition to the industrial valleys, BBC Wales drew on history to express the distinct sense of national identity in Wales. Foremost among these heroes was Owain Glyndŵr. On St David's Day, 1948, The Welsh Home Service made Glyndŵr the subject of a large-scale feature program and planned a rebroadcast for March 19. Watkin Jones sent a copy of the script to Godfrey Adams in London and asked that it be considered for the Basic Home Service. The Features Department complimented the quality and structure of the program, but also concluded:

> There are plenty of knocks at the English … and since the script is so intensely nationalistic … I can't decide whether the English want to hear a whole hour's programme on what to them must be a little-known hero.[131]

Adams replied that while *Glyndŵr* might make "an extremely successful Welsh broadcast," he rejected it for the Basic Home Service because their (i.e. English) "listeners would not have the same latent interest in the central figure and might … tire of the intense nationalism."[132] This episode is notable not just because it demonstrates that the Welsh Home Service broadcast Welsh patriotic programs but also because it shows the mutability of national figures such as Glyndŵr. During the war the BBC presented Glyndŵr as a hero in the cause of freedom—a distinctly "British" interpretation—as the Glyndŵr revolt of 1400 was co-opted to fit the propaganda themes of the war. Three years later, the Welsh Home Service produced a much more Welsh nationalist version of his life.

With the BBC's Charter set to expire in 1951, and with no substantial examination of the state of broadcasting since 1936, the Labour government appointed a committee of inquiry under the chairmanship of Sir William Beveridge. Beveridge was distrustful of the BBC monopoly and intensely interested in regional broadcasting. Oldfield-Davies reported that when Beveridge visited Cardiff, he "expected to find an anti-London bias," and was surprised when that turned out not to be the case.[133] Oldfield-Davies himself argued against a Welsh broadcasting corporation, and he urged Welsh MPs to back away from a memorandum, submitted in their name, calling for the complete devolution of broadcasting in Wales.

As they had in 1936, the regional staff remained, by and large, loyal to the BBC. But the Beveridge inquiry did open up opportunities for critics of the BBC, including *Plaid Cymru*, which reiterated its demand for an independent broadcasting system for Wales. The Welsh Advisory Council also chimed in, but was divided on the future of broadcasting in Wales. Unable to arrive at a consensus opinion, the Advisory Council used equivocal language when it told the Beveridge Committee: "Wales should not be considered as a region of the BBC ... [but] as a national broadcasting unit within the pattern of British broadcasting."[134]

In its report, the Beveridge Committee recommended that Welsh broadcasting continue within the fold of the BBC, but with greater devolution. Wales was to have its own Broadcasting Council. The new council would be responsible for oversight of program content, finance, accommodation, and staff. They would be like a Board of Governors for the Welsh Home Service, not merely an advisory body. Furthermore, the Chairman of the Broadcasting Council for Wales would sit on the Board of Governors, to insure that the Board had at least one member with specialized knowledge of Wales. Significantly, the Beveridge Committee's report largely placated nationalist groups like *Undeb Cymru Fydd* and *Plaid Cymru*, and won the broad acceptance of Welsh public opinion.[135] The Conservative government largely adopted the recommendations of the Beveridge Committee on regional matters. In July, it was announced that the first Welsh Governor for the BBC would be Lord Macdonald of Gwaenysgor. He was a Wesleyan, a Welsh-speaker, and a member of the former Labour government—a man well suited to represent the interests of Wales. "His appointment," John Davies notes, "won widespread approval."[136]

The government's acceptance of the Beveridge Committee's recommendations on regional broadcasting affirmed the importance of maintaining robust Welsh broadcasting in Wales. Although still part of the BBC, Welsh broadcasters had considerable freedom and power to broadcast what they liked. Although the nationalist's dream of an independent Welsh corporation was still in the distant future, BBC Wales flourished in the 1950s and 1960s under the leadership of Oldfield-Davies. In terms of its autonomy and its ability to reflect the culture and society of Wales, Welsh radio had come a long way from the days when it had to share a transmitter with the west of England region. The goal of Welsh broadcasting since its inception, to forge a common sense of self among the disparate communities of Wales—north and south, Welsh-speaking and English-speaking—could be more fully achieved after 1952 than at any time in the history of Welsh radio.

The Welsh Home Service fell short of the independence in broadcasting some in Wales desired. London could still cramp Cardiff's ability to represent the Welsh nation. As with the Scottish National Party, *Plaid Cymru* candidates were barred from giving party political broadcasts until the 1960s. The justification for this policy was that *Plaid Cymru* did not have enough support to warrant the same access to the microphone as the Conservative and Labour parties. The rub was that the BBC used *Plaid Cymru*'s support within the entire United Kingdom, not Wales, as the measure of its popular support. The BBC's exclusion of *Plaid Cymru* had the backing of both the Labour and Conservative parties, neither of which supported the claims of Welsh nationalism. Yet it says something about the objectives and means of Welsh broadcasters that members of *Plaid Cymru*, most notably Saunders Lewis, broadcast on the Welsh language, Welsh history, and Welsh culture. Although political nationalism was beyond the pale, BBC Wales embraced a measure of cultural nationalism.

The government's decision to provide further devolution to Wales and the other national regions consummated the long struggle by Welsh broadcasters to provide a genuinely Welsh service to its listeners, with a minimal amount of interference from London. It is ironic then, that the moment of victory for Welsh radio broadcasters—the inclusion of a large measure of devolution into the BBC's charter—occurred at the beginning of what would become a tectonic shift in the habits of their listeners. For just as Wales achieved even greater autonomy in radio broadcasting, television began to penetrate the Welsh valleys. But, as had been the case with radio, the BBC forced Wales to share its television transmitter at Wenvoe with the west of England. And the arrival of commercial television in Wales in the late 1950s further fractured the Welsh television audience. The south was served by Television Wales and the West, while Manchester-based Granada television served the north. The western part of Wales received no television service until the establishment of Wales (West and North) Television in 1962, which failed, for financial reasons, a year later.[137] This hardly obviates the work of Welsh radio broadcasters in the years following 1952, but debates about broadcasting would be dominated by television, a medium that was still highly centralized in London.

Notes

1 Alun Oldfield-Davies, quoted in Davies, *BBC in Wales*, 190.
2 John Davies, *A History of Wales* (London: Penguin, 1993), 565.
3 Prys Morgan, "From a Death to a View: The Hunt for the Welsh Past in the Romantic Era," in *The Invention of Tradition*, Hobsbawm and Ranger, eds, 43–100.
4 Ibid.
5 Dai Smith, *Wales! Wales?* (London: Allen & Unwin, 1984).
6 Gwyn A. Williams, *When Was Wales?* (London: Penguin, 1985), 176, 202.
7 Davies, *BBC in Wales*, 1.
8 Glasgow was by far the largest conurbation in Scotland and Aberdeen was unrivalled in population and status in northeast Scotland.
9 Davies, *BBC in Wales*, 4–5.
10 Ibid., 34.
11 Ibid., 5, 1.
12 J. C. W. Reith, quoted in Ibid., 16.
13 The BBC limited the amount of Welsh material on Daventry, including the use of the Welsh language, because Daventry was available to listeners across Britain. Ibid., 36.
14 Rowland Lucas, *Voice of a Nation? A Concise Account of the BBC in Wales, 1923–1973* (Llandysul: Gomer Press, 1981), 24.
15 Davies, *BBC in Wales*, 32–3; Lucas, 24–6.
16 *Radio Times*, April 16, 1926, 165. The *Radio Times* boasted "Welsh music has suffered from the apathy of its musical historians and recorders in the past, and this programme is the first occasion on which many of the airs have been collected together and arranged for pianoforte accompaniment."
17 *Radio Times*, December 11, 1925, 563. It is not clear if the Glyndŵr program was broadcast over Daventry because it was considered to be of national (i.e. British) interest or so that listeners in central and north Wales could hear it. The program, written by Appleton, was the first of a series entitled *Heroes of Britain*.
18 *Radio Times*, October 22, 1926, 220.
19 *Radio Times*, June 16, 1933, 681. E. R. Appleton remained hopeful that "with the quickening of interest in broadcasting, due to the opening of the new transmitting station, better results may be attained this year."
20 Lucas, 24.
21 Ibid.
22 *Radio Times*, January 14, 1927, 100.
23 Davies, *BBC in Wales*, 40.
24 Pegg, 22–35.
25 *BBC Yearbook 1934*, 189.
26 *Radio Times*, June 16, 1933, 681.

27 E. R. Appleton to Charles Siepmann, August 1, 1933, BBC WAC, R51/631/1.

28 *Radio Times*, August 25, 1932, 418.

29 *Radio Times*, June 16, 1933, 681.

30 *Radio Times*, August 25, 1933, 418.

31 Siepmann to J. T. Sutthery, October 3, 1933, BBC WAC, R51/631/1.

32 Appleton to Siepmann, September 14, 1933, Ibid.

33 Sutthery to Talks Executive, November 1, 1933, Ibid. Ultimately, the discussion on cultural nationalism took place with Lord Raglan and Stephen J. Williams. *Radio Times*, January 12, 1934, 104. The BBC West region also had some difficulty finding someone to chair the discussions. See Sutthery to Francis Worsley, October 27, 1933; Talks Executive to Appleton, October 30, 1933; Sutthery to Siepmann, November 8, 1933, BBC WAC, R51/631/1.

34 *Radio Times*, January 12, 1934, 104. The Lewis introduction was allowed at the request of Sutthery. See Sutthery to Worsley, October 27, 1933, R51/631/1. In spite of his antipathy towards the BBC, Lewis was a frequent broadcaster.

35 *Radio Times*, February 7, 1930, 352; *Radio Times*, June 27, 1930, 749.

36 *Radio Times*, April 3, 1931, 53.

37 *Radio Times*, January 22, 1932.

38 *Radio Times*, April 29, 1932.

39 *BBC Handbook 1934*, 95.

40 *Radio Times*, March 23, 1934, 920. See also *Radio Times*, February 21, 1930, 457.

41 *Radio Times*, December 5, 1930, 709; *Radio Times*, September 29, 1933, 768. On this occasion the BBC produced *Danger* from London.

42 Siepmann to Appleton, November 13, 1936, and Parry to Siepmann, November 23, 1936, BBC WAC, R19/1428/1.

43 *Radio Times*, February 4, 1938, 79.

44 *Radio Times*, August 12, 1938, 14.

45 *Radio Times*, September 21, 1938, 55.

46 *Radio Times*, May 12, 1939, 11.

47 *Radio Times*, October 30, 1934, 380; Davies, *BBC in Wales*, 9.

48 *Radio Times*, February 22, 1924, 339.

49 *Radio Times*, February 27, 1925, 440.

50 *Radio Times*, February 11, 1927, 308; *Radio Times*, February 25, 1927, 425.

51 Lindsay Wellington to Appleton, August 15, 1929, BBC WAC, R34/237/1. Wellington continued, "The national angle of such concerts always seem to me to be both accidental and purely incidental."

52 Ernest Jenkins to Wellington, August 16, 1929, Ibid.

53 *Radio Times*, February 14, 1930, 421.

54 Appleton to Reith, March 28, 1930, BBC WAC, R34/237/1.

55 *Radio Times*, February 19, 1932, 442.

56 *Radio Times*, February 17, 1933, 390.

57 *Radio Times*, February 23, 1934, 586; *Radio Times*, February 22, 1935, 68. John Davies characterizes the 1934 St David's Day programs as "weird Welsh kitsch by the former archdruid, Wil Ifan, and an 'awful script' by A. G. Prys-Jones." The 1935 program was well-received by the *Western Mail*. Davies, *BBC in Wales*, 86.

58 Appleton to Talks Executive, February 4, 1935. It is unclear whether a talk about Wales in English counted as Welsh material, or of general interest, merely by virtue of the language in which it was broadcast. Later in the memorandum Appleton refers to the eight to ten hours per week of "general material" produced by his region, including "Western Studio Orchestra, talks, etc. [and] … Outside Broadcasts from Monmouthshire and South Wales."

59 Lucas, 48. Almost from its inception, local authorities, *Plaid Cymru*, and Welsh MPs made regular, though separate, approaches to the BBC to discuss the nature of broadcasting for Wales. This dissatisfaction was given a single voice in 1928 when the University of Wales formed a council to treat with the BBC on Welsh broadcasting. The Council included W. N. Bruce, Sir Walford Davies, William George (brother of Lloyd George), and W. J. Gruffydd. In 1929 the Council requested that the BBC establish a high-power transmitter exclusively for Wales and include the Welsh language more in its programs. Lucas, 41, 44.

60 The following account is based on Lucas, 52–8.

61 Ibid., 51.

62 Ibid., 52.

63 Ibid., 54.

64 Ibid., 58.

65 In 1935, the BBC's existing Welsh staff consisted of Ernest Jenkins, Edgar Jones, Sam Jones, Dafydd Gruffydd, Owen Parry, and Elwyn Evans. Davies, *BBC in Wales*, 71.

66 Ibid.

67 In 1932 he called the BBC an "essentially English Corporation." Ibid., 78.

68 Ibid.; Lucas, 71–2.

69 *Coast to Coast*, BBC WAC, Scripts, Welsh Regional Talks, Reel 23.

70 Davies, *BBC in Wales*, 109.

71 "An Anglo-Welshman's Point of View," BBC WAC, Scripts, West Region Talks.

72 *Radio Times*, March 26, 1937, 72.

73 Lucas, 91.

74 *Radio Times*, January 28, 1938, 7.

75 Laurence Gilliam to John Tudor Jones, September 17, 1937; Moray McLaren to Tudor Jones, February 10, 1938, BBC WAC, R19/1428/1.

76 Rhys Hopkin Morris to Val Gielgud, August 16, 1937, Ibid.

77 Provisional Talks Schedule, Welsh Region, BBC WAC, R51/631/2.

78 In other ways, the BBC in Wales reinforced these divisions, despite their best efforts. The tendency for English-language programs to be "modern" and Welsh-language programmes to focus on the past has been noted above. John Davies, citing *Crugybar* as an example, notes that Welsh-language plays tended to deal with religion while English-language plays were more secular in subject matter. Davies, *BBC in Wales*, 118.

79 The following is taken from Davies, *BBC in Wales*, 123–31.

80 Ibid., 127.

81 In a memo to Basil Nicolls, Hopkin Morris wrote "I am satisfied from my own

experience that without your advocacy the case of Wales would not have been met as it has, and certainly not in as generous a measure. Wales is indebted to you." Ibid., 125–6.

82 Ibid., 127.

83 BBC Monitoring did take notice when Hamburg broadcast, in English, to "the distressed areas of South Wales." Ibid.

84 Ibid., 130.

85 A. Watkin Jones to Richard Maconachie, December 11, 1939, BBC WAC, R51/631/3.

86 The BBC devised a plan by which each region would provide talks for the Home Service, usually one or two a week. And, as noted in Chapter 4, London scheduled most regional talks during the early morning or afternoon.

87 Watkin Jones to Harman Grisewood, June 7, 1940, BBC WAC, R51/631/3.

88 Grisewood to George Barnes, June 7, 1940, Ibid.

89 Watkin Jones to Grisewood, January 24, 1941 and Watkin Jones to Grisewood, February 21, 1941, BBC WAC, R34/945/3.

90 Aneirin Talfan Davies to Barnes, December 31, 1942, BBC WAC, R51/631/3.

91 Ibid.

92 See, for example, Director of Programme Planning to Programme Organizer (Home), March 20, 1942, and Nicolls to Cecil Graves, April 1, 1942, BBC WAC, R34/945/3.

93 Welsh Programme Director to Laurence Gilliam, September 21, 1939, BBC WAC, R19/1426/1.

94 Watkin Jones to Maconachie, January 18, 1940, BBC WAC, R51/631/3.

95 Watkin Jones to Maconachie, June 9, 1941; Christopher Salmon to Maconachie, June 14, 1941; Salmon to Watkin Jones, June 17, 1941, BBC WAC, R34/945/3.

96 Watkin Jones to Presentation Director, July 9, 1940, Ibid.

97 Memorandum, "Programmes from Wales," n.d., BBC WAC, R34/945/3; T. Rowland Hughes to Assistant Director Features, April 28, 1943, BBC WAC, R19/1426/1.

98 Assistant Director School Broadcasting to Assistant Controller (Home), February 11, 1942, BBC WAC, R34/945/3. This seems to have caused suspicion among some at Head Office because the script of the Welsh-language broadcast was not sent to London to be vetted.

99 Davies, *BBC in Wales*, 128–9.

100 *Radio Times*, April 25, 1941, 2.

101 The two had collaborated to produce *Best Welsh* in 1938. See above.

102 *Radio Times*, January 6, 1940, 3.

103 For an analysis of the film *The Proud Valley*, see Richards, *Films*, 77–9.

104 For an analysis of the importance of Goliath as a black hero in the film version, see Richards, *Films*, chapter 2.

105 *The Proud Valley*, BBC WAC, Script Library, 9.

106 Ibid., 3.

107 Rowland Hughes in the *Radio Times*, February 23, 1940, 8.

108 *The Proud Valley*, BBC WAC, Script Library, 13.

109 Ibid., 16.

110 *Radio Times*, February 23, 1940, 8.

111 *The Proud Valley*, BBC WAC, Script Library, 27.

112 Moray McLaren to Rowland Hughes, October 20, 1941, BBC WAC, R19/1428/1.

113 For the film version of *How Green Was My Valley*, see Richards, *Films*, 216–22.

114 Dai Smith, "Myth and Meaning in the Literature of the South Wales Coalfield—the 1930s," *The Anglo-Welsh Review*, 56 (1976): 40.

115 *How Green Was My Valley*, BBC WAC, Script Library, 6.

116 Ibid., 8.

117 Ibid., 21–6.

118 Ibid., 33.

119 Lucas, 141.

120 Ibid., 142.

121 Davies, *BBC in Wales*, 180.

122 Watkin Jones, quoted in Davies, *BBC in Wales*, 158. A similar development occurred in Scotland before the war. See Chapter 5.

123 Rowland Hughes to Director Variety, April 29, 1941, BBC WAC, R34/945/3.

124 Ibid.

125 See Davies, *BBC in Wales*, 148–53, 160–4.

126 P. H. Burton to Wellington, August 29, 1945, BBC WAC, R19/1428/2.

127 Davies, *BBC in Wales*, 187.

128 Watkin Jones to Gilliam, Wellington, August 20, 1947, BBC WAC, R19/1426/2.

129 Davies, *BBC in Wales*, 187.

130 HWP to Controller, Home Service, November 9, 1949, BBC WAC, R19/1426/2.

131 Dorothy Baker to Gilliam, March 16, 1948, Ibid.

132 Godfrey Adams to Watkin Jones, March 22, 1948, Ibid.

133 Davies, *BBC in Wales*, 178.

134 Ibid., 179.

135 Jamie Medhurst, "'Minorities with a Message:' The Beveridge Report on Broadcasting (1949–1951) and Wales," *Twentieth Century British History*, 19 (2008): 229, 230.

136 Davies, *BBC in Wales*, 183.

136 Jamie Medhurst, "'Wales Television—Mammon's Television'? ITV in Wales in the 1960s," *Media History*, 10 (2004): 119–31.

7

This Is Northern Ireland: regional broadcasting and identity in "Ulster"

This chapter makes three interconnected claims. First, that BBC Northern Ireland (hereafter BBC NI) played a vital role in maintaining a strong *British* national consciousness in Northern Ireland. Second, that BBC NI self-consciously sought to also construct a unifying "Ulster" identity for the new province. As with Scotland and Wales, the BBC's projection of "Ulsterness" did not represent the abandonment of unionism or British identity but was rather an attempt to assert the distinctiveness of Ulster culture within Great Britain as well as distinguish it from the rest of Ireland. Finally, this chapter argues that BBC NI was not able to fully distance itself from Orangeism. Although reluctant to embrace populist Protestantism in the 1930s, BBC NI, by the Second World War, was becoming more open to promoting, or at least tolerating, some of the more unsavory aspects on unionism in its programs.

First and foremost, the BBC represented a vital link to "mainland Britain" for the geographically disconnected statelet of Northern Ireland. Because, like all BBC regions, Northern Ireland received the National Programme, and later the Home Service and Light Programme, the BBC allowed Northern Irish listeners to indulge in British culture, news, and moments of national importance. The ability of radio broadcasting to create a sense of simultaneity and shared experience was particularly important in this regard. Belfast listeners could hear the same broadcast at the same time as their fellow Britons in Glasgow, or Manchester, or London, and be reminded that Northern Ireland was part of a larger national community. Also, and perhaps of greater importance, they were simultaneously reminded that Northern Ireland was *not* part of the Irish Free State. The ability to more completely integrate Northern Ireland into the national community of Britain dovetailed with the Protestant community's strong sense of Britishness. The most revered acts of Northern Irish patriotism—the formation of the Ulster Volunteers in 1912, the Larne gun running of 1914, the service of the Ulster regiments in the First World War—represented for the Protestant community their will to maintain the British connection, not to attain independence for Northern Ireland.[1] The power of radio to literally connect Northern Ireland to rest of Britain combined with the British identity of the majority community shaped the BBC's approach to broadcasting in the region. As George Marshall, head of the BBC's Northern Ireland station for much of the 1930s and 1940s wrote in an article for the *Radio Times*, "broadcasting not only tried to reflect the native culture of the Region; it has played a large part in its development. For one thing, it has been a constant link with the remainder of the British Isles."[2] Here Marshall expresses a kind of cultural unionism which, of course, unpinned political unionism. It was not that BBC NI helped to develop the local culture and provided a link to Britain, but rather that it developed the local culture because it maintained that vital link. Further, while BBC NI refused to endorse the more bigoted aspects of unionism, especially before the Second World War, it did adopt a decidedly unionist point of view. From its inception the BBC in Northern Ireland, despite occasional clashes, embraced the unionist establishment and the Stormont government. The first two station directors of BBC NI, Marshall and his predecessor Gerald Beadle, were Scottish and English, respectively, and strangers in Northern Ireland. But they were quickly co-opted into the social elite of the province.[3] Finally, the partition of Ireland provided the *raison d'être* for the BBC's presence in Northern Ireland; it would have been difficult for the BBC to have anything other than a pro-unionist position.

Besides maintaining the British connection, BBC NI also endeavored to construct a national/regional identity specific to Northern Ireland. Despite the sectarian divide, and an initial reluctance to celebrate unionist culture, BBC NI did contribute significantly to the development of an Ulster identity in Northern Ireland. It accomplished this in a variety ways. The BBC presented the region, on a daily basis, as a bounded, knowable community, distinct from the Irish Free State (after 1937, Eire). The very act of establishing a BBC station in Belfast for "Ulster" listeners contributed to the process whereby the unionists of Northern Ireland could regard themselves as Britons and Ulstermen (and women), and not Irish. The BBC reinforced this communal re-imagining through news, talks, and entertainment programs that presented Ulster to itself. Much of the content of these broadcasts was banal; but such programs familiarized listeners with the terrain and boundaries of "their" province of Northern Ireland, a relatively new creation. Tourism talks, which BBC NI began to broadcast in the late 1930s in consultation with the

Northern Ireland government, had the same impact. The tourist programs also encouraged a sense of local pride, as did the numerous programs produced by BBC NI on Northern Ireland's most famous sons and daughters. What BBC NI attempted to construct with its programs was a dual identity, "Ulster-Britishness." Although there are contemporary fractures within the Protestant community in Northern Ireland between unionists, whose primary allegiance is to Britain, and loyalists, who identify not with Britain but rather with Ulster, these distinctions derive from The Troubles and the British government's various responses to sectarianism in the province.[4] Before the 1960s, an Ulster regional identity and British national identity were seen as complementary, not antagonistic or mutually exclusive. To embrace Ulsterness was not to reject Britishness, but rather to reject Irishness.

Finally, this chapter demonstrates that BBC NI's attitude towards Protestant patriotism changed significantly during the period 1924–1954. The extreme caution that characterized the BBC's relationship with Orangeism in the 1920s began to erode by the middle of the 1930s, as BBC NI became more confident in its own ability to judge what constituted good broadcasting in Northern Ireland. Indeed, BBC Head Office had to check the ambitions of BBC NI and intervene to stop potentially inflammatory broadcasts. However, the key shift, especially among the staff in Northern Ireland, took place during the Second World War. While the staff of BBC NI always had given little consideration to the Catholic community in Northern Ireland and the competency of their counterparts at Eire's Radio Eireann, Ireland's neutrality during the Second World War hardened these attitudes.[5] Some staff members at BBC NI, including Marshall, became openly hostile to both Eire and the Catholic community in the North. And the BBC's overall propaganda strategy of attracting southern Irish listeners by taking a friendly stance towards Eire only exacerbated the feelings of the staff of BBC NI. BBC NI never wrangled with Head Office so much as it did during the war. As the conflict dragged on, Marshall and his Programme Director Ursula Eason increasingly came to share the unionist world-view. For example, it was during the Second World War that the BBC noted in its programs, for the first time, the Twelfth of July.[6]

After 1945, the BBC increasingly accommodated a more sectarian unionism in its programs. This was due in part to the fact that after the war regional broadcasters were given more autonomy. The BBC in London could do little to prevent BBC NI from celebrating the Twelfth, or any other heroic moment from the Protestant community's past, such as the Siege of Derry. BBC NI also hired more "natives" from Northern Ireland after the war, including John

Boyd, Sam Hanna Bell, John Hewitt, and William Rogers.[7] BBC NI committed itself to breaking from its guarded past, and reflecting fully the history of
Northern Ireland. As a result, BBC NI began to confront some of the problems
of Northern Ireland in ways not possible before the war, even encouraging
discussion of the sectarian divisions that wracked the region. Yet, in attempting to reflect Ulster in the full, BBC NI necessarily accommodated the basest
characteristics of unionist identity. This is the great irony of the BBC's development in Northern Ireland. Just as it began to attempt to bridge the sectarian divide in Northern Ireland, and, as a consequence, give more air time to
the region's Catholics, it also provided a privileged voice for militant popular
Protestantism. Of course, the willingness of BBC NI to push the envelope
with regard to unionist culture and give some voice to the Catholic community had a common origin: the newfound confidence of the unionist elite in
Northern Ireland, which included the management of BBC NI. In the 1920s,
the very existence of Northern Ireland remained a political question mark. By
1945, after twenty-four years of independence capped by unwavering loyalty
during the Second World War, the unionist community could be sure that
there would be no change to the constitutional status of Northern Ireland
without the consent of the Protestant majority.

The challenges of broadcasting in Northern Ireland

Regional broadcasting in Northern Ireland faced many of the same hurdles
and issues as regional broadcasting in Scotland and Wales. To an even greater
extent than those two regions, BBC NI suffered from the arrogance of Head
Office and, before 1945, limitations on the amount and type of programming
it produced. Both BBC Head Office and the English and Scottish administra-
tors who managed the BBC's Northern Ireland station lamented the quality
of the local talent and, consequently, locally produced programs. Northern
Ireland was the smallest of the BBC's broadcasting regions, with the smallest
number of license holders per head. More than any other BBC regional station,
BBC NI had to struggle against Head Office for a measure of broadcasting
independence. However, the most serious challenge for BBC NI was the origin
and nature of the state itself.

The modern origins of Northern Ireland are to be found in the 1880s and
the vehement opposition of Irish Protestants to any form of devolution or
Home Rule for Ireland. These Protestant "unionists" found political allies in
the Conservative Party and a sizeable portion of the Liberal Party—a coalition

that wrecked William Gladstone's plans for Ireland. When the Liberals, now led by H. H. Asquith, pursued Home Rule in the 1910s the unionists again swung into action, this time adopting extra-parliamentary means such as military drilling and arms smuggling. When Irish nationalists responded in kind, it seemed as if Ireland might be on the brink of a civil war.

The British declaration of war against Germany in 1914 tabled Home Rule as a political issue, but it did nothing to mitigate sectarian hostility in Ireland. Rather, the postponement of Home Rule yet again encouraged an armed rebellion in Dublin on Easter Monday, 1916. Although unsuccessful, the Easter Rising further embittered Protestant unionists towards the Catholic nationalist majority. By 1920 the British government, unable to hold Ireland militarily or politically, but unwilling to abandon those unionists concentrated in the northeast of Ireland, partitioned the island. The south and west became the Irish Free State, a Dominion in the British empire. The northeast remained part of the United Kingdom but, ironically, had its own devolved parliament which met at Stormont, just outside Belfast.

The new province of Northern Ireland was created in such a way as to insure Protestant dominance. The border with the Irish Free State did not correspond to the historic province of Ulster, but was cropped so that two-thirds of the population of Northern Ireland was Protestant. Electoral districts were gerrymandered to insure the political dominance of the unionists in the Stormont parliament. Catholics, most of whom opposed partition, were discriminated against in terms of jobs and housing. Northern Ireland became an anomaly within liberal Britain, a region where a Protestant majority could lord their power over a large, disenfranchised, and resentful minority.

Unlike the Scottish, Welsh, and English regions, BBC NI served a distinct political entity within the United Kingdom. The creation of the BBC's Northern Ireland region was in no small part a political decision to massage the egos of the political class and broader unionist community of Northern Ireland. Although the cultural, class, and linguistic diversity of Wales and Scotland complicated the BBC's representation of those regions, the Catholic/Protestant divide in Northern Ireland ran deeper and aroused more passion. The BBC might have been reluctant to broadcast on contentious subjects such as separatist nationalism in Scotland and Wales, but the regional stations ultimately covered these topics. In Northern Ireland the BBC ignored the nationalist community and the systematic discrimination against the Catholic minority. Furthermore, while a broadcast on Scottish nationalism might arouse controversy, Scottish and Welsh broadcasters did not have to worry that such a program might incite a riot. A broadcast by a Catholic, or a triumphalist Protestant program, had the potential to cause violence in Northern Ireland. Faced with such a possibility, and aware of the power of historical memories in Northern Ireland, the BBC, unlike its practice in Scotland and Wales, was initially reluctant to commemorate important festivals, anniversaries, and "great men" from Northern Ireland's history.

The BBC in Northern Ireland: constructing Ulster

Perhaps the most important function the new medium of radio played in the construction of an Ulster-British identity in the new state of Northern Ireland was to create a sense of national community, territory, and space which included the province. The BBC, by committing itself to broadcasting the great ceremonies of state, sporting events, and the best of British culture, constructed a national community of British listeners that included the Northern Irish in a way that other types of media, such as the press, could not. But, because the BBC was organized on a regional, as well as a national basis, the BBC not only integrated Northern Ireland into the broader national community but also helped to define Northern Irish identity; to be Northern Irish meant, in part, to consume the only wholly Northern Irish medium at the time, BBC NI. Once the BBC established its first station in Belfast the new statelet found itself endowed with a powerful means by which its citizens, or at least the Protestant majority, could be defined and socialized into the imagined community of "Northern Ireland."

The first BBC station in Northern Ireland opened in 1924, in Belfast. 2BE was one of the original nine main stations established by the BBC in the 1920s. While 2BE served the most densely populated part of Northern Ireland, its range was limited to the city limits of Belfast. Like the other main stations 2BE broadcast locally produced material and carried its share of programs from London and the English regions. In these ways, the BBC NI served as a conduit for the expression of both British and Northern Irish, or at least Belfast, identity and culture. But the BBC could not be heard throughout the province until the opening of a medium-wave transmitter in Northern Ireland at Lisnagarvey in 1936. Since 2BE was the only BBC station in Northern Ireland, the implementation of the regional scheme did not mean, as was the case in Scotland and Wales, the consolidation and closure of studios and transmitters. Production remained centered in Belfast, but the Lisnagarvey transmitter allowed BBC NI to reach a wider audience.

Significantly, this audience, the imagined community that BBC NI helped to define was "Ulster," not "Northern Ireland," and certainly not the "six counties." Though technically the name of the BBC's service in Northern Ireland was, at different times, the Northern Ireland Regional Programme, the Northern Ireland Programme, and after World War II, the Northern Ireland Home Service, the name "Northern Ireland" was rarely used for, or in, programs. Notable broadcasts such as Denis Johnston's *Six Counties at War*, or Sam Hanna Bell's *This Is Northern Ireland* are the exceptions that prove the rule. Indeed, as early as 1930, Gerald Beadle, director of the BBC's Belfast station, referred to it as the "Ulster Broadcasting Station."[8]

An examination of BBC NI's schedules demonstrates that "Ulster" was far and away the preferred term for the province. For example, in 1936, BBC NI proposed to Head Office nine series of talks, to start in January 1937. These included *How Ulster Is Governed, Ulster Speaks, All Things Considered*, "a fortnightly review of Ulster news," and *For Ulster Farmers*.[9] The Northern Ireland Programme Director did not propose a single talk series containing the words "Northern Ireland." The following autumn, BBC NI submitted a provisional talks schedule to Head Office that included *And So Ulster Was Made, Ulster Scientists, News Comes to Ulster, Does Ulster Contribute to Irish Culture?*, and *Made in Ulster*. The only reference to "Northern Ireland" in the schedule was a lone talk, *How Northern Ireland Helped With Weather Forecasts*.[10] During the Second World War, Northern Ireland was represented in the Home Service by two series, *Ulster Magazine*, and a news program, *Today in Ulster*. When regional broadcasting was restored after the war, BBC NI continued with its almost exclusive use of "Ulster." Regularly scheduled programs for Northern Irish listeners included *Ulster Sport, Arts in Ulster, Ulster Magazine, Ulster Commentary*, and *Ulster Mirror*.

Although program producers do not seem to have been given a direct order to use "Ulster" instead of "Northern Ireland" (i.e. there are no memoranda directing producers to certain terminology), the prevalence of its use strongly suggests that it was used purposely and officially sanctioned; as already noted, the Belfast Station Director referred to BBC NI as the "Ulster Broadcasting Station." Two other incidents further indicate that BBC NI's use of "Ulster" was intentional and done at the behest of the Stormont government. In 1942, the Overseas Service began broadcasting a program for soldiers from Northern Ireland entitled *Six Counties Half Hour*. The Stormont government protested against the name of the show, forcing a change to *Ulster Half Hour*.[11] Then there was the Northern Ireland contribution to a Light Programme series *World of Work*, broadcast in October of 1946. It is not the content of the program, a description of the economic crisis in Northern Ireland, that is noteworthy, but rather that in the script each mention of "Northern Ireland," is crossed out and replaced with "Ulster." The editor of the program even substituted "Ulster Government" for "Northern Ireland Government."[12]

"Ulster" was the preferred unionist term for Northern Ireland.[13] Ulster is one of the four historic provinces of Ireland, and some unionists argued that Ulster possessed an organic unity as well as a distinct history and culture that naturally separated it from the rest of Ireland. Some unionist intellectuals, such as the BBC's own W. R. Rogers, argued that Ulster's divergence from the rest of Ireland pre-dated the plantations of the seventeenth century.[14] "Northern Ireland," in contrast, was a recent invention whose boundary was the result of a sordid political compromise; "six counties" was even worse, as it carried the implication that the North was still fundamentally a part of Eire. Of course it mattered little to the Stormont government or the BBC that Northern Ireland and Ulster were not coterminous; three of the historic counties of Ulster were and remain part of Eire.[15]

While BBC NI, before the Second World War, was considerably restricted in the types of programs it could produce in regard to the history, culture, and government of Northern Ireland, it did seek to represent the identity of the region. Anti-Catholic bigotry was outside the bounds of Reithian public-service broadcasting, but emphasizing the differences between Northern Ireland and Eire and the fostering of local pride certainly were not. The staff of BBC NI, like those at BBC Wales and BBC Scotland, chafed at the sometimes overbearing and condescending attitudes of their colleagues and superiors in London. The Head Office/regional dynamic discussed with regards to Scotland and Wales certainly existed in Northern Ireland, but they were complicated by the existence of independent Eire. The BBC in London wanted to use its presence in Northern Ireland to tap the cultural resources of the whole of Ireland for programs. BBC NI staff resented the fact that rather than serving their own community with programs, they were being asked to act as the conduit by which Irish culture—the culture of, in their eyes, a foreign and hostile people—penetrated Britain. But for the London staff, Eire programs, other than ones with the potential to be politically controversial, were no different from any other program contribution from the empire.

By the end of the 1930s the staff of BBC NI successfully resisted the tendency of the BBC in London to "regard the BBC in Northern Ireland as the BBC in Ireland."[16] A rapid Ulsterization of the output of BBC NI was put into effect. George Marshall's proposal in 1937 for a "series of four Irish national lectures ... in order to foster the idea of a cultural unity in Ireland and ... enable Ulster to make use of some of the talent in the South," is notable because such sentiments were rarely expressed at BBC NI at the time.[17] Although BBC NI largely ignored the religious/political divide within Northern Ireland, it could, and did, construct an image for Northern Ireland that emphasized its differences—historical, cultural, ethnic—from Eire. The BBC in Northern Ireland proved to be instrumental in the "construction of a partitionist mentality."[18]

One way in which BBC NI attempted to encourage pride in Northern Ireland was through programs that recounted the exploits of famous men from the province or that employed notables from the region. In 1934 BBC NI proposed a series of talks titled *London Line*, which would feature prominent personalities with a Northern Ireland connection, but living in England, discussing some aspect of the province. In addition to demonstrating Northern Ireland's contribution to national culture and politics, *London Line* highlighted the links between Northern Ireland and the rest of Britain. However, as often happened with proposals from Northern Ireland, Head Office rejected the program, fearing that it would inevitably spill over into politics. "I cannot see," noted Charles Siepmann upon refusing the program, what "prominent Ulstermen in London can have to say to Northern Ireland that could be of genuine interest to your listeners outside of politics, which clearly would have to be avoided."[19] The following year BBC NI proposed *Six Men Went Forth*, a series of vignettes on the lives of six "Ulstermen ... [who] went forth from Ulster to achieve fame elsewhere," including John Lawrence, Lord Castlereagh, Colonel Robert Ross, and Lord Dufferin. Later that year BBC NI proposed another series of talks, similar to *London Line*, but based on the nostalgic recollections of well-known personalities from Northern Ireland, entitled *Back To*. *Back To*, like *Six Men Went Forth*, drew attention to Northern Ireland's participation in the broader British nation and empire, and it was specifically designed to appeal to the local pride of those towns that would shortly be within range of the new Lisnagarvey transmitter. In 1937, BBC NI produced another series of talks called *I Remember*, which included contributions from Harold Nicolson and St John Ervine. The idea behind the series, noted Marshall, "was to continue our process of arousing Northern Ireland to the fact that it has some famous men."[20] *I Remember*, yet another reincarnation of the old *London Line* proposal, reflected the dual purpose of the BBC in Northern Ireland: it encouraged listeners to take pride in their region while also reminding them of their national and imperial connections.

If BBC NI tried to foster regional pride in the contribution of Ulster to the United Kingdom and the empire, it also developed another way to project the province—tourist programs. Such programs could hardly be called patriotic or even unionist, but they did serve the purpose of the Stormont government. These programs, in reporting the exploits of travelers through Ulster, or advertising the noted holiday spots of Ulster, gave Northern Ireland, a province created by the stroke of a pen only in 1921, an imaginative cohesion and unity. Further, when these types of programs were broadcast for British listeners throughout the United Kingdom, they served as a potent reminder of Northern Ireland's inclusion in Britain.

By the mid 1930s, BBC NI began running several travel and tourism programs, encouraging people to explore and visit Northern Ireland. These started out simply enough—a series entitled *Weekend Out of Doors,* which, each week, highlighted a different Ulster pleasure spot. In 1936, BBC NI produced an innovative series of talks based on the travels of an unemployed worker given £3 by the Corporation. In 1937, it instituted another weekly travel program, *Ulster Holiday,* intended, according to Marshall, to "advertise in a mild way the charms of Northern Ireland."[21]

These programs were important in that they reflected the land and people of Northern Ireland, or at least the unionist community, back to themselves; equally important to the unionists of Northern Ireland were those programs that reflected Northern Ireland's membership in the United Kingdom to both Irish and British listeners. During the 1930s, the unionist government in Northern Ireland strongly asserted that the North was British, and consistently sought ways to demonstrate this fact including tourism and advertisement. The Stormont government established the Ulster Tourist Development Association in 1924 in part to improve the public image of the province and project Ulster's Britishness.[22] By the late 1930s, BBC NI also looked to "advertise the charms" of Ulster not only to the Northern Irish, but to the rest of the United Kingdom as well. Their initial attempts to place tourist programs in the National Programme, like so many of their ideas, were initially rebuffed by Head Office. The BBC did not want to appear as if it was favoring Northern Ireland after refusing similar requests from other regions. Happily for Marshall, however, Northern Ireland was included in an all-Britain tourist series titled *Summer over the British Isles.*[23] Another series of tourist programs ran for Northern Ireland listeners in the summer of 1938, *Undiscovered Ulster,* "a series of six talks … on the side of Ulster that does not appear in guidebooks."[24] The culmination of these efforts was *Holiday in Ulster,* a series of four talks, made with the cooperation of "the authorities in Northern Ireland," and broadcast on the National Programme. They were written and delivered by the noted Ulster writer Lynn Doyle.[25]

The desire of the unionist community in Northern Ireland to see Ulster represented as both distinct from Eire and part of the United Kingdom reached its height during the Second World War. For, while Northern Ireland responded to the war with more than its share of recruits and production, the war had the potential to underscore the differences between Northern Ireland and the rest of the United Kingdom. The British state never introduced conscription into Northern Ireland, demonstrating the weakness of the British presence in the province. It might, unionists worried, give the appearance that Northern Ireland was not doing its fair share for the war effort. The fact that key war industries such as steel, coal, and armaments were not located in Northern Ireland exacerbated these anxieties. Finally, the unionist elite feared that the British government might offer Northern Ireland to neutral Eire in return for a declaration of war. This fact made it imperative for unionists to create an image of Ulster as loyal, vital to the war effort, and sharing in the same dangers as London, or Glasgow, or Coventry.

For unionists, the Second World War was an opportunity to reassert their commitment to the British state (unlike the Southern Irish), and the BBC happily accommodated them. Programs such as *Go To It*, *Keep At It*, and *They Went At It*, designed to represent the war effort in Britain's various regions, always included a contribution from Northern Ireland. In *Go To It* and *Keep At It*, listeners overheard the conversations of Belfast factory workers. The programs reflected the official anxiety of the Stormont government in arguing that Northern Ireland contributed to the war effort even though its factories did not churn out tanks, or airplanes, or weapons. "It wouldn't be bad making them [linen tablecloths] just for wages, now—but they say that it's more we're doin' don't they," says one woman worker, while another claims "you can work out *our* war effort based on overtime [emphasis text]." In all of these programs one of the women factory workers has a son serving in the British Expeditionary Force.[26] In another all-regions program, *The Old Country*, the unionist community again asserted their affinity for Britain and willingness to defend their British homeland. In the broadcast, subtitled *The Blue Hills of Antrim*, Scotland, not Eire, is referred to as " [our] nearest neighbor, friend, and kin." The program, broadcast a month after Churchill's "Battle of Britain" speech, also invoked the powerful historical memory of the Spanish Armada. "The Hills of Antrim are not always blue," the narrator of the broadcast concluded, but "in the inky night they show the teeth invaders fear."[27] This mythic moment was even more potent for Northern Ireland because it represented not just deliverance from foreign invasion but also Protestant England's divine deliverance from Catholic Spain. With the inclusion of Northern Ireland in such regional programs, as well as BBC NI's regular contributions to the shared Home Service, *Ulster Magazine* and *Today in Ulster*, BBC NI made British listeners aware of Northern Ireland's commitment to the war effort.

The "Ulsterization" of St Patrick's Day

Talks and magazine programs were the staples of broadcasting in Northern Ireland, but equally important were those programs broadcast annually, to commemorate special holidays or anniversaries. As noted in Chapters 5 and 6 in regard to St Andrew's and St David's Days, the BBC, from its earliest days, committed itself to a policy that public occasions and days of particular significance should be recognized with appropriate program material. This included St Patrick's Day. Because St Patrick was the patron saint of Ireland, BBC Head Office held the opinion that the Belfast station ought to produce a special program in honor of the saint. This proved to be one of the most difficult responsibilities shouldered by BBC NI during period from 1924 to the 1950s. "Saint Patrick" in the words of one BBC producer, was "regarded by a large proportion of their (i.e. northern Ireland's) inhabitants as nothing to do" with the province.[28] Ironically, despite the lack of affection for St Patrick amongst the unionist community, BBC NI continued to prepare and broadcast grandiose programs for March 17. This policy did not represent an attempt to mollify the Catholic minority or find some common cultural ground with Eire. Rather, the staff at BBC NI gave considerable attention to the annual St Patrick's Day broadcast because it represented one of the few opportunities for a program from Northern Ireland to be heard by listeners throughout the British Isles and empire. Regardless of the reason for the program, the unionist establishment wanted them to be of the highest quality so that Northern Ireland was properly represented in the National Programme. Rex Cathcart vividly recounts the anger and resentment a poorly executed St Patrick's Day broadcast could cause in Northern Ireland in the 1930s.[29]

The purpose here in not to rehash Cathcart's discussion of the public reactions to the St Patrick's Day programs produced by BBC NI, but rather to trace their development from broadcasts first designed as nostalgia for Irish emigrants and their descendants throughout the United Kingdom, to programs intended to represent Protestant, unionist, Ulster.[30] Not only did the

St Patrick's Day programs rely less and less on material from Eire, as BBC NI preferred to represent Protestant Ulster, but also, by the late 1940s and early 1950s, the St Patrick's Day broadcasts projected an explicitly unionist ideology. By 1950, references to St Patrick himself in the programs were infrequent or absent altogether.

From the opening of the Belfast station in 1924, the BBC was conscious of the potential problems posed by the St Patrick's Day program. It kept the tone of the program, which usually consisted of representative tunes from Northern and southern Ireland, light. The 1931 broadcast was typical, consisting largely of musical performances relayed from the Ulster Hall in Belfast and St Patrick's (Anglican) Cathedral in Armagh.[31] It was, according to station director Gerald Beadle, little more than "a knock-about variety show."[32] And although the program was uncontroversial and thought to be popular with listeners in England and Scotland, Beadle reported that its content and style grated on listeners in Northern Ireland. The following year, hesitant to offer a similar show, Beadle noted to Head Office that "Irish people are not awfully pleased with the idea of devoting St. Patrick's night to the stuff of which none of them are particularly proud."[33]

BBC NI's approach towards the St Patrick's Day program began to change shortly after the arrival of Marshall at the Belfast station, and he did not waste any time in trying to establish St Patrick's Day as an exclusively Ulster affair. The program, which usually drew on artists from Eire or included a broadcast from Dublin, began to use less and less material from the south. The St Patrick Day's program became Ulsterized and increasingly regarded as an opportunity to provide an aural snapshot of Northern Ireland. After Marshall's first year as Director of the Northern Ireland station, BBC NI proposed a program that some Head Office staff criticized for focusing too much on Belfast and too little on Eire. Lindsay Wellington reassured Marshall that the program was acceptable, although his comments hardly constitute a strong endorsement of the show: "I do not think it inappropriate that the Northern capital should get the lion's share of publicity," adding, in a subsequent memo, "we may be criticized for talking about Belfast at greater length than about Dublin, but … the BBC's connection is with Belfast … [this] is probably sufficient justification."[34] Perhaps encouraged by Wellington's comments, Marshall proposed an even more exclusively Northern Irish program for the following year. Although Marshall's original proposal has been lost, subsequent comments suggest that Marshall wanted the program to largely, if not exclusively, focus on Northern Ireland. Marshall's plans were not favorably received at Head Office. "The St.

Patrick's Day programme was discussed" at Programme Board, wrote Wellington to the Northern Ireland Programme Director, and "it was strongly suggested that it should include some kind of relay from Dublin, [and] *the idea of 'selling Ulster' in any way did not find favor* [emphasis mine]."[35]

Despite this rebuff, BBC NI came back the following year with an ambitious program that again sought to put Ulster at the center of the St Patrick's Day broadcast. Early in 1935, the Northern Ireland Programme Director outlined his ideas for Wellington:

> As to St. Patrick's night itself, we have considered this question very carefully, and are feeling some alarm at the rate at which all the obvious ways of celebrating a Saint's Day are being worked out in the various regions ... What we have in mind this year is to try to give a cross section of Ulster life today, making the occasion for its presentation St. Patrick's Day, rather than trying to present St. Patrick as an emblem of Ireland as a whole. [36]

BBC producers in Northern Ireland further cited the possibility of religious controversy arising out of a program that focused on St Patrick himself, while "anything presenting Ireland as a whole is politically fraught with pitfalls ... [it's] as well to be frankly Ulster." [37] Unlike the previous year, this new program was acceptable to the BBC in London because of Marshall's assurance that it would avoid religious divisiveness and its non-controversial content. Nor did it try to "sell Ulster," in a propagandist manner, which is not to say that it did not appeal to the unionist mind. For one, Eire had no presence in the program, reinforcing the idea of Ulster as a historical community with its own traditions, customs, and patterns of work and leisure. Further, the "range of subjects" that made up the program, based on "those in which Ulster is predominant today," included ship-building, linen, motor racing, rose growing and rope making.[38] BBC NI's Ulster was predominantly modern and industrial, in contradistinction to rural, peasant Eire.

Before the war there was a limit on how far Northern Ireland could Ulsterize the content of the St Patrick's Day program. Buoyed by the acquiescence of London in 1935, Marshall proposed a more overtly unionist program for 1936. Whereas the 1935 broadcast "dealt with the life and industry of the Province of Northern Ireland," the 1936 version was to consider "the character of the Province and the people who live in it." The outline presented by Marshall asserted, "Ulster is part of Great Britain," and proposed a section on the plantation of Ulster and the Scots influence.[39] London quickly scotched Marshall's plans. Telling him to assemble an alternative broadcast, Cecil Graves wrote, "I don't think ... the ... programme is suitable [and] I am sure it is dangerous."[40] BBC NI was reduced to providing a musical variety program for the day, similar to what they had offered in the 1920s. However, in 1938, they put together a rather ambitious broadcast that must have been quite pleasing to unionist ears, a celebration of Ulster that included a trans-Atlantic broadcast by Ulster immigrants in Canada. Like the St Andrew's Day program broadcast by Scotland a few years before, the 1938 St Patrick's Day broadcast ably demonstrated Northern Ireland's contribution to building, and continuing presence in, the empire.

The development of the St Patrick's Day program into a fête for Northern Ireland ended abruptly with the start of the Second World War. As noted above, British propaganda towards Eire was designed to conciliate the south into benevolent neutrality, and perhaps attract recruits for the British armed forces, or at least for British munitions factories.[41] To both BBC Head Office and the Ministry of Information, St Patrick's Day broadcasts appeared to be an ideal opportunity to foster goodwill with Eire, and they demanded that Northern Ireland produce the appropriate material. In 1941 Andrew Stewart, seconded from the BBC to the MOI during the war, asked BBC NI for a St Patrick's Day program "emphasizing the solidarity between the two countries [Eire and Northern Ireland]." "It would be useful," he continued, to show "fraternization and joint celebration along the Ulster border, with British soldiers taking part in local St. Patrick's Day festivities."[42] Marshall was incredulous. His response is worth quoting at length:

> Am I to understand that the suggested programme is to be for both Home and Overseas and that it will [present] Ireland as a whole for, if this is so, I have grave doubts as to how it could be carried out to the satisfaction of all concerned. Northern Ireland is part of the United Kingdom, [and] is quite distinct from Eire (a neutral country). St. Patrick's Day is not celebrated here to any extent, except by the Catholic minority … Apart from the above, am I to understand that the St. Patrick's Day programme is to be composed by this Region? … Miss Eason, as you know, has already written to you regarding this programme and one of the suggestions she made was for the incorporation of a citizen of Eire serving in His Majesties Forces, thereby illustrating the support being given by individuals in that country to the war effort … Any St. Patrick's Day feature in the Home or Overseas Programmes should be confined to Northern Ireland from which we could present something appropriate to the occasion, but not along the lines suggested by MOI. If Eire must be represented, then the programme should, I suggest, be taken from Dublin.[43]

In the end, Marshall agreed to a program produced jointly by BBC NI and Radio Eireann, but he complained to Basil Nicolls and criticized his peers in Dublin.[44]

Marshall and his Programme Director, Ursula Eason, resented the friendly attitude adopted by BBC Head Office towards Eire during the war. In 1942 Eason, in an attempt to refocus the St Patrick's Day program on Northern Ireland, proposed the "Ulster play," *Apollo in Mourne*, and a talk by a Northern Ireland speaker; she suggested Basil Brooke, the future Prime Minister of Northern Ireland, for the *Postscript* to the nine o'clock news. Head Office found these unacceptable, the latter, ironically, because "the date [March 17] is not particularly appropriate to a *N. Ireland* talk [emphasis in original]."[45] In 1943, Marshall, becoming almost paranoid about any implication of cooperation between BBC NI and Eire, fought off a suggestion from BBC Head Office that the St Patrick's Day schedule include a broadcast from the Shamrock Club. Because "the idea of the club is to provide a meeting place and amenities for Irishmen and women, irrespective of whether they come from Northern Ireland or Eire," Marshall worried that "the impression might easily be given in America and Overseas generally that Ireland had united or at least was a stage further in this direction."[46] Instead, the BBC broadcast a play, *St. Patrick Was a Gentleman*. Though Head Office complained that the program was "a humdrum affair [that] lacked any distinction," Marshall reflected, with some relief, that "this was the first St. Patrick's Day program since I came to Northern Ireland eleven years ago that was not greeted with a flood of criticism from one point of view or another."[47]

The war proved to be an only temporary return to lighter, less controversial programs for St Patrick's Day. Not long after the war ended BBC NI returned to producing programs for St Patrick's Day designed specifically for the Protestant unionist community. In 1948, BBC NI staffer Henry McMullan chose to broadcast, on St Patrick's Day, *Lillibulero*, Dennis Johnston's dramatic reconstruction of the Siege of Derry. Johnston's story of the successful, almost miraculous, defense of Derry by Protestant forces against the Catholic King James II in 1689 embittered the Catholic community in Northern Ireland, especially as it was broadcast on March 17. McMullan, who had defended the program, later admitted that broadcasting it on St Patrick's Day was a mistake.[48] But the episode demonstrates the eagerness of BBC NI to get back to making St Patrick's Day a celebration of Ulster, and not, as it had been during the war, an expression of goodwill towards Eire. BBC NI canceled its planned St Patrick's Day programs in 1949, on account of political tensions in Northern Ireland, but in 1950 it came back with an eloquent and thoughtful expression of Ulster unionism, Sam Hanna Bell's *This Is Northern Ireland*.

This Is Northern Ireland was among the finest programs produced by BBC

NI in the first thirty years of its existence. Described by McMullan as "quite the best picture of Northern Ireland which has gone on the air in the last twenty five years," it was first broadcast to celebrate the fifteenth anniversary of the BBC in Northern Ireland.[49] It was innovative in that Bell used the working class to represent Northern Ireland, and he made extensive use of working-class voices in the program.[50] *This Is Northern Ireland* was also one of the first programs made by BBC NI to mention, albeit in passing, the religious divide in Northern Ireland, although it hardly acknowledged the full scope of the discrimination against the Catholic minority.[51] Above all, *This Is Northern Ireland* was a powerful presentation of Ulster nationalism, if not Protestant-ism, and represented the climax of BBC NI's efforts to Ulsterize the St Patrick's Day broadcast. For, not only was Eire expunged altogether from the BBC NI program, *This Is Northern Ireland* represented the statelet as a distinct cultural unit with a common destiny, an organic, historic community. Bell's implicit argument in *This Is Northern Ireland* is that the people of Northern Ireland have more in common with each other than with Catholics or Protestants in Eire, by virtue of their shared Ulsterness.

The opening narration of the program creates for Northern Ireland a natural, well-defined, fixed border; Northern Ireland occupies its own space, distinct from Eire. "This is our map," the program begins:

> Here see is the scalloped border that *binds* our Province. Half of it over moun-tains, loughs and farmlands; half under cliffs, over strands, through the oil and sludge of busy ports. Along the coast of Down, under the feet of Armagh, Tyrone and Fermanagh, over the seaward heads of Derry and Antrim, until it meets and clasps in the city of Belfast … Here the ford is bridged, *the clip clasped* [emphasis mine].[52]

Bell litters *This Is Northern Ireland* with suggestions that the citizens of North-ern Ireland possess a cultural and historical unity more powerful than their sectarian differences. One scene, describing ship workers leaving the Belfast docks, concludes, "they walk, they do not march, for they are not an army, but a People." The program describes Northern Irish speech as having "dryness and economy of words," while the voices of southern Ireland reveal the "cadence and idiom of an older tongue." Turning to religious differences, Bell posits, "it may be only the thickness of a page of India paper that divides us."[53] The broadcast closed as it opened, in Belfast, "the clip clasped," in a passage that more than any other invokes the commonality of all Northern Irish people. *This Is Northern Ireland* concludes: "tonight, where each man stands and looks out, whether it be on darkling lough, or creaming surf, or city street, this is our common heritage—this is Northern Ireland."[54] The shame of *This Is Northern Ireland* is that Bell's message is a liberal re-imagining of a secular Northern Ireland where national and regional loyalties trump religious differences. Unfortunately, in order to construct this image of Northern Ireland, the program must ignore the political and social origins of Catholic discontent, thereby giving legitimacy to the policies of the Stormont regime. Similarly, it must deny the Irish character of the North. In the context of the 1950s Bell's noble call for both communities to recognize their common way of life only gave cultural support to partition and unionism.

Constructing Ulsterness at the BBC: unionist myths and unionist heroes

National history and national myth, the story of the community, its origins, its deliverance from enemies, and its glories, constitute a key facet of national identity.[55] For the unionist community in Northern Ireland two myths were of particular import: the victory of the forces of the Calvinist William III over those of the Catholic James II in the late seventeenth century, and Sir Edward Carson's adamantine opposition to Irish Home Rule in the early twentieth century. Both serve as foundational myths for the unionist community. The events comprising the former, notably the relief of the Siege of Derry and the Battle of the Boyne, preserved Britain's Protestant monarchy and Protestant domination of Ireland; the latter led directly to the creation of the Northern Irish state and the Stormont parliament. Both myths have an atavistic quality, informing events, politics, and social attitudes long after their occurrence. During the 1912–14 Ulster crisis Edward Carson "fabricated a genealogy for … Ulster Unionism by evoking comparisons with William III." Ever since, unionist politicians have tried to present themselves as inheritors of Carson's legacy.[56]

Despite its policy to reflect the culture and traditions of the region it served, the BBC, in London and in Northern Ireland, was reluctant, at first, to celebrate unionist history, especially anything having to do with William III or Carson. The BBC's *modus operandi* in Northern Ireland was to cater to unionist sentiments without provoking the Catholic community. It recognized that programs smacking of Protestant triumphalism would alienate the Catholic population of the province, regardless of how popular they might have been with unionist listeners. Recognizing national holidays or major events caused the BBC few problems in Scotland and Wales, but in Northern Ireland, celebrating the history of the majority meant denigrating the minority, a fact that made the BBC reluctant to broadcast popular unionist events like the celebrations of the Derry Apprentice Boys. This tentativeness demonstrates how problematic it was for the BBC, a British institution that was tolerant (within limits) of political and religious difference, to completely represent sectarian Northern Ireland.

The BBC's policy regarding the Twelfth of July celebrations in honor of William's victory at the Battle of the Boyne changed considerably from the 1930s to the 1950s. Before the Second World War, the BBC, especially Head Office, resisted both public and government pressure to broadcast special programs in honor of the Battle of the Boyne. In a memo that recounts the BBC's history of refusing to mark the Twelfth with special programs, and perhaps reveals Marshall's desire to revise this policy, the Northern Ireland Director explained the situation to Stephen Tallents, the BBC's Controller of Public Relations: "each year, as you probably know, attempts are made to get us to broadcast a commentary on the Twelfth of July procession, and this year even stronger representations were made by such people as Cabinet ministers."[57] Similarly, the BBC received angry letters from listeners and censure from the unionist press in Northern Ireland for failing to suitably recognize the Twelfth. *The Belfast Telegraph*, a frequent critic of the BBC, accused it of neglecting the wishes of its audience while affirming the role of the Twelfth of July celebrations as an important and legitimate expression of British nationalism. "To regard the Orange Order," it claimed,

> merely as a political institution, is to make a grievous fundamental error. Never an Orange demonstration is held without its participants renewing their allegiance to the King and Constitution. Is this a political crime in the eyes of the *British* [emphasis in text] Broadcasting Corporation? If the loyal population of Northern Ireland chooses to express its patriotism through the legitimate form of its "Twelfth" celebrations, what sound and valid reason is there against their interpretation over the air to an interested listening public?[58]

Nevertheless, because of the potential controversy, and violence, the BBC refused to recognize the Twelfth on either the National Programme or the Northern Ireland Regional Programme.

The Second World War saw an important shift in BBC policy towards the Twelfth. No announcement of a formal change in policy came from London, and the Twelfth remained off the list of holidays, circulated by Basil Nicolls, that the BBC was required to recognize—a list that included American Independence Day, Belgian National Day, and Queen Wilhelmina's Birthday.[59] Most likely, the BBC simply wanted to reward, in a small, unofficial way, Northern Ireland's loyalty by finally acknowledging the anniversary of the Battle of the Boyne. The Director of Programme Planning at Head Office notified Marshall in 1941 that in honor of Ulster's "great National Day," (the Twelfth) the BBC was broadcasting "a short programme of Ulster airs."[60] Two years later, the BBC broadcast a program on the Twelfth of July that lauded Northern Ireland's contribution to the war effort. While these programs did not compare, in time or cost, to those the BBC produced for Saint Patrick's Day, they mark an important step in accommodating unionism and popular patriotism.

This trend continued, albeit unevenly, after the war. On July 12, 1950, Lynn Doyle, an experienced broadcaster, gave a talk on his childhood memories of the Twelfth, while a year later the unionist historian Cyril Falls lectured on the Battle of the Boyne.[61] These rather straightforward talks hardly celebrated a bigoted unionism, but they mark a further step by BBC NI in admitting the importance of July Twelfth. Finally, in 1953, the coronation year, BBC NI broadcast what unionists had long asked for—a running commentary of an Orange Parade. After 1953 commentaries on Orange celebrations for the Twelfth became a fixture in the schedule of BBC NI.

The BBC NI's reluctance to give voice to more popular, and less tolerant, forms of unionism extended beyond the Twelfth itself to include programs dealing with the more sectarian aspects of Northern Ireland's history. Despite his status as a national hero, BBC NI neglected to commemorate the legacy of William III with a large-scale feature program. Wales and Scotland made extensive use of their history and tradition as fodder for feature programs. Scotland produced a number of features on the Jacobite rebellions, Mary, Queen of Scots, Wallace, and Robert the Bruce; many Welsh features focused on the local heroes of the mining communities and the Welsh rebel Owain Glyndŵr. In contrast, BBC NI made little use of Ulster's history, particularly moments etched in the collective memory of the Protestant community, for features. The great exception, Denis Johnston's acclaimed *Lillibulero*,[62] demonstrates the extent to which the BBC had to take extraordinary care in the manner in which it represented Northern Ireland.

Johnston's *Lillibulero*, its title taken from a triumphalist Protestant song, recreated the Siege of Derry. The siege, which resulted in the deliverance of the Protestant city from Catholic forces, is among the most important of the unionist's foundational myths. During the Home Rule crisis of 1912, Ulster unionists took up the cry of "no surrender," attributed to the defenders of Derry. The day is still marked in Derry with a march by the Apprentice Boy's clubs, founded in memory of the young men who closed the gates of Derry to James II's Catholic allies in 1688.[63]

When Henry McMullan, the Programme Director for BBC NI, first sent a script of *Lillibulero* to Head Office, it met with immediate approval for its artistry, but concern on political grounds. The Assistant Director of Features told McMullan that reading the script was "almost pure pleasure," and that he would "recommend it most strongly … for inclusion at a suitable time." But, he warned, "how you are going to get it over amongst your own people without an appalling amount of controversy I don't know."[64] The proposed feature quickly came to the attention of the highest levels of management within the BBC. Both the Controller of Programmes and the Controller of Public Relations read the script. The latter liked the program, but was wary of the possible reaction in Northern Ireland. He asked Marshall if the script had the backing of a "reliable authority … such as a Professor of History."[65] Marshall successfully diffused the concerns of Head Office by stressing Johnston's own scholarship and care in constructing the feature. Nevertheless, the BBC's advance publicity for the program reveals the worries of Head Office, as it tried to diffuse any controversy surrounding the program by emphasizing its authenticity and historical objectivity. *Lillibulero,* it proclaimed, "involved six months of research among over 50 works of reference, original documents, papers, in such sources as the National Library of Ireland, the Bodleian, the Derry Cathedral Chapter House, the Linenhall Library and the private papers of the Dean of Derry."[66]

Johnston's *Lillibulero* was the end result of BBC NI's self-perceived role to reflect the image of Northern Ireland held by the unionist community and the Stormont government, but to do so without antagonizing Catholics. Dedicated "to the memory and in honor of the illustrious men who distinguished themselves in the Siege of Londonderry," *Lillibulero* appealed to the national pride of unionists and tapped into the British, as well as regional, aspects of their identity. It began with paean to the sincere loyalty of Ulster during the Glorious Revolution, while stressing the importance of the siege to British history.

> Sixteen hundred and eighty-eight … When William, Prince of Orange, set his foot / Upon the ruddy soil of Devon / and with drum and fife, buckler and sword, invokes / The liberties of England and the Protestant Faith / While yet the prudent Lords of Albion / Lurk in their homes and wait upon event / One corner of these islands sheds the mask / And gives a shout of gladness at his coming. / Far in the cold north-west, Ulstermen gather in the glens / And plan resistance to the sceptered Stuart … These planters gather on their hard-won lands / And rend the bonds of their allegiance.[67]

Although not blatantly bigoted, Johnston portrayed Catholics according to Protestant stereotypes. The "men of the South and West" are "wild laughing men. Warm-hearted fighters galloping to war."[68] Johnston starkly contrasts the character of the southern, Catholic Irish to the "Ulsterman" when he fades the bawdy camp song of James's men into the Reverend Walker's earnest prayer for Derry's deliverance.[69]

The first broadcast of *Lillibulero* was a triumph for BBC NI. Even the Catholic *Irish News* gave it praise. It became one of the most frequently re-broadcast programs BBC NI ever produced; in the domestic services alone it was broadcast twice in 1938, once in 1939, and twice again in 1948. Yet the history of this troublesome program demonstrates how difficult it was for BBC NI to fulfill its "state-building" role in Northern Ireland. BBC NI simply could not tap into Ulster history in the same way that BBC Scotland and BBC Wales mined history for entertaining and meaningful programs.

In 1947 McMullan decided to broadcast a revival of *Lillibulero* for St Patrick's Day, 1948. Although some in the BBC expressed surprise at McMullan's choice, it was the logical consequence of BBC NI's policy, discussed above, to make its big St Patrick's Day program a reflection of Northern Ireland or some aspect of Ulster identity. The Home Service refused to carry it, and Head Office staff remarked that the program was "a very odd choice and nothing whatsoever to do with Saint Patrick." But, given the greater autonomy of the regions after the Second World War, Head Office could not prevent BBC NI from broadcasting *Lillibulero* on March 17.[70] When McMullan offered the program to the other BBC regional stations, they also responded with skepticism. David Gretton, of the Midland region, questioned the decision to "choose Saint Patrick's Day for beating the Orange drum."[71] Nevertheless, all the regional stations broadcast *Lillibulero* on St Patrick's Day 1948.

The public reaction to the broadcast of *Lillibulero* in 1948 was markedly different from the acclaim the program enjoyed in 1939. Gretton was correct to question the wisdom of such a broadcast on St Patrick's Day. Nationalists and Catholics in Northern Ireland regarded the broadcast of *Lillibulero* on St Patrick's Day as an affront and accused BBC NI of "malice," and "belittling those of nationalist sympathies."[72] In contrast, Protestants interpreted the program as a gesture of solidarity with the regime and the unionist world-view. One pleased listener wrote, "the significance of making such a broadcast … will not be lost on the Unionists of Derry and their loyalist friends elsewhere."[73] McMullan later acknowledged his mistake, as well as the danger of dabbling in Northern Ireland's contentious history. "The choice of *Lillibulero*," he admitted in retrospect, "which was fighting Ulster history, was unfortunate for the Saint's day."[74] This was last performance of Johnston's *Lillibulero* on the BBC.

Honoring Edward Carson: the limits of the BBC in constructing Ulster identity

If the BBC was slow to employ unionist history and myth in the form of the Battle of the Boyne and the Siege of Derry, it was even more reluctant to deal with the events of 1912, "the creation myth for Unionism in the twentieth century."[75] As important as the Battle of the Boyne and the Siege of Derry were to unionist history, they were, at least, events of the distant past.[76] The year 1912 was still within the living memory of most people when BBC NI first proposed a feature program on the Ulster Volunteer Force in 1937.[77] Head Office, unsurprisingly, rejected it.

The BBC's refusal to promote the cult of Edward Carson demonstrates again the limits of the BBC's ability to construct a unionist identity in Northern Ireland. Carson was "an Orange icon,"[78] the George Washington of Northern Ireland, and he could not easily be ignored. The unveiling of a statue of Carson before the Stormont parliament in 1933, and his state funeral in 1935, were among the most important ceremonial occasions in Northern Ireland in the 1930s.[79] Yet, as leader of the Ulster Volunteer Force, he organized armed resistance to the British parliament and nearly precipitated a civil war in Ireland. BBC NI's attitude to the popular hero of the unionists remained, at best, equivocal.

As with William III, only more so, any program on Edward Carson was likely to antagonize Northern Ireland's Catholics. When Carson died, BBC NI allowed his successor, Lord Craigavon, to broadcast an appreciation. In his speech the Prime Minister of Northern Ireland referred to Carson as a "patriot" whose "greatest triumph [was] saving Ulster for the Empire."[80] BBC NI also provided live coverage of Carson's state funeral. Yet it was prepared to do little else to mythologize a man who epitomized the sectarian divide in Northern Ireland.

In 1940, the BBC was preparing a series of programs titled *These Men Were Free*. As with so much wartime programming, Head Office wanted to include contributions from all the regions. Ursula Eason suggested Carson for Northern Ireland's contribution, calling him "the obvious man." Anticipating resistance, she articulated, in the most frank language, the unionist vision of Northern Ireland and the BBC's role in the province:

"Trouble" need not be anticipated. Any objections—so far as Ireland is concerned— would come from a small body of irresponsible people whose opinion is worthless and who are, in any case, avowed enemies of England, so they don't matter in the least. The whole loyal population of the six counties would more than welcome a Carson feature.

"It would be hard," she concluded, "to exaggerate the importance of such a feature in Northern Ireland."[81] That Eason even proposed such a program demonstrates the extent to which broadcasters in Northern Ireland adopted the unionist world-view. Her stated justification for the program also shows the extent to which the war, and Eire's neutrality, drove a wedge between BBC NI and the Catholic community. Eason equated Catholic nationalists who opposed the lionization of Carson with traitors before utterly marginalizing them. Head Office's reply in turn reflected their desire to avoid any divisive program material during the war. They rejected Eason's proposal outright, and no Carson feature appeared at any time during the war.

After the war, BBC NI again attempted to honor the unionist hero with a feature program in 1949, but it proved, from its inception, to be a matter of controversy.[82] Although BBC NI originally commissioned Denis Johnston to write a program on Carson, they refused to broadcast it after Johnston delivered the script. McMullan claimed that the station lacked the talent and resources to produce Johnston's Carson feature.[83] He also, in a memo to Laurence Gilliam, accused Johnston of "pulling his punches," and writing a poor program.[84] Johnston was furious at McMullan's attempt to back out of the Carson broadcast. He guessed correctly that it was a matter of timidity on the part of BBC NI. Johnston, commenting on McMullan's refusal of the program to a Features producer in London noted: "when it [BBC NI] says now that it has not got the facilities or the cast, I really must take alarm, because as an old BBC man myself, I know the use that is usually made of that kind of reason, and frankly do not believe that is the real one."[85] Johnston's correspondence also suggests that he did not "pull his punches," as McMullan claimed, but rather the opposite. It seems BBC NI was concerned about how Catholic Northern Ireland might perceive a celebratory program about Carson. "Surely," he wrote to Laurence Gilliam, "a program about Carson ought to be accepted by Northern Ireland as their full responsibility, or else not done at all? Or am I wrong?" A month later Johnston, still upset, wrote a telling letter to Geoffrey Bridson in which he explained that he agreed to write the feature in the "belief that Northern Ireland was at last prepared to go a step further than it did with regard to the Siege of Derry, and tell about its own particular hero."

Johnston refused to consider doing the broadcast from London, a compromise that might have ended the impasse, claiming his program was "intimately the concern of Northern Ireland," and offering to return his fee. He concluded: "A programme on Carson the lawyer and his celebrated cases by all means [could be broadcast from London]. But this is not what I understand is wanted."[86] Johnston's feature, which for him seems to have been a conscious attempt at myth-making for the unionist community, was never broadcast. McMullan can hardly be blamed for his decision. Political tensions in Northern Ireland in 1948 had already convinced him to cancel the region's St Patrick's Day program for 1949.[87] A Carson feature would have only added fuel to the fire.

Conclusion

Although BBC NI served as the voice of the Protestant community in Northern Ireland it could never fully embrace popular unionism. As it evolved in the 1930s and 1940s BBC NI became more willing to explore and project the more overtly political aspects of unionism and Ulster identity, but circumstances meant that certain themes remained off-limits. The fear that sectarian broadcasts really would lead to violence in the streets was an important mitigating factor, as was the fundamental liberalism that characterized the BBC during the first decades of its existence; it proved difficult to harness public service broadcasting to ethno-centrism and religious bigotry. The BBC rightly earned the suspicion of the Catholic community in Northern Ireland, but it often tried to avoid antagonizing the minority, albeit with mixed success.

In several important ways, however, BBC NI reinforced the unionist community's British identity and helped to build a complementary Ulster identity that could be employed to differentiate Northern Ireland from the south. The BBC was a link to the rest of the United Kingdom, one that allowed the Northern Irish to participate in the broader cultural life of Britain; the National Programme and later the Home Service and the Light Programme reinforced their sense of kinship with the rest of the United Kingdom by including them in the imagined community of Britain. And whenever a BBC NI program appeared on one of the other BBC networks it served to remind British listeners that part of Ireland did indeed remain within the United Kingdom. BBC NI also played an important, albeit limited, "state-building" role in Northern Ireland. It was, after all, instituted to reflect the life and culture of the province. Not unlike the BBC's national networks, BBC NI could gather together all the inhabitants of Northern Ireland as listeners into the imagined community of Ulster, an entity it helped to define through its programs. As in Scotland and Wales, the BBC, through its dual structure (with national and "regional" stations) and its programs, encouraged the development of a dual identity in Northern Ireland—both British and Ulster. It is notable that this duality mirrors discourse about identity and political allegiance in contemporary Northern Ireland.[88] This is not to claim a direct causal relationship between BBC programs and the formation of unionist identity, but it does suggest that the BBC, along with other institutions, played a formative role in the creation of the unionist world-view.

Although BBC NI could not go as far as its counterparts in Scotland and Wales, its contribution to forging an identity for Northern Ireland ought not be underestimated. It gave a cohesion, boundedness, and history to a region that only came into existence in 1922. Beginning in the 1930s, it increasingly asserted itself against the intrusions of London and committed itself to providing a more accurate, if still somewhat skewed, representation of Northern Ireland. But, whereas the development of regional broadcasting in Wales and Scotland can be read as a success story, where these regional stations gradually created a certain amount of freedom of action for themselves, Northern Ireland's development towards broadcasting autonomy is marred by the fact that it meant giving in, to a degree, to a more conservative, triumphalist, and bigoted unionism.

Notes

1   On the British self-identity of the Protestants of Northern Ireland, see James Loughlin, *Ulster and British National Identity* (London: Pinter, 1995).

2   *Radio Times*, November 9, 1935, 455.

3   Rex Cathcart, *The Most Contrary Region: The BBC in Northern Ireland* (Belfast: Blackstaff, 1984), 36.

4   Brian Graham, "The Place of Ulster: Alternate Loyalist Identities," in *History, Nationhood, and the Question of Britain*, Brocklehurst and Phillips, eds, 99–111.

5   On the neutrality of Eire during the Second World War, see Dermot Keogh and Mervyn O'Driscoll, eds, *Ireland in the Second World War: Neutrality and Survival* (Douglas Village, Cork: Mercier, 2004); T. Ryle Dwyer, *Irish Neutrality and the USA, 1939–47* (Totowa, NJ: Rowan and Littlefield, 1977). For Northern Ireland during the war, see John W. Blake, *Northern Ireland in the Second World War* (Belfast: Blackstaff Press, 2001); Brian Barton, *The Blitz: Belfast in the War Years* (Belfast: Blackstaff Press, 1989).

6   July 12 marks the anniversary of the Battle of the Boyne, in which the Protestant William of Orange defeated the Catholic James II in a decisive battle. It is one of the most important festivals for the Protestant community in Northern Ireland,

and is celebrated with triumphalist marches routed, in the past, through tradition-ally Catholic neighborhoods.

7 Cathcart, 169. See also Heather Clark, "Regional Roots: The BBC and Poetry in Northern Ireland, 1945–55," *Eire-Ireland: Journal of Irish Studies*, 38 (2003): 87–105.

8 *BBC Yearbook 1930*, 111

9 Memo, Northern Ireland Programme Director to Richard Maconachie, October 2, 1936, BBC WAC, R51/356/1.

10 Memo, Northern Ireland Programme Director to George Barnes, September 6, 1937, BBC WAC, R51/356/2.

11 Cathcart, 129.

12 *World At Work*, BBC WAC, Northern Ireland Regional Scripts, Reel 126/127.

13 Oliver MacDonagh, *States of Mind: Two Centuries of Anglo-Irish Conflict* (London: Pimlico, 1992), 26–7.

14 Loughlin, 142–4. Rodgers worked in the Features Department of BBC NI from 1946 to 1952 and after continued to contribute to BBC programmes as a script-writer and performer.

15 On partition, and the efforts of the Protestants of Derry, Cavan and Monaghan to be included in the new Northern Irish state, see Michael Laffan, *The Partition of Ireland* (Dundalk: Dundalgan Press, 1983).

16 Cathcart, 5. On Irish broadcasting, see Richard Pine, *2RN and the Origins of Irish Radio* (Dublin: Four Courts Press, 2002); John Horgan, *Irish Media: A Critical History* (London: Routledge, 2001), 6–76; Martin McLoone, ed., *Culture, Iden-tity, and Broadcasting in Ireland* (Belfast: Institute of Irish Studies, 1991); Maurice Gorham, *Forty Years of Irish Broadcasting* (Dublin: Talbot Press, 1967).

17 George Marshall to Maconachie, June 2, 1937, BBC WAC, R51/356/2.

18 Martin McLoone, "The Construction of a Partitionist Mentality: Early Broad-casting in Ireland," in *Broadcasting in a Divided Community: Seventy Years of the BBC in Northern Ireland*, McLoone, ed. (Belfast: Queen's University Press, 1996). McLoone's essay examines the process by which two separate broadcasting authori-ties were established in Ireland, the BBC and Radio Eireann.

19 Charles Siepmann to Gerald Beadle, December 28, 1934, BBC WAC, R51/356.

20 Marshall to Maconachie, January 11, 1937, BBC WAC, R51/356/2.

21 Marshall to Maconachie, January 29, 1937, Ibid.

22 Loughlin, 108–10.

23 Maconachie to Marshall, April 19, 1937; Laurence Gilliam to Director of Program Planning, June 18, 1937, BBC WAC, R51/356/2.

24 Northern Ireland Programme Director to Maconachie, June 24, 1938, Ibid.

25 Northern Ireland Programme Director to Director of Programme Planning, November 8, 1938, Ibid.

26 *Go To It*; *Keep At It*, BBC WAC, Northern Ireland Regional Scripts, Reel 144/145.

27 *The Old Country: The Blue Hills of Antrim*, Ibid.

28 Moray McLaren to Gilliam, May 29, 1937, BBC WAC, R34/239/2.

29 Cathcart, 44, 63–4.

30 This was not unlike the process by which the St David's and St Andrew's Day programs developed into days for the expression of Welsh and Scottish patriotism. See Chapters 5 and 6.

31 *Radio Times*, March 13, 1931, 637.

32 Beadle to Lindsay Wellington, March 23, 1931, BBC WAC, R34/239/1.

33 Beadle to Wellington, November 24, 1931, Ibid. Beadle's exact meaning is unclear. He is referring most likely to the fact that the show appeared too vulgar or lowbrow to BBC NI's middle-class listeners. However, it might be a reference to the inclusion of "southern Irish" material in the program.

34 Wellington to Marshall, February 13, 1933; February 23, 1933, Ibid.

35 Wellington to Mair, January 17, 1934, BBC WAC, R34/239/2. See also Program Board Minutes, January 16, 1934, BBC WAC, R34/600/6.

36 Northern Ireland Programme Director to Wellington, January 15, 1935, BBC WAC, R34/239/2.

37 Ibid.

38 Ibid.

39 J. T. Sutthery to Cecil Graves, January 1936, Ibid.

40 Graves to Marshall, January 24, 1936, Ibid.

41 On BBC propaganda for Eire during the war, see BBC WAC, R34/371/1 and R34/371/2. See also Cathcart, 114–17.

42 Andrew Stewart to Godfrey Adams, January 25, 1941, BBC WAC, R34/239/3.

43 Marshall to Adams, January 29, 1941, Ibid.

44 Marshall to Basil Nicolls, March 18, 1941, Ibid.

45 Ursula Eason to Nicolls, January 16, 1942; Eason to Barnes, January 16, 1942; Barnes to Maconachie, January 16, 1942, Ibid. It should be noted that Brooke, as well as Northern Ireland Prime Ministers Lord Craigavon and J. M. Andrews, were given several opportunities to broadcast during the war.

46 Marshall to Adams, January 25, 1943, Ibid.

47 Adams to Marshall, March 20, 1943; Marshall to Adams, March 23, 1943, Ibid.

48 See below.

49 Henry McMullan to Wellington, October 27, 1949, BBC WAC, NI4/197/2. Bell's biographer, Sean McMahon, includes it as one of Bell's finest pieces. See Sean McMahon, *Sam Hanna Bell, A Biography* (Belfast: Blackstaff: 1999).

50 Some members of the audience, reported BBC Listener Research, "thought the broadcast concentrated too much on the geographical and industrial aspects [of Northern Ireland], to the exclusion of the historic and the legendary." Listener Research Report LR/50/570, *This Is Northern Ireland*, March 29, 1950, Ibid.

51 *This Is Northern Ireland* includes the following description of Armagh: "Armagh, ecclesiastical capital of Ireland, with its two Cathedrals, Protestant and Roman Catholic, raised over against each other on opposing hills, like the horns of a dilemma … we are a dogmatic churchgoing people, knowing not only why we go to our places of worship, but why we don't go to that of our neighbours." *This Is Northern Ireland*, BBC WAC, Script Library, 12.

52 Ibid, 1.

53 Ibid, 3, 11, 12.

54 Ibid, 37.

55 Anthony Smith, *National Identity* (London: Penguin, 1991), 36–41.

56 Alvin Jackson, "Unionist Myths 1912–1985," *Past and Present*, 136 (1992): 170.

57 Marshall to Stephen Tallents, June 23, 1939, BBC WAC, R34/224.

58 *Belfast Telegraph*, June 22, 1939. See Ibid.

59 Nicolls, circulating memo, n.d., BBC WAC, R34/190/3.

60 Adams to Marshall, May 31, 1941, BBC WAC, R34/347/1.

61 See BBC WAC, Northern Ireland Regional Scripts, Reel 128.

62 According to Cathcart, *Lillibulero* was "hailed as … 'the most ambitious radio pro-
    gramme ever to be produced in Belfast.'" Cathcart, 82.

63 William Kelly, ed., *The Sieges of Derry* (Dublin: Four Courts Press, 2001); Ian
    McBride, *The Siege of Derry in Ulster Protestant Mythology* (Dublin: Four Courts
    Press, 1997).

64 McLaren to McMullan, January 3, 1938, BBC WAC, R19/660.

65 Tallents to Nicolls, January 24, 1938, Ibid.

66 Marshall to Assistant Controller (Public Relations), March 8, 1938, Ibid.

67 *Lillibulero*, BBC WAC, Northern Ireland Regional Scripts, Reel 144.

68 Ibid.

69 Ibid. Walker's prayer reads: "Hear, Lord, O hear the cries of the hungry and thirsty
    that daily call upon thee within these walls. And send us relief, O Lord, and timely
    redemption in this out time of trouble. That we may yet live to praise thy holy
    name for all thy miraculous deliverances to this city."

70 McMullan to Wellington, November 27, 1947, BBC WAC, R34/239/3.

71 David Gretton to McMullan, January 20, 1948, BBC WAC, NI4/118/6.

72 See BBC WAC, NI4/118/7.

73 Letter, M. W. Dewar, to BBC, March 17, 1948, BBC WAC, NI4/118/7.

74 McMullan to Stewart, November 7, 1949, BBC WAC, NI4/197/2.

75 Jackson, 166.

76 Ursula Eason tartly noted, "The fact that Carson lived more recently than Wolfe
    Tone makes little difference in this country where people's memories are long and
    where, in Northern Ireland at any rate, political feeling still hinges on the Battle of
    the Boyne in 1688." BBC WAC, R19/839/1.

77 See BBC WAC R19/1534.

78 Jackson, 166.

79 McIntosh, 36–50.

80 *Broadcast Appreciation of the Late Lord Carson*, BBC WAC, Northern Ireland
    Regional Scripts, Reel 118/119.

81 Eason to Gilliam, September 17, 1940, BBC WAC, R19/839/1.

82 The following is based on BBC WAC, Rcont, Johnston, Denis.

83 Denis Johnston to Geoffrey Bridson, August 18, 1949, Ibid.

84 McMullan to Gilliam, July 21, 1949, Ibid.

85 Johnston to Bridson, August 18, 1949, Ibid.

86 Ibid.

87 See BBC WAC, NI4/197/2.

88 Graham, "The Place of Ulster;" John McGarry and Brendan O'Leary, *Explaining Northern Ireland: Broken Images* (Oxford: Blackwell Publishers, 1995), 105–21; Jennifer Todd, "The Limits of Britishness," *The Irish Review*, 5 (1988): 11.

Conclusion

In October 1955, Harman Grisewood, the BBC's Director of the Spoken Word, presented a paper, "The Status of the BBC as the National Instrument of Broadcasting in the United Kingdom," to the BBC's Board of Management. The paper provides a window into the mind-set of the upper echelons of the BBC in the mid-1950s. Two facets of Grisewood's paper stand out: his insistence on the special role of the BBC in society but also his concern about the challenge of commercial television. Grisewood insisted on the distinctiveness of the BBC, particularly because of its status as a public service corporation. For Grisewood, the BBC's nature and purpose were intimately bound to the idea of the nation, and rooted in its history of projecting and preserving national culture. The BBC, Grisewood concluded, should continue to "serve the national interest at all points—throughout the wide range of every diverse activity and enjoyment which broadcasting can reflect and stimulate."[1] In a follow-up memo, he expounded similar opinions:

> Our status should be that of a *unique* [emphasis text] organization ... We alone devote all our resources—money, skill, and energy—to good broadcasting. We have no other motive ... We alone among broadcasting agencies in Britain exist to serve the national interest ... since all we do—entertainment, information, education—is done in the service of the public and with no other interest in view.[2]

For Grisewood, the uniqueness of the BBC was to be found in its public service mission, but his idea of public service was very much bound to the idea of Britishness. Grisewood claimed that, unlike commercial television, the BBC played an important role in education and it continued to coordinate propaganda campaigns with the government. The BBC, he also noted, remained responsible for the Overseas Services, which broadcast to the world "on behalf of Britain."[3] Finally, the BBC was, in Grisewood's words, the "interpreter of the British genius."[4]

Yet Grisewood's assertions reveal not confidence but rather anxiety about the position of the BBC. As he saw it, the arrival of commercial broadcasting had completely altered the landscape of broadcasting in Britain and undermined the importance of the BBC in the eyes of the public. Above all, Grisewood wanted to remind the government and the Director-General, Ian Jacob, of the BBC's public service mission. He pressed Jacob to obtain official recognition from the government of the BBC's special status, hardly a sign of self-assurance. Grisewood's greatest fear was that the public "may come to think of the BBC as little more than the non-commercialised alternative to the I.T.A. [Independent Television Authority]"[5]

Subsequent events would prove that Grisewood was right in sounding the tocsin about the challenge of commercial broadcasting.[6] Less than a year after Grisewood presented his paper, 1.5 million viewers could receive ITV; by 1960, over 10 million had access to ITV. Worse for the BBC, those who were able to receive both stations overwhelmingly chose ITV. In September 1957, Kenneth Clark, the Chairman of the Independent Television Authority, claimed that the ratio of ITV viewers to BBC viewers was 79 to 21. Because ITV dominated in terms of viewership, competition had an enormous impact on the BBC. In order to justify its receipt of the license fee, the BBC had to become more competitive with ITV in terms of audience share. To the horror of an old hand like Grisewood, the BBC accomplished this by imitating the populist fare of ITV. Ironically, the very thing that enabled Reith to adopt policies of mixed programming and cultural uplift—the license fee—forced the BBC to further modify its idea of "public service" and abandon what remained of its Reithian principles. Competition, as Grisewood suspected, undermined the BBC's authority to represent Britishness: broadcasting in Britain no longer spoke with one voice.

From its founding in 1922 until its monopoly was broken in 1954, the BBC was the central site where national identity in Britain was produced, projected, and contested. Due to its nature and structure, the BBC did project a unitary and consensual version of Britishness. The BBC's national networks, the pre-war National Programme and the post-war Light Programme, reached nearly every corner of the British Isles. Through these networks, the BBC reinforced Britishness by creating a community of listeners who could experience programs, especially important national events, simultaneously. In the age of radio Britishness meant, in part, paying your license fee and listening to the BBC.

The very name of the network, the British Broadcasting Corporation, provided a gentle but constant reminder to listeners of their membership in the British nation.[7]

The national structure of the BBC was also reflected in its program policy, which could be said to be officially unionist. Programs that seemed to question the essential unity of Britain were heavily scrutinized, edited, or simply disallowed. Discussion of Scottish and Welsh nationalism had to be carefully balanced with unionist voices. Any program that even remotely called into question the constitutional status of Northern Ireland and its relation to Eire would never make it on the air. The BBC also placed great importance on broadcasting for national holidays and state occasions. Every year the BBC provided special broadcasts for Empire Day, Armistice Day, Christmas, as well as a host of other noteworthy anniversaries with national significance such as Trafalgar Day and Shakespeare's birthday.

The BBC also constructed a unitary British national identity by its extensive promotion of empire. Empire programs reminded Britons of their shared heritage and destiny. Further, the BBC, like other forms of popular culture, presented empire as the representative achievement of the British character. Imperialism was the natural outgrowth of British pluck, courage, and racial superiority. The BBC's promotion of empire in its programs, well into the 1950s, strongly suggests that imperialism remained an integral part of Britishness for longer than most scholarship recognizes. Imperial culture in Britain was not critically undermined by the First World War or even the Second World War. Rather, new media such as cinema and radio perpetuated imperialism "at home." Even after Indian independence, empire, in variegated forms, remained entrenched in the BBC's schedules, from discussions of imperial policy on the Third Programme to adaptations of juvenile fiction into radio serials on the Light Programme. The BBC may not have educated its listeners about empire, but it did help to maintain empire as a central part of the British world-view.

Monarchy served a similar function for the BBC. The BBC's coverage of the deaths of George V and George VI and coronations of George VI and Elizabeth II was extensive, with coronation-related programs appearing several weeks or even months before the actual events. Other important moments for the monarchy, from the opening of the Empire Exhibition to the royal tour of Africa, received similar, fawning attention. Further, the BBC did not merely promote the monarchy, it did so in a way that emphasized its role in symbolizing the national diversity of Britain. As with empire, the BBC stressed the ways in which monarchy unified Britain due to its historic ties to Scotland, Wales, and Northern Ireland. In supporting the monarchy, the BBC helped to construct a consensual and tolerant sense of Britishness that was inclusive of all of the peoples of Britain.

To argue that the BBC was committed to a unitary Britishness centered on the empire and the monarchy is not, however, to argue that the BBC projected an anglicized or homogenized Britishness that conflicted with or subsumed other regional or local identities. In contrast to the prevailing scholarship, this book has argued that the BBC constructed Britishness as an inclusive, pluralistic identity and that the Corporation created spaces for the expression of multiple national identities in Britain. The BBC made room for these alternative expressions of national identity in Scotland, Wales, and Northern Ireland through its structure and its programs. The fact that the BBC established high-power regional stations in Scotland, Wales, and Northern Ireland was itself a recognition of Britain's national diversity. Like the BBC's National Programme, these stations strengthened national identity in the regions by providing them with an institution purpose-built for the expression of their national-regional culture and by creating bounded communities of listeners in these areas. This was especially important in Wales, which, other than its National Library in Aberystwyth, had few national institutions, and Northern Ireland, whose very creation as a political unit preceded the establishment of the BBC by only a year. Even in Scotland, which retained its own educational system, legal code, and established Church, the very existence of BBC Scotland served to reinforce distinctions between Scotland, England, and Britain.

In addition to bringing into being new national listening-communities in Scotland, Wales, and Northern Ireland, the BBC also mined the geography, history, and culture of the regions for its programs. There were certainly debates about whether or not regional broadcasting accurately reflected life in the regions. Like the BBC in London, regional broadcasters often brought middle-class biases to their programs. And regional broadcasters were acutely aware of the dangers of becoming too provincial. Similarly, nationalists in both Wales and Scotland proved to be the harshest critics of the BBC, regarding it as a threat to the national language or culture of Wales or Scotland. The regional BBCs, in their opinion, were poor substitutes for the fully independent broadcasting organizations that Wales and Scotland, as nations, merited.

That said, it is perhaps best not to give too much weight to the opinions of Scottish and Welsh nationalists when assessing the BBC's projection of British (and Welsh, Scottish, and Northern Irish) national identity. By the late 1930s, the regional networks in Scotland, Wales, and Northern Ireland offered a range of programs, during most of the peak evening listening hours, designed to reflect the life of their regions. These programs were not overtly nationalist, but they did not have to be. Something as simple as a series of programs on tourism in Scotland, Wales, or Northern Ireland powerfully reinforced for regional listeners that the mountains, rivers, and lakes described in such programs were *their* mountains, *their* rivers, *their* lakes. Such broadcasts, along with history programs, celebrations of national holidays, and radio adaptations of the work of famous regional authors and writers, created a sense of space, place, and community for regional listeners.

It would be misleading to argue that the BBC, during the first thirty years of its existence, strengthened or undermined Britishness. Rather, the BBC reinforced a particular kind of Britishness, and in doing so, it helped to transform it, pushing the boundaries of what it meant to be British. The BBC made British national identity more flexible and accommodating of the diversity of the peoples of the British Isles. It particularly helped to reinforce the dual identities so characteristic of Britons during the twentieth century. In providing national radio networks to British listeners the BBC enabled any Briton to partake in British life; but by providing the regional networks the BBC also made room for expression of Scottishness, Welshness, or Ulsterness. Furthermore, the connection of regional broadcasting to the larger BBC structure prevented regional broadcasting from sinking into a kind of insular provincialism. A weighty amount of scholarship has focused on the ways in which the BBC standardized certain aspects of British culture. For example, the BBC's insistence, until the Second World War, that its announcers and newsreaders use only received pronunciation is often cited as an example of broadcasting's attempt to create a uniform version of English, as well as its middle-class and metropolitan biases. While there is more than a grain of truth to these arguments, more consideration must be given to the ways in which the BBC helped to refashion Britishness and British institutions such as the empire and especially the monarchy in ways that increasingly recognized the multi-national character of Britain.

Scholars of nationalism often comment that the weakness of Britishness is that, unlike Englishness, it does not correspond to any ethnic community. Tom Nairn's derisive reference to Britain as "Yookay" and "Ukania," is emblematic of such criticisms.[8] But what has been often regarded as a weakness might prove to be the greatest strength of Britishness. As Britain continues to evolve into a multi-cultural society, Britishness may become increasingly important.

Members of Britain's West Indian and Asian communities, or more recent immigrants from Europe and Africa, who could find it difficult to embrace ethnically based identities such Englishness or Scottishness, might be able to accommodate themselves to the more institutionally based national identity that Britishness offers. And these are, much like those of the Scottish and Welsh, dual identities—Black British or British-Asian—reaffirming the historic function of Britishness in integrating the various communities of Britain. Undoubtedly the BBC will play a central role in the continuing evolution of Britishness, whether by giving greater freedom to the regional BBCs in the wake of political devolution in Scotland, Wales, and Northern Ireland, or by providing more programs and opportunities for members of the Black and Asian communities in Britain.

Notes

1 Harman Grisewood, "The Status of the BBC as the National Instrument of Broadcasting in the United Kingdom," October 22, 1955, Barnes Papers, File Misc 72/58, Archive Centre, King's College, Cambridge.

2 Grisewood to Ian Jacob, November 7, 1955, Ibid.

3 Ibid.

4 Grisewood, "Status of the BBC," Ibid.

5 Ibid.

6 For British broadcasting after the end of the BBC monopoly, see Briggs, *Competition*. See also Colin Seymour-Ure, *The British Press and Broadcasting Since 1945* (Oxford: Basil Blackwell, 1991); Bernard Sendall, *Independent Television in Britain*, vol. 1, *Origin and Foundation 1946–1962* (London: Macmillan, 1982); Curran and Seaton, 159–234; Crisell, 89–104.

7 For the ways in which mass media provide subtle but powerful reminders of nationhood, see Michael Billig, *Banal Nationalism* (London: Sage, 1995).

8 Tom Nairn, *The Break-up of Britain*, 2nd ed. (London: Verso, 1994).

Select bibliography

Archives

BBC Written Archives Centre, Caversham.
British Library, A. P. A. C., India Office Records, London.
Archive Centre, King's College, Cambridge.
Churchill College Archives, Cambridge.
The National Archives: Public Records Office, Kew.

Newspapers and journals

Listener, The
Radio Times

Printed primary sources

BBC Annual
BBC Handbook
BBC Yearbook
Black, Peter. *The Biggest Aspidistra in the World*. London: British Broadcasting Corporation, 1972.
Bridson, Geoffrey. *Prospero and Ariel*. London: Gollancz, 1972.
Burnett, George, ed. *Scotland on the Air*. Edinburgh: Moray Press, 1938.
Eckersley, Peter. *The Power Behind the Microphone*. London: Jonathan Cape, 1941.
Eckersley, Roger. *The BBC and All That*. Marston, 1946.
Gamlin, Lionel. *You're on the Air: A Book about Broadcasting*. London: Chapman and Hall, 1947.
George VI. *George VI to His Peoples, 1936–1951: Selected Broadcasts and Speeches*. London: John Murray, 1952.
Gilliam, Laurence. *BBC Features*. London: Evans Brothers, 1950.
Grisewood, Freddy. *My Story of the BBC*. London: Odhams Press, 1959.
Lambert, R. S. *Ariel and All His Quality*. London: Victor Gollancz, 1940.
Lockhart, Howard. *On My Wavelength*. Aberdeen: Impulse Books, 1973.
Orwell, George. *Burmese Days*. San Diego: Harcourt Brace and Company, 1962.

Reith, J. C. W. *Broadcast Over Britain*. London: Hodder and Stoughton, 1924.
——. *Into the Wind*. London: Hodder & Stoughton, 1949.
——. *The Reith Diaries*. Charles Stuart, ed. London: Collins, 1975.
Silvey, Robert. *Who's Listening? The Story of BBC Audience Research*. London: George Allen and Unwin, 1974

Secondary Sources

Anderson, Benedict. *Imagined Communities: Reflections on the Origin and Spread of Nationalism*. London: Verso, 1986.
Ascherson, Neal. *Stone Voices: The Search for Scotland*. New York: Hill and Wang, 2004.
Avery, Todd. *Radio Modernism: Literature, Ethics, and the BBC, 1922–1938*. Aldershot, Hampshire: Ashgate, 2006.
Barton, Brian. *The Blitz: Belfast in the War Years*. Belfast: Blackstaff Press, 1989.
Bell, Ian. "Publishing, Journalism and Broadcasting." In *Scotland: A Concise History*. Paul H. Scott, ed. (Edinburgh: Mainstream Publishing, 1993).
Billig, Michael. *Banal Nationalism*. London: Sage, 1995.
Bivona, Daniel. *British Imperial Literature: Writing and the Administration of Empire*. Cambridge: Cambridge University Press, 1998.
Blake, John W. *Northern Ireland in the Second World War*. Belfast: Blackstaff Press, 2001.
Bourke, Joanna. "Heroes and Hoaxes: The Unknown Warrior, Kitchener and 'Missing Men' in the 1920s." *War and Society*, 13 (1995): 41–63.
Boyle, Andrew. *Only the Wind Will Listen: Reith of the BBC*. London: Hutchinson, 1972.
Bradford, Sarah. *The Reluctant King: The Life and Reign of George VI 1895–1952*. New York: St Martin's Press, 1989.
Bradshaw, Brendan, and Peter Roberts, eds. *British Consciousness and Identity, 1533–1707*. Cambridge: Cambridge University Press, 1998.
Brewer, Susan. *To Win the Peace: British Propaganda in the United States During World War II*. Ithaca NY: Cornell University Press, 1997.
Briggs, Asa. *The History of Broadcasting in the United Kingdom*, 5 vols.—1. *The Birth of Broadcasting;* 2. *Sound and Vision;* 3. *The War of Words;* 4. *The Golden Age of Wireless;* 5. *Competition*. Oxford: Oxford University Press, 1961–95.
——. "Local and Regional in Northern Sound Broadcasting." *Northern History*, 10 (1975): 165–87.
——. "Problems and Possibilities in the Writing of Broadcast Histories." *Media, Culture, and Society*, 2 (1980): 5–13.
——. *The BBC: The First Fifty Years*. Oxford: Oxford University Press, 1985.
Brocklehurst, Helen, and Robert Phillips, eds. *History, Nationhood and the Question of Britain*. Basingstoke: Palgrave Macmillan, 2004.
Brockliss, Laurence, and David Eastwood, eds. *A Union of Multiple Identities: The British Isles, 1750–1850*. Manchester: Manchester University Press, 1997.
Browne, Donald R. "Radio Normandie and the IBC Challenge to the BBC Monopoly." *Historical Journal of Film, Radio and Television*, 5 (1985): 3–18.
Brubaker, Rogers. *Nationalism Reframed: Nationhood and the National Question in the*

New Europe. New York: Cambridge University Press, 1997.

Bruce, Steve. *The Edge of the Union: The Ulster Loyalist Political Vision*. Oxford: Oxford University Press, 1994.

Burton, Antoinette. *Burdens of History: British Feminists, Indian Women, and Imperial Culture, 1865–1915*. Chapel Hill, NC: University of North Carolina Press, 1994.

——, ed. *After the Imperial Turn: Thinking With and Through the Nation*. Durham, NC: Duke University Press, 2003.

Butler, L. J. *Britain and Empire: Adjusting to a Post-Imperial World*. London: I. B. Tauris, 2002

Calder, Angus. *The People's War*. London: Jonathan Cape, 1969.

——. *The Myth of the Blitz*. London: Pimlico, 1992.

Cannadine, David. *Ornamentalism: How the British Saw Their Empire*. Oxford: Oxford University Press, 2001.

Cardiff, David, and Paddy Scannell, "Radio in World War II." *U203 Popular Culture*, Block 2 Unit 8. Milton Keynes: The Open University Press, 1981.

Castle, Kathryn. *Britannia's Children: Reading Colonialism Through Children's Books and Magazines*. Manchester: Manchester University Press, 1996.

Cathcart, Rex. *The Most Contrary Region: The BBC in Northern Ireland*. Belfast: Blackstaff, 1984.

Clark, Heather. "Regional Roots: The BBC and Poetry in Northern Ireland, 1945–55." *Eire-Ireland: Journal of Irish Studies*, 38 (2003): 87–105.

Colley, Linda. "Britishness and Otherness: An Argument." *Journal of British Studies*, 31 (1992): 309–29.

——. *Britons: Forging the Nation 1707–1837*. London: Pimlico, 1992.

Colls, Robert. *Identity of England*. Oxford: Oxford University Press, 2004.

Crisell, Andrew. *An Introductory History of British Broadcasting*. 2nd ed. London: Routledge, 2002.

Cull, Nicholas John. *Selling War: The British Propaganda Campaign Against American Neutrality in World War II*. Oxford: Oxford University Press, 1995.

Curran, James, and Jean Seaton. *Power Without Responsibility: The Press, Broadcasting, and the New Media in Britain*. 6th ed. London: Routledge, 2003.

Davies, John. *A History of Wales*. London: Penguin, 1993.

——. *Broadcasting and the BBC in Wales*. Cardiff: University of Wales Press, 1994.

Davies, Norman. *The Isles: A History*. New York: Oxford University Press, 1999.

Dwyer, T. Ryle. *Irish Neutrality and the USA: 1939–47*. Totowa, NJ: Rowan and Littlefield, 1977.

Ellis, John S. "Reconciling the Celt: British National Identity, Empire, and the 1911 Investiture of the Prince of Wales." *Journal of British Studies*, 37 (1998): 391–418.

Ellwood, David W, and Rob Kroes, eds. *Hollywood in Europe: Experiences of Cultural Hegemony*. Amsterdam: VU University Press, 1994.

English, Richard, and Graham Walker, eds. *Unionism in Modern Ireland: New Perspectives on Politics and Culture*. New York: St Martin's Press, 1996.

Finlay, Richard J. "'For or Against?': Scottish Nationalists and the British Empire." *Scottish Historical Review*, 71 (1992): 184–206.

——. "Pressure Group or Political Party?: The Nationalist Impact on Scottish Politics." *Twentieth Century British History*, 3 (1992): 274–97.

——. *Independent and Free: Scottish Politics and the Origin of the Scottish National Party 1918–1945*. Edinburgh: John Donald Publishers, 1994.

————. "The Rise and Fall of Popular Imperialism in Scotland, 1850–1950." *Scottish Geographical Magazine*, 113 (1997): 13–21.

Forsyth, David S. "Empire and Union: Imperial and National Identity in Nineteenth-Century Scotland." *Scottish Geographical Magazine*, 113 (1997): 6–12.

Geertz, Clifford. *The Interpretation of Cultures: Selected Essays*. New York: Basic Books, 1973.

Gellner, Ernest. *Nations and Nationalism*. Ithaca, NY: Cornell University Press, 1983.

Gorham, Maurice. *Forty Years of Irish Broadcasting*. Dublin: Talbot Press, 1967.

Grant, Alexander, and Keith Stringer, eds. *Uniting the Kingdom? The Making of British History*. London: Routledge, 1995.

Greenfield, Liah. *Nationalism: Five Roads to Modernity*. Cambridge MA: Harvard University Press, 1992.

Hajkowski, Thomas. "The BBC, the Empire, and the Second World War." *Historical Journal of Film Radio and Television*, 22 (2002): 135–56.

Hajkowski, Thomas. "Red on the Map: Empire and Americanization at the BBC." In Joel Wiener and Mark Hampton, *Anglo-American Media Interactions*. Basingstoke: Palgrave, 2007.

Hall, Catherine, ed. *"White, Male, and Middle Class:" Explorations in Feminism and History*. London: Routledge, 1992.

————. *Cultures of Empire: A Reader*. New York: Routledge, 2000.

————. *Civilising Subjects: Metropole and Colony in the English Imagination, 1830–1867*. Chicago: University of Chicago Press, 2002.

Harling, Philip. "The Centrality of Locality: The Local State, Local Democracy, and Local Consciousness in Late-Victorian and Edwardian Britain." *Journal of Victorian Culture*, 9 (2004): 216–34.

Harvey, Sylvia, and Kevin Robins, eds. *The Regions, the Nations and the BBC*. London: British Film Institute, 1993.

Harvie, Christopher. *Scotland and Nationalism: Scottish Society and Politics, 1707 to the Present*. London: Routledge, 1995.

Hechter, Michael. *Internal Colonialism: The Celtic Fringe in British National Development*. Berkeley, CA: University of California Press, 1975.

Heyck, T. W., and Stanford Lehmberg. *The Peoples of the British Isles: A New History*. 3 vols. Belmont, CA: Wadsworth, 1992.

Hobsbawm, Eric. *Nations and Nationalism Since 1780: Programme, Myth, Reality*. Cambridge: Cambridge University Press, 1990.

Hobsbawm, Eric, and Terence Ranger, eds. *The Invention of Tradition*. Cambridge: Cambridge University Press, 1983.

Jackson, Alvin. "Unionist Myths 1912–1985." *Past and Present*, 136 (1992): 164–85.

James, Lawrence. *The Rise and Fall of the British Empire*. New York: St Martin's Press, 1996.

Jenkins, Geraint H. and J. Beverley Smith, eds. *Politics and Society in Wales, 1840–1922*. Cardiff: University of Wales Press, 1988.

Kaul, Chandrika. "Monarchical Display and the Politics of Empire: Princes of Wales and India 1870–1920s." *Twentieth Century British History*, 17 (2006): 464–88.

————, ed. *Media and the British Empire*. Basingstoke: Palgrave Macmillan, 2006.

Kearney, Hugh. *The British Isles: A History of Four Nations*. Cambridge: Cambridge University Press, 1989.

Kelly, William, ed. *The Sieges of Derry*. Dublin: Four Courts Press, 2001.

Keogh, Dermot, and Mervyn O'Driscoll, eds. *Ireland in the Second World War: Neutrality and Survival.* Douglas Village, Cork: Mercier, 2004.

Kuhn, William. *Democratic Royalism: The Transformation of the British Monarchy.* New York: St Martin's Press, 1996.

Kumar, Krishan. *The Making of English National Identity.* Cambridge: Cambridge University Press, 2003.

Lacey, Robert. *Monarch: The Life and Reign of Elizabeth II.* New York: The Free Press, 2002.

Leavis, F. R. *Mass Civilisation and Minority Culture.* Cambridge: Minority Press, 1930.

LeMahieu, D. L. *A Culture for Democracy: Mass Communication and the Cultivated Mind in Britain between the Wars.* Oxford: Oxford University Press, 1988.

Levine, Philippa. *Prostitution, Race and Politics: Policing Venereal Disease in the British Empire.* London: Routledge, 2003.

Loughlin, James. *Ulster and British National Identity.* London: Pinter, 1995.

Lucas, Rowland. *Voice of a Nation? A Concise Account of the BBC in Wales, 1923–1973.* Llandysul: Gomer Press, 1981.

MacDonagh, Oliver. *States of Mind: Two Centuries of Anglo-Irish Conflict.* London: Pimlico, 1992.

MacDonald, Robert H. *The Language of Empire.* Manchester: Manchester University Press, 1994.

MacKenzie, John M. *Propaganda and Empire.* Manchester: Manchester University Press, 1984.

——. "Essay and Reflection: On Scotland and the Empire." *The International History Review*, 15 (November 1993): 714–39.

——. *Orientalism: History, Theory and the Arts.* Manchester: Manchester University Press, 1995.

——. "Empire and National Identities: The Case of Scotland." *Transactions of the Royal Historical Society* sixth series, 8 (1998): 215–31.

——, ed. *Imperialism and Popular Culture.* Manchester: Manchester University Press, 1986.

——, ed. *Imperialism and the Natural World.* Manchester: Manchester University Press, 1990.

——, ed. *Popular Imperialism and the Military, 1850–1950.* Manchester: Manchester University Press, 1992.

Mandler, Peter. *The English National Character: The History of an Idea from Edmund Burke to Tony Blair.* New Haven, CT: Yale University Press, 2006.

Mangan, J. A., ed. *"Benefits Bestowed?" Education and British Imperialism.* Manchester: Manchester University Press, 1988.

——, ed. *The Imperial Curriculum: Racial Images and Education in the British Colonial Experience.* London: Routledge, 1993.

Mansell, Gerard. *Let the Truth Be Told: 50 Years of BBC External Broadcasting.* London: Weidenfeld and Nicolson, 1982.

Marr, Andrew. *The Battle for Scotland.* London: Penguin, 1990.

Marshall, P. J. "Imperial Britain." *Journal of Imperial and Commonwealth History*, 23 (1995): 379–94.

Marwick, Arthur. *A History of the Modern British Isles, 1914–1999: Circumstances, Events and Outcomes.* Oxford: Blackwell Publishers, 2000.

McBride, Ian. *The Siege of Derry in Ulster Protestant Mythology.* Dublin: Four Courts

Press, 1997.

McClintock, Anne. *Imperial Leather: Race, Gender, and Sexuality in the Colonial Contest.* London: Routledge, 1995.

McDonald, Catriona M. M., ed. *Unionist Scotland 1800–1997.* Edinburgh: John Donald Publishers, 1998.

McDowell, W. H. *The History of BBC Broadcasting in Scotland, 1923–1983.* Edinburgh: Edinburgh University Press, 1992.

McGarry, John, and Brendan O'Leary. *Explaining Northern Ireland: Broken Images.* Oxford: Blackwell Publishers, 1995.

McIntosh, Gillian. *The Force of Culture. Unionist Identities in Twentieth Century Ireland.* Cork: Cork University Press, 1999.

McIntyre, Ian. *The Expense of Glory: A Life of John Reith.* London: Harper Collins, 1994.

McLoone, Martin. "Music Hall Dope and British Propaganda? Cultural Identity and Early Broadcasting in Ireland." *Historical Journal of Film, Radio and Television,* 20 (2000): 301–16.

———. *Film, Media and Popular Culture in Ireland.* Dublin: Irish Academic Press, 2008.

———, ed. *Culture, Identity, and Broadcasting in Ireland.* Belfast: Institute of Irish Studies, 1991.

———, ed. *Broadcasting in a Divided Community: Seventy Years of the BBC in Northern Ireland.* Belfast: Queen's University Press, 1996.

McMahon, Sean. *Sam Hanna Bell, A Biography.* Belfast: Blackstaff, 1999.

Medhurst, Jamie. "'Wales Television—Mammon's Television'? ITV in Wales in the 1960s." *Media History,* 10 (2004): 103–17.

———. "'Minorities with a Message': The Beveridge Report on Broadcasting (1949–1951) and Wales." *Twentieth Century British History,* 19 (2008): 217–33.

Midgley, Clare, ed. *Gender and Imperialism.* Manchester: Manchester University Press, 1998.

Morley, David, and Kevin Robins, eds. *British Cultural Studies.* Oxford: Oxford University Press, 2001.

Nairn, Tom. *The Break-up of Britain,* 2nd ed. London: Verso, 1994.

———. *The Enchanted Glass: Britain and Its Monarchy.* London: Vintage, 1994.

Nicholas, Siân. *The Echo of War: Home Front Propaganda and the Wartime BBC, 1939–45.* Manchester: Manchester University Press, 1996.

———. "'Brushing Up Your Empire:' Dominion and Colonial Propaganda on the BBC's Home Services, 1939–1945." *Journal of Imperial and Commonwealth History,* 31 (2003): 207–30.

Olechnowicz, Andrzej, ed. *The Monarchy and the British Nation 1780 to the Present.* Cambridge: Cambridge University Press, 2007.

Pederson, Susan, and Peter Mandler, eds. *After the Victorians.* London, 1994.

Pegg, Mark. *Broadcasting and Society, 1918–1939.* London: Croom Helm, 1983.

Perkin, Harold. *The Rise of Professional Society: England Since 1880.* New York: Routledge, 1989.

Pittock, Murray G. H. *The Invention of Scotland: The Stuart Myth and Scottish Identity, 1638 to the Present.* London: Routledge, 1991.

———. *Inventing and Resisting Britain: Cultural Identities in Britain and Ireland, 1685–1789.* Basingstoke: Palgrave Macmillan, 1996.

Plunkett, John. *Queen Victoria: First Media Monarch*. Oxford: Oxford University Press, 2003.

Pocock, J. G. A. "'British History:' A Plea for a New Subject." *Journal of Modern History*, 47 (1975): 601–21.

Porter, Bernard. *The Absent-Minded Imperialists: Empire, Society, and Culture in Britain*. Oxford: Oxford University Press, 2004.

Potter, Simon. *News and the British World: The Emergence of an Imperial Press System*. Oxford: Oxford University Press, 2003.

———. "The BBC, the CBC, and the 1939 Royal Tour of Canada." *Cultural and Social History*, 3 (2006): 424–44.

Prebble, John. *The King's Jaunt: George IV in Scotland, August 1822 "One and Twenty Daft Days"*. London: Collins, 1988.

Price, Richard. *An Imperial War and the British Working Class: Working-Class Attitudes and Reactions to the Boer War, 1899–1902*. London: Routledge and Keegan Paul, 1972.

———. "One Big Thing: Britain, Its Empire, and Their Imperial Culture." *Journal of British Studies*, 45 (2006): 602–27.

Prochaska, Frank. *Royal Bounty: The Making of a Welfare Monarchy*. New Haven: Yale University Press, 1995.

Richards, Jeffrey. *The Age of the Dream Palace: Cinema and Society in Britain, 1930–1939*. London: Routledge and Kegan Paul, 1984.

———. *Films and British National Identity From Dickens to Dad's Army*. Manchester: Manchester University Press, 1997.

———, ed. *Imperialism and Juvenile Literature*. Manchester: Manchester University Press, 1989.

Robbins, Keith. *Nineteenth Century Britain, England, Scotland, and Wales: The Making of a Nation*. Oxford: Oxford University Press, 1989.

———. *Great Britain: Identities, Institutions, and the Idea of Britishness*. London: Longman, 1998.

———, ed. *The British Isles*. Oxford: Oxford University Press, 2002.

Rose, Jonathan. *The Intellectual Life of the British Working Class*. New Haven, CT: Yale University Press, 2001.

Rose, Sonya. *Which People's War? National Identity and Citizenship in Wartime Britain, 1939–1944*. Oxford: Oxford University Press, 2003.

Rush, Anne Spry. "Imperial Identity in Colonial Minds: Harold Moody and the League of Coloured Peoples, 1931–40." *Twentieth Century British History*, 13 (2002): 356–83.

Said, Edward. *Orientalism*. New York: Vintage Books, 1979.

———. *Culture and Imperialism*. New York: Alfred A Knopf, 1993.

Samuel, Raphael, ed. *Patriotism: The Making and Unmaking of British National Identity*, vol. 1, *History and Politics*. London: Routledge, 1989.

———, ed. *Island Stories: Unravelling Britain*, vol. 2 *Theatres of Memory*. London: Verso, 1998.

Scannell, Paddy, and David Cardiff. *A Social History of British Broadcasting: 1922–1939*, vol. 1, *Serving the Nation*. Oxford: Blackwell Publishers, 1991.

Schwoch, James. "Crypto-Convergence, Media, and the Cold War: The Early Globalization of Television Networks in the 1950s." Unpublished paper delivered at the MIT Media-In-Transitions Conference, 2002.

Scullion, Adrienne. "BBC Radio in Scotland, 1923–1939: Devolution, Regionalism and Centralisation." *Northern Scotland*, 15 (1994): 63–93.

Sendall, Bernard. *Independent Television in Britain*, vol. 1, *Origin and Foundation 1946–1962*. London: Macmillan, 1982.

Seymour-Ure, Colin. *The British Press and Broadcasting Since 1945*. Oxford: Basil Blackwell, 1991.

Shaw, Tony. *Eden, Suez and the Mass Media: Propaganda and Persuasion During the Suez Crisis*. London: I. B. Tauris, 1995.

Sinha, Mrinalina. *Colonial Masculinity: The "Manly Englishman" and the "Effeminate Bengali" in the Late Nineteenth Century*. Manchester: Manchester University Press, 1995.

Smith, Anthony D. *National Identity*. London: Penguin, 1991.

Smith, Dai. *Wales! Wales?* London: Allen & Unwin, 1984.

Thompson, Andrew. *The Empire Strikes Back? The Impact of Imperialism on Britain from the Mid-Nineteenth Century*. Harlow: Pearson Longman, 2005

Tidrick, Kathryn. *Empire and the English Character*. London: I. B. Tauris, 1990.

Todd, Jennifer. "The Limits of Britishness." *The Irish Review*, 5 (1988): 11–16.

Ward, Paul. *Britishness Since 1870*. London: Routledge, 2004.

——. *Unionism in the United Kingdom, 1918–1974*. Basingstoke: Palgrave Macmillan, 2005.

Ward, Stuart, ed. *British Culture and the End of Empire*. Manchester: Manchester University Press, 2001.

Webster, Wendy. "Domesticating the Frontier: Gender, Empire and Adventure Landscapes in British Cinema, 1945−59." *Gender & History*, 15 (2003): 85–107.

Webster, Wendy. *Englishness and Empire, 1939–1965*. Oxford: Oxford University Press, 2005.

Weight, Richard. *Patriots: National Identity in Britain, 1940–2000*. London: Macmillan, 2002.

Wheeler-Bennett, John W. *King George VI: His Life and Reign*. New York: St Martin's Press, 1958.

Wiener, Joel, and Mark Hampton, eds. *Anglo-American Media Interactions, 1850–2000*. Basingstoke: Palgrave Macmillan, 2007.

Williams, Gwyn A. *When Was Wales?* London: Penguin, 1985.

Williams, Raymond. *Culture and Society, 1780–1950*. New York: Harper and Row, 1958.

Wilson, Kathleen. *Island Race: Englishness, Empire and Gender in the Eighteenth Century*. London: Routledge, 2002.

Woolacott, Angela. *To Try Her Fortune in London: Australian Women, Colonialism, and Modernity*. Oxford: Oxford University Press, 2001.

Index